Noise and Noise Law

Francis McManus dedicates this book to the UK Noise Association

Noise and Noise Law

A Practitioner's Guide

FRANCIS McMANUS with ANDY McKENZIE

EDINBURGH
University Press

Edinburgh University Press is one of the leading university presses in the UK. We publish academic books and journals in our selected subject areas across the humanities and social sciences, combining cutting-edge scholarship with high editorial and production values to produce academic works of lasting importance. For more information visit our website: edinburghuniversitypress.com

Edinburgh University Press Ltd
The Tun – Holyrood Road
12(2f) Jackson's Entry
Edinburgh EH8 8PJ

Typeset in Adobe Caslin
by Cheshire Typesetting Ltd, Cuddington, Cheshire, and
printed and bound by CPI Group (UK) Ltd
Croydon, CR0 4yy

A CIP record for this book is available from the British Library

ISBN 978 1 3995 0504 8 (hardback)
ISBN 978 1 3995 0505 5 (paperback)
ISBN 978 1 3995 0506 2 (webready PDF)
ISBN 978 1 3995 0507 9 (epub)

Contents

Foreword – Sir Crispin Agnew of Lochnaw Bt vi
Preface vii
Table of Cases ix
Table of Legislation xv

1 Introduction 1
Francis McManus

2 Basic Acoustics and Human Sound Perception 9
Andy McKenzie

3 The Measurement and Assessment of Noise 17
Andy McKenzie

4 Common Law Nuisance 31
Francis McManus

5 Statutory Nuisance 45
Francis McManus

6 Neighbourhood Noise 63
Francis McManus

7 Noise and Human Rights 99
Francis McManus

8 Transport Noise 111
Francis McManus

9 Noise Mapping 129
Francis McManus

10 Planning and Noise 141
Francis McManus

11 Noise in the Workplace 167
Francis McManus

Appendix 177
Index 185

Foreword

Noise has long been the Cinderella pollution for people and the environment, mainly because there are so many different characteristics to account for, different sources of noise from house parties and hi-fi systems to industrial noise, and different impacts on people because of their different sensibilities. The damage noise causes to employees in the workplace began to be recognised along with health and safety at work, but in the wider environment, the fact that over the years the courts looked at noise in the context of its relevant locality has tended to mask the invidious impact of noise on individuals. The EU Environmental Noise Directive eventually recognised the impact of noise on human health and well-being and the World Health Organisation has recognised that noise can affect human health.

This book, by Francis McManus, who has had a long-term interest in the law of nuisance, including noise nuisance, with Andy McKenzie, who has had a forty year career in noise consultancy and acoustics research, brings together the law and science of the impact of noise on human beings. This book is a very valuable contribution to this neglected area of the law. Lawyers need to understand the science behind noise, including basic acoustics and the perception of sound and measuring sound, and its impact, before they can properly advise. The detailed historical background to noise legislation is well informed and set the current law in context with very helpful chapters on subjects such as neighbourhood noise, traffic noise, human rights and the role of planning and noise.

While this book deals with noise in the human context there is increasing evidence that noise impacts on wildlife and ecosystems, but that is for another day.

This book is highly commended and should be on the bookshelf of every lawyer who deals with the environment and is likely to act for clients where noise is an issue, as it is increasingly in the planning field.

Sir Crispin Agnew of Lochnaw Bt, LVO, QC
Honorary Research Fellow, University of Dundee, Law School
August 2022

Preface

Noise is not a topic which, thus far, has commanded the attention of environmentalists in a way that more emotive issues, such as climate change, have done. However, it is beyond dispute that noise has the capacity to have a negative impact on human health and, indeed, the natural environment, as a whole. Noise emanates from a variety of sources and human activities, ranging from heavy industry to traffic noise, noise from recreational activities, noise in the workplace and also to neighbourhood noise. This state of affairs has required Parliament, over the years, to deal with the corresponding impact of noise on society in different ways, by passing a mosaic of legislation that has required balancing the rights of the noise maker with that of the recipient of the noise.

At the time of writing, the UK has left the EU, which had been active in certain areas, including addressing noise from transport, environmental assessment and noise mapping. It will be interesting to observe how noise law and policy will develop in the absence of the EU.

Environment is a devolved function in the UK and, therefore, under the control of the relevant national legislatures and governments. However, the substantive law (for example, the law relating to common law nuisance, statutory nuisance, environmental assessment and planning), which is discussed in this book, does not differ significantly over the four jurisdictions. The book concentrates on noise law as it relates to England, Scotland and Wales. The authors have refrained from discussing the law relating to Northern Ireland, since it is considered that this merits separate treatment.

The book is intended to provide practitioners and students with an introduction to the scientific background to noise, as well as a comprehensive and detailed account of the substantive law relating to the control of noise. *Noise and Noise Law* includes an account of common law nuisance, statutory nuisance, neighbourhood noise, noise and human rights, transport noise, noise mapping, town and country planning and noise in the workplace.

Francis McManus wrote the legal chapters, namely chs 1 and 4–11, inclusive. Andy McKenzie wrote the technical and scientific chapters, namely, chs 2 and 3.

Francis McManus would like to thank the following for their help in the production of this book, namely; Ronald E Conway, Jim Kerr, Nigel Rodgers, John Stewart, Henry Thoresby, Val Weedon, the Ministry of Defence and the Health and Safety Executive. However, any errors or other shortcomings in the book rest firmly with the authors. The authors would also like to thank Edinburgh University Press for their help over the past eighteen months.

Andy McKenzie would like to dedicate his chapters to Marcus Trinick KC, with the greatest respect, and with whom he has had the pleasure, on many occasions, of discussing the complexities of noise generation, perception and control, over a glass or two, often until the early hours of the morning!

The law is stated in force on 1 July 2022. However, it has been possible to take account of some developments at a later date.

Francis McManus
Andy McKenzie
July 2022

Table of Cases

National Cases

Adam (Scotland) Ltd v Bearsden and Milngavie District Council 1996 SLT (Sh. Ct) 21 64
AG British Columbia ex rel Eaton (1963) 39 DLR (2d) 48 121
AG v Hastings Corp (1950) 94 Sol Jo. 225 1
Al Nashiri v Poland (2015) 60 EHRR 16 1
Al Nashiri v Romania (2019) 68 EHRR 3 1
Allen v Gulf Oil Refining Ltd [1981] AC 1001 .... 41, 126
Anderson v City of Dundee Council 2000 SLT (Sh Ct) 134 .... 48, 52
Ashdown Forest Economic Development LLP v Secretary of State for Local Government [2015] EWCA Civ 681; [2014] EWHC 406 152
Attorney General v PYA Quarries Ltd [1957] 2 QB 169 .... 84, 121

Baker v Quantum Clothing Group Ltd [2011] 1 WLR 1003; 168
Bamford v Turnley (1862) 31 LJQB 286 .... 34, 36
Baxendale v MacMurray (1867) LR 2 Ch 790 42
Baxter v Camden LBC [1999] 4 All ER 449 98
Baxter v Camden LBC (No 2) [2001] 1 AC 1 .... 31, 32, 40, 99
Bellew v Cement Ltd [1948] IR 61 33
Berkeley v Secretary of State for the Environment, Transport and the Regions [2001] 2 AC 603 .... 147, 149
Bolton v Stone [1951] AC 850 168
Bowen-West v Secretary of State for Communities and Local Government [2012] Env LR 22 143
Brentwood BC v City and Country (Warley) Ltd [2010] JPL 1443 64
Bridlington Relay Ltd v Yorkshire Electricity Board [1965] Ch 436 37
British Airports Authority v Secretary of State for Scotland 1979 SC 200 164
Budd v Colchester BC [1999] Env LR 739 54
Bux v Slough Metals Ltd [1973] 1 WLR 1358 169
Bybrook Barn Garden Centre Ltd v Kent County Council [2000] Env LR 30 39

Cala Homes (South) Ltd v Secretary of State for Communities and Local Government 77 [2012] EWCA Civ 639 153
Caledonian Railway Co v Baird (1876) 3R 839 40
Camden LBC v Easynet Ltd [2002] EWHC 2929 54
Camden LBC v Gunby [2000] 1 WLR 465; [1999] 4 All ER 602 51
Camden LBC v London Underground [2000] Env LR 369 54
Christie v Davy [1893] 1 Ch 316 34
Collins v Hamilton (1837) 15 S 902 42

Colville v Middleton 27 May 1817, FC 42–3
Cooke v Adatia (1989) 153 JP 129 48
Coventry CC v Doyle [1981] 1 WLR 1325 55
Cowan v Kinaird (1865) 4 M 236 42
Crouch v British Rail Engineering Ltd [1988] IRLR 404 169
Cunningham v Birmingham City Council [1998] Env LR 1 48

De Keyser's Royal Hotel Ltd v Spicer Bros Ltd (1914) 30 TLR 257 36
Delaware Mansions Ltd v Westminster City Council [2001] 1 AC 321 39
Dennis Rye Ltd v Bolsover DC [2013] EWHC 1041 48
Dennis v Ministry of Defence [2003] Env LR 741; [2003] EHLR 17 .... 33, 100, 120
Dobson v Thames Water Utilities Ltd [2011] EWHC 3253 41
Duke of Buccleuch v Cowan (1866) 5M 214 42
Dunn v Hamilton (1837) 15 S 853 40

Earl of Kintore v Pirie (1903) 5 F 818 .... 42, 43
East Northamptonshire DC v Fossett [1994] Env R 388 49
Elvington Park Ltd v City of York Council [2010] Env LR 10 54

Fearn v Tate Modern Modern Galleries [2020] EWCA Civ 104 .... 31, 32
Fleming v Hislop (1882) 10 R 426; (1886) 13 R (HL) 43 32

Gateshead Metropolitan BC v Secretary of State for the Environment [1995] Env LR 37 .... 161–2, 163
Gathercole v Suffolk CC [2020] EWCA Civ 1179 150
Geddis v Proprietors of Bann Reservoir (1887–1888) LR 3 App. Cas. 430 41
Glasgow City Council v Ferguson 2009 SLT (Sh Ct) 47 1
Godfrey v Conwy CBC [2001] Env LR 38 49
Goldman v Hargrave [1967] 1 AC 645 39
Goldscheider v Royal Opera House Covent Garden Foundation [2020] ICR 1 .... 172, 173

Haddon v Lynch [1911] VLR 230 32
Hammersmith and City Railway Co v Brand (1869–1870) LR 4 HL 171 41
Harrison v Southwark Water Co Ltd [1891] 2 Ch 409 33
Heath v Brighton Corporation (1908) 24 TLR 414 37
Hill v Wood (1863) 1 M 360 43
Hollywood Silver Fox Farm Ltd v Emmet [1936] 2 KB 468 34
Hope Butuyuyu v Hammersmith and Fulham LBC [1997] Env LR D 13 56
Hopkins Development Ltd v First Secretary of State and North Wiltshire DC [2007] Env LR 14 162–3
Houldsworth v Wishaw Magistrates (1887) 14 R 920 43
Howarth v Canadian Red Cross Society [1943] 2 WWR 692 32
Hunter v Canary Wharf Ltd [1997] AC 655; [1997] Env LR 488 .... 31, 37, 38, 43, 45, 99

Inglis v Shotts Iron Co (1881) 8 R 1006 34

James v Dover DC [2022] EWHC 961 163–4
Jones v Ministry of Defence [2021] EWHC 2276 .... 100–1, 120

Kent v First Secretary of State [2005] Env LR 30 149–50
Kenyon v Secretary of State for Housing, Communities and Local Government [2020] EWCA Civ 302 150
King v Advocate General for Scotland 2009 CSOH 169 .... 33, 120
Kruse v Johnson [1898] 2 QB 91 .... 2, 94

Lambert (A) Flat Management Ltd v Lomas [1981] 1 WLR 898 49
Lawrence v Fen Tigers Ltd [2014] AC 822 .... 35–6, 41, 42, 43, 49
Lawrence v Fen Tigers Ltd (No 2) [2015] AC 106 40
Leakey v National Trust for Places of Historic Interest or Natural Beauty [1980] QB 485 39
Liverpool Corp v Coghill and Son Ltd [1918] 1 Ch 307 42
Lovell v Blundells and T Albert Crompton and Co Ltd [1944] KB 502; 169
Lowe Watson v South Somerset DC [1998] Env LR 143 54

MacBean v Scottish Water [2020] CSOH 55 32
McDonald v Indigo Sun Retail Ltd [2022] SAC (Civ) 15 .... 167, 171
McGillivray v Stephenson [1950] 1 All ER 942 55
MacIntyre Bros v McGavin [1893] AC 268 42
McIntyre v Strathclyde RC 1944 SLT 933 169
Managers of the Metropolitan Asylum District v Hill (1880–1881) LR 6 App Cas 193, HL 41
Marcic v Thames Water Utilities [2004] 2 AC 42 38
Miller v Jackson [1977] QB 966 .... 33, 43
Milne v Stuartfield Windpower Ltd [2019] SC ABE 25; [2018] 5 WLUK 717 .... 46, 48, 49
Mitchell v Glasgow City Council [2009] 1 AC 874 1
Morris v Curran 2019 GWD 31-496 37
Mutter v Fyffe (1848) 11 D 303 32
Myatt v Teignbridge DC [1995] Env LR 78 54

Naismith v London Film Productions Ltd [1939] 1 All ER 794 167
NCB v Thorne [1976] 1 WLR 543 46
Network Housing Association v Westminster City Council [1995] Env 176 .... 51, 52, 54
Newbury DC v Secretary of oS for the Environment [1981] AC 578 .... 163–4, 164
Newham LBC v White (12 March 2015, unreported) 48
Nolan v Dental Manufacturing Co [1958] 1 WLR 936 169
Nor Video Services Ltd v Ontario Hydro (1978) 84 (3d) 221 37
North Lincolnshire County Council v Act Fast North Lincolnshire CC (CIC) [2014] Env LR 7; [2014] JPL 371 54

Oakley v Birmingham City Council [2001] 1 AC 617 46–7

Pape v Cumbria CC [1992] ICR 132 168
Paris v Stepney BC [1951] AC 367 169
Peires v Bickerton's Aerodromes Ltd [2017] 1 WLR 2865 111–12
Pettigrew v Inverclyde Council 1999 Hous. L.R. 31 52
Pike v Sefton MBC [2000] Env LR D31 46
Powell v May [1946] KB 330 94
Pyx Granite Co Ltd v Ministry of Housing and Local Government [1958] 1 QB 554 163

Qualcast (Wolverhampton) Ltd v Haynes [1959] AC 743 169

R (Anne) v Test Valley BC [2002] Env LR 22 48
R (Baker) v Bath and North East Somerset Council [2009] EWHC 595 142
R (Bateman) v Cambridgeshire DC [2011] EWCA Civ 157 .... 146, 147
R (Birchall Gardens LLP) v Hertfordshire CC [2017] Env LR 17 .... 146–7, 147
R (Blewett) v Derbyshire CC [2004] Env LR 29 149
R (Buckinghamshire CC) v Secretary of State for Transport [2014] 1 WLR 324 .... 152, 154–5
R (Cooperative Group Ltd) v Northumberland CC [2010] Env LR 40 146
R (Elvington Park Ltd) v York Crown Court [2011] EWHC 2213 55
R (Fisher) v Durham CC [2020] Env LR 28 53
R (Friends of Basildon Golf Course) v Basildon DC [2011] Env LR 16 147
R (Friends of the Earth, England, Wales and Northern Ireland Ltd) v The Welsh Ministers [2016] Env LR 1 .... 152, 155
R (Friends of the Earth UK Ltd) v Secretary of State for Housing, Communities and Local Government [2019] Env LR 26 155
R (Hackney LBC) v Rottenberg [2007] Env LR 24 .... 48, 49
R (McGuigan) v Chief Constable of the Police Service of Northern Ireland [2017] NIQB 96 1
R (Save Britain's Heritage) v Secretary of State for Communities and Local Government 2014 Env LR 9 143
R (St Albans City and District Council) v Patel [2009] Env LR 22 56
R (Thakeham Village Action Ltd) v Horsham DC [2014] Env LR 21 .... 146, 147
R v Birmingham Justices ex p Guppy (1988) JP 159 55
R v Bolton MBC ex p Kirkman [1998] JPL 787 .... 162, 163
R v Bristol City Council ex p Everett [1999] 1 WLR 1170 47
R v Carrick DC ex p Shelley [1996] Env LR 273 51
R v Crown Court at Canterbury [2001] Env LR 36 54
R v Falmouth and Truro Port Health Authority ex p South West Water Services Ltd [2001] QB 445 .... 51, 54
R v Fenny Stratford Justices [1976] 1 WLR 1101 55
R v Jones v Mansfield DC [2004] Env LR 21 146
R v North Yorkshire CC ex p Brown [1999] Env LR 623 at 630 (per Lord Hoffman) 143
R v Parlby (1889) 22 QBD 520 46
R v Secretary of State [1994] 1 WLR 74 117
R v Swale BC ex p Royal Society for the Protection of Birds [1991] JPL 39 143
R v Tunbridge Wells Justices [1996] Env LR 88 55
Re Young & Harston's Contract (1885) 31 Ch D 168 51
Robb v Dundee City Council 2002 SC 301; 2002 SLT 853 .... 46, 48, 49, 51, 52
Rochford Rural DC v Port of London Authority [1914] 2 KB 916 52
Roper v Tussauds Theme Parks Ltd [2007] Env LR 31 .... 49, 54
Rose v Miles (1815) 4 M and S 101; 105 ER 773 121
Rushmer v Polsue and Alfieri Ltd [1907] AC 121 34

Salford City Council v McNally [1976] AC 379 .... 46, 47
Sandwell MBC v Bujok [1990] 1 WLR 1350 55
Sedleigh-Denfield v O'Callaghan [1940] AC 880 38–9
Slater v McLellan 1924 SC 854 38
Smith v Scott [1973] Ch 314 .... 38, 40
Southwark LBC v Ince (1989) 21 HLR 504 47
Speed v Thomas Swift and Co [1943] KB 557 168
Spurrier v Secretary of State for Transport [2019] EWHC 1070 156

St Helens Smelting Co v Tipping (1865) 11 HL Cas 642 35
Stokes v Guest, Keen and Nettlefold (Bolt and Nuts) Ltd [1968] 1 WLR 1776 at 1783 168
Strathclyde Regional Council v Tudhope 1983 SLT 22 .... 54, 55, 64
Sturges v Bridgman (1879) 11 Ch D 22 42
Surrey Free Inns v Gosport BC [1999] Env LR 750 54
Swinton v Pedie (1837) 15 S 775 34
Swire v Ashford BC [2021] EWHC 702 146

Tate and Lyle Industries Ltd v Greater London Council [1983] 2 AC 509 41
Tesco Stores Ltd v Secretary of State for the Environment [1995] 1 WLR 759 .... 151, 163
Tetley v Chitty [1986] 1 All ER 663 40
The Barns (NE) Ltd v Newcastle upon Tyne City Council [2006] Env LR 25 59
Thompson v Smith's Ship Repairers (North Shields) Ltd [1984] QB 405 168
Tower Hamlets LBC v Manzoni and Walder [1984] JPL 436 48
Trotter v Farnie (1830) 9S 144 34

Vale of White Horse DC v Allen [1997] Env LR 212 59
Vaughan v Taff Vale Railway (1860) 5 H and N 679 41
Vella v London Borough of Lambeth [2006] Env LR 33 .... 46, 47

Walter Lilley and Co Ltd v Westminster CC [1994] Env LR 380 64
Waltham Forest LBC v Mitoo [2017] Env LR 9 56
Walton v The Scottish Ministers 2013 SC (UKSC) 67 153–4
Watkins v Aged Merchant Seaman's Homes [2019] Env LR 2 59
Watt v Jamieson 154 SC 56 .... 31–2, 38
Webster v Lord Advocate 1984 SLT 13; reversed in relation to interdict granted, 1985 SC 173 .... 33, 36, 37, 40, 42, 43
Wellingborough BC v Gordon [1993] Env LR 218 .... 48, 55–6
Western Silver Fox Ranch v Ross and Cromarty CC 1940 SLT 144 32
Westminster City Council v French Connection Retail Ltd [2005] Env LR 42 66
Westminster City Council v McDonald [2005] Env LR 48
Wilson and Clyde Coal Co Ltd v English [1938] AC 57 169
Wilson v Tyneside Window Cleaning Co [1958] 2 QB 110 167
Wiltshire Construction (London) Ltd v Westminster City Council [1997] Env LR 321 64
Wincanton Rural District Council v Parsons [1905] 2 KB 34 52

Zeb v Birmingham City Council [2010] Env LR 30 146

European Union Cases

Commission v Spain [2004] ECR 1-08253 142
Hoofdsedilyk Gewest v Vlaams Gewest [2012] Env LR 9 142
Inter-Environment Bruxelles ASBL v Region de Bruxelles-Capitale Case 567/210; [2010] Env LR 30 153

European Court of Human Rights

Dees v Hungary (2013) 57 EHRR 12 104–5
Dmitriyev v Russia App. No. 17840/06, judgement 1 December 2020 102
Fadayeva v Russia (2007) 45 EHRR 10 .... 102, 104

Gomez v Spain 2005) 41 EHRR 40 103–4
Hatton v United Kingdom (2003) 37 EHRR 28 101–2
Kapa v Poland App. No. 75031/13, judgement 14 October 2021 .... 103, 104
Lopez Ostra v Spain (1995) 20 EHRR 277 102–3
Oluic v Croatia App. No. 61260/08, judgement 20 May 2010 106–8
Powell and Rayner v United Kingdom (1990) 12 EHRR 355 101–2
Pugliesi v National Capital (1977) 3 CCLT 18 32
Zammit Meampel v Malta App. No. 24202/10, judgement 22 November 2011 108–9

Table of Legislation

Statutes

Anti-social Behaviour, Crime and Policing Act 2014 .... 4, 78–9
s 1(1) 79
s 1(2) 79
s 1(3) 79
s 1(4) 79
s 1(5) 79
s 1(6) 79
s 1(7) 79
s 1(8) 80
s 2(1) 79
s 2(2) 79
s 43 4–5
s 76 80
s 76(1) 80
s 76(2) 80
s 76(3) 80
(a) 80
s 76(4) 80
s 76(5) 80
s 76(6) 80
s 76(7) 80
s 77(1) 81
s 77(2) 81
s 77(4) 81
s 77(5) 81
s 78 81
s 79 .... 81, 83
s 80 .... 80, 82
(1) 81
(2) 81
(3) 81
(5) 81
(6) 81
(7) 82
(8) 82
s 81 .... 82, 83
(1) 82
(2) 82
s 82(1) 82
s 82(2) 82
s 82(3) 82
s 82(4) 82
s 82(7) 83
s 83 83
s 84 83
s 85(1) 83
s 85(2) 83
s 85(3) 83
s 85(4) 83
s 86(1) 83
s 86(2) 83
s 86(3) 83
s 86(4)–(6) 83
Antisocial Behaviour etc. (Scotland) Act 2004 (ABSA) 4, 73, 74
Part 2 .... 4, 73
s 4(1) 73
s 4(2) 73
s 18 73
Part 5 .... 4, 74, 78
s 41(1) 74
s 41(2) 74
s 41(3) 74
s 41(5) 74
s 41(6) 74
s 42(1) 74
ss 43–47 74
s 43(1) 75
s 43(2) 75
s 43(3) 75
s 43(4) 75
s 43(5) 75
s 44 75

Antisocial Behaviour etc. (Scotland) Act 2004 (ABSA) (*cont.*)
s 44(1) 75
(2) 75
(3) 75
(4) 76
(5) 76
(6) 76
s 45 76–7
(1) 76
(2) 76
(3) 76
(5) 76
s 46 76
(1) 77
(2) 76
(3) 77
(4) 77
(5) 77
(6) 77
(7) 77
s 47(1) 77
s 47(2) 58, 77, 78
s 47(3) 77
s 47(4) 77
s 47(5) 78
s 47(6) 78
s 47(7) 78
s 48 75
s 49(1) 76
s 49(2) 76
s 50(1) 78
s 51(2) 77
s 53(1) 74, 75
s 143(1) 73
s 143(2) 73
Schedule 1 58

Building (Scotland) Act 2003 65

Civic Government (Scotland) Act 1982 ... 67
s 41 87
(1) 86
(2) 86
(3) 86
s 49(1) 68
s 54(1) 67–8, 68
s 54(2) 68
s 54(2A) 68
s 54(2B) 68

Civil Aviation Act 1971
s 29 118
Civil Aviation Act 1982 .... 111, 115
s 3 114
s 5 114
(1) 114
(2) 114
s 38A 118
(2) 119
(11) 118
s 38B(2) 119
s 38B(5) 119
s 38C(2) 119
s 38C(4) 119
s 38C(5) 119
s 60(3) 112
(r) 113
s 62 111
s 76(1) 111–12
s 77(1) 115
s 77(2) 115, 124
s 78 118
(1) 115
(2) 115
(3) 115–17
(4) 116
(5) 116–17
(6) 117
(6A) 117
(8) 117–18
(9) 118
s 79 .... 118, 119
s 80 115
Schedule 14 118
Civil Aviation Act 2012
s 84(1) 120
s 84(2) 120
s 84(7) 120
Clean Neighbourhoods and Environment Act (Northern Ireland) 2011 46
Control of Pollution Act 1974 (COPA) 3
Part III 3, 64
s 58(4) 56
s 60 .... 57, 58, 63, 64, 65, 67, 126
(1) 63, 65
(2) 63
(3) 64
(4) 64

(5) 64–5
(6) 65
(7) 65
(8) 65, 66
s 61 .... 57, 58, 66, 126
(2) 65
(3) 65
(4) 65
(5) 65
(6) 65
(7) 66
(8) 66
(9) 66
(10) 66
s 62 68
(1) 66, 67
(a) 66
(b) 66
(1A) 66
(1B) 66
(2) 66–7
(3) 67
(3A) 67
s 65 57
s 66 57
s 67 57
s 68(1) 67
s 68(3) 67
Crime and Disorder Act 1998 4
Criminal Justice and Public Order Act 1994 86
s 63 .... 87–8, 88–9
(1) 86–7, 88
(1A) 87
(2) 87, 88, 88–9
(3) 87, 88
(4) 87
(6) 87
(7) 87
(7A) 87
(7B) 87
(9) 87
(10) 87
s 64 88
(1) 88
(2) 88
(4) 88, 89
(b) 88
s 64(5) 88
s 64(5A) 88
s 64(6) 88
s 65 89
(1) 89
(2) 89
(3) 89
(4) 89
(5) 89
(6) 89
s 66(1) 89
s 67 89

Environment Act 2021 7
s 1(1) 7
s 8(1) 7
s 8(2) 7
s 17(1), (2) 7
s 17(5) 7
s 44 7
s 45 7
Environmental Assessment (Scotland) Act 2005 159
Environmental Protection Act 1990 (EPA) 161–2
s 35(3) 95
s 35(6) 95
Part III 3, 50, 120
s 79 126
(1) 45–6, 50, 121
(a) 46–7, 48
(g) 48–9, 50, 52, 56, 57, 58, 60, 61, 80
(ga) 49–50, 53, 57–8, 58, 59, 60, 61
(2) 48
(6) 111
(6A) 50, 111, 121
(7) 46, 48, 49, 51
(9) 56
(10) 50
s 80 .... 50, 54, 126
(1) 51, 52
(a) 57
(2) 51, 52
(2A) 52
(a) 53
(2B) 53
(2C) 53
(2E) 53
(3) 53, 55
(4) 55, 56, 57, 58

Environmental Protection Act 1990 (EPA) (*cont.*)
s 80(4A) ... 56, 58
(5) ... 56
(6) ... 56
(7) ... 56
(8) ... 56
(aa) ... 57
(9) ... 57
(10) ... 57
s 80A ... 50
(1) ... 53
(2) ... 53
(b) ... 53–4
(2D) ... 53
(3) ... 53
(4) ... 53
(5) ... 53
(6) ... 53
(7) ... 54
(8) ... 54
s 80ZA ... 56
s 81(1) ... 57
s 81(1A) ... 57
s 81(1B) ... 58
s 81(3) ... 58
s 81(3A) ... 58
s 81(3B) ... 58
s 81(3C) ... 58
s 81(4) ... 58
s 81(5) ... 58
s 81(6) ... 58
s 81(7) ... 59
s 82 ... 47, 66, 80
(1)–(4) ... 60
(1) ... 59
(2) ... 59, 60
(3) ... 60
(4) ... 60
(5) ... 60
(5A) ... 60
(6) ... 60
(7) ... 60
(8) ... 60, 61
(9) ... 61
(10) ... 61
(11) ... 61
(12) ... 61
(13) ... 61
Schedule 3 ... 59
para 6 ... 54
Equality Act 2010 ... 53

Factories Act 1961 ... 67
Fireworks Act 2003 ... 89
s 1(1) ... 89
s 2(1) ... 89
s 2(2) ... 91
s 11(1) ... 89
Fireworks and Pyrotechnic Articles (Scotland) Act 2022 ... 92

Gulf Oil Refining Act 1965 ... 41

Health and Safety at Work etc. Act 1974 ... 170
s 2(1) ... 170
s 2(2)(a) ... 170
s 3(1) ... 170
s 47(1) ... 170
High-Speed Rail (London-West Midlands) Act 2017 ... 126
Hovercraft Act 1968
s 1(1) ... 120
Human Rights Act 1998 (HRA) ... 53, 99
ss 1, 2 ... 99

Land Compensation Act 1973 ... 124
s 1(1) ... 124
s 1(2) ... 124
s 1(3) ... 124
s 1(4) ... 124
s 1(5) ... 124
s 1(6) ... 124
s 2 ... 124
s 20 ... 125
(1) ... 125
Land Compensation (Scotland) Act 1973 ... 125
Land Reform (Scotland) Act 2003 ... 88
Licensing Act 2003 ... 68, 83–4
s 1(1)(c) ... 87
s 2(7A) ... 68
s 4(1) ... 85
s 4(2) ... 84
s 5(1) ... 85
s 5A(1) ... 85
s 18(2) ... 85
s 72(2) ... 85
s 136 ... 87

(1) ... 85
s 160(1) ... 85
s 160(2) ... 85
s 160(3) ... 85
s 160(4) ... 85
s 160(5) ... 85–6
s 160(6) ... 86
s 173(1) ... 85
s 182 ... 84
Schedule 1 ... 84
Licensing (Scotland) Act 2005 ... 86
s 27(6) ... 86
Local Government Act 1972
s 222 ... 122
s 235(1) ... 94
s 235(3) ... 94
Local Government (Scotland) Act 1973
s 201(1) ... 94

Motor Cycle Noise Act 1987
s 1(1) ... 123

Noise Abatement Act 1960 ... 2, 66, 93
Noise Act 1996 ... 4, 68, 74, 78
ss 2–9 ... 71
s 2(1) ... 68
s 2(2) ... 68
s 2(3) ... 68
s 2(4) ... 69
s 2(5) ... 69
s 2(6) ... 68
s 2(7A) ... 68
s 3 ... 69
(1) ... 69
(2) ... 69
(3) ... 69
(3A) ... 69
(4) ... 69
(5) ... 69
(6) ... 70
s 4 ... 71, 72
(1) ... 70
(2) ... 70
(3) ... 70
s 4A ... 71, 72
(1) ... 70
(2) ... 70
s 5 ... 68
(1) ... 70
(2) ... 70
(3) ... 71
(4) ... 71
s 6(1) ... 71
s 6(2) ... 71
s 6(3) ... 71
s 8 ... 71
(1) ... 71
(2) ... 71
(3) ... 71
(4) ... 71
(5) ... 71
s 8A ... 71
s 9(2) ... 72
s 9(2A) ... 72
s 10(1) ... 72
s 10(2) ... 72, 73
s 10(3) ... 72
s 10(4) ... 72, 73
s 10(5) ... 73
s 10(6) ... 73
s 10(7) ... 73
s 10(8) ... 73
s 11(2) ... 68, 70
Noise and Statutory Nuisance Act 1993 ... 3–4
s 8 ... 67
Schedule 2 ... 67

Planning Act 2008
s 14(1)(k) ... 126
s 25(1) ... 126
s 31 ... 126
s 158(1), (2) ... 126
Planning and Compulsory Purchase Act 2004
s 38(6) ... 161
Planning (Scotland) Act 2019
s 13(2) ... 166
Police Reform Act 2002
s 59(1) ... 123
s 59(2) ... 123
s 59(3) ... 123
s 59(4) ... 123–4
s 59(5) ... 124
s 59(9) ... 123
Pollution Prevention and Control Act 1999
s 2 ... 50
Public Health Act 1848 ... 45
Public Health Act 1875 ... 45

Public Health Act 1936 .... 2, 45
s 92 47
s 99 47
Public Health (Scotland) Act 1867 45
Public Health (Scotland) Act 1897 .... 2, 45

Road Traffic Act 1988
s 41 122
(1) 122
(2) 122
(2A) 122
s 42 122
s 54 122
(1) 122
s 55(1) 122
s 55(2) 122
Road Traffic Regulation Act 1984
s 1(1) 123
Roads (Scotland) Act 1984
s 7 154

Scotland Act 1998 .... 122, 165

Town and Country Planning Act 1947 160
Town and Country Planning Act 1990 (TCPA 1990) 161, 163, 165, 166
s 55 143
s 70(1) 163
s 70(2) 161
s 106 118
s 288 .... 162, 163
Town and Country Planning (Scotland) Act 1947 160
Town and Country Planning (Scotland) Act 1972
s 233 164
Town and Country Planning (Scotland) Act 1997 (TCPSA 1997) 166
s 3A(6) 155
s 24 166
s 26 143
s 37 166
s 37(1) 166
s 37(2) 166
s 41A 166
s 41A(1) 166
s 41A(2) 166
Transport Act 2000
s 70(2) 120
Transport and Works (Scotland) Act 2007
s 1 .... 41, 126

Vehicle Excise and Registration Act 1994 51

Statutory Instruments

Aeroplane Noise Regulations 1999 (SI 1999/1452)
reg 4 113
Air Navigation (Environmental Standards for Non-Part 2121 Aircraft) Order 2008 (SI 2008/3133) 114
art 3 114
art 4(1) 114
art 4(2) 114
art 7(2) 114
Air Navigation Order 2016 (SI 2016/765)
art 218(1) 115
art 249(1) 112
art 265 112
Airports (Noise-related Operating Restrictions) (England and Wales) Regulations 2018 (SI 2018/785) 164–5
reg 3 165
reg 3(1) 165
Antisocial Behaviour (Noise Control) (Scotland) Regulations 2005 (SSI 2005/43)
reg 3 75
reg 5 76

Building Regulations 2010 (SI 2010/2214) 96
reg 4(1) 96
reg 4(2) 96
reg 6(1)(f) 96
reg 6(2)(b) 96
reg 41(4) 97
reg 45 97
Schedule 1 96
Part E1 96–7
Part E2 96
Part E3 96
Part E4 96

Building (Scotland) Regulations 2004 (SI 2004/406)
Schedule 5 para 1 ... 97
Schedule 5 para 2 ... 97
Civil Aviation (Designation of Aerodromes) Order 1981 (SI 1981/651) ... 118
Civil Aviation (Notices) Regulations 1978 (SI 1978/1303) ... 115
reg 2 ... 115
Control of Appeals (Scotland) Regulations 1983 (SI 1983/1455)
reg 5 ... 65
Control of Noise (Appeals) Regulations 1975 (SI 1975/2116)
reg 5 ... 65
Control of Noise at Work Regulations 2005 (SI 2005/1643) ... 19, 170
reg 2(1) ... 170–1
reg 3(1) ... 170
reg 4 ... 175
(1) ... 171
(2) ... 171
(3) ... 171
(5) ... 171
reg 5(1) ... 171
reg 5(2) ... 171
reg 5(3) ... 171
reg 5(4) ... 171
reg 5(5) ... 172
reg 5(6) ... 172
reg 6 ... 172, 173, 174
(1) ... 172
(2) ... 172
(3) ... 172
(4) ... 172, 175, 176
(6) ... 173
reg 7 ... 172, 174, 175
(1) ... 173–4, 175, 176
(2) ... 171, 173–4, 175, 176
(3) ... 173, 176
(4) ... 173
(5) ... 173
reg 8 ... 174
(1) ... 172, 174
(2) ... 174, 175
reg 9 ... 175
(1) ... 174
(2) ... 174
(4) ... 174
(5) ... 174
reg 10 ... 172
(1) ... 175
(2) ... 175
(3) ... 175
reg 11(1) ... 175
reg 11(2) ... 175
reg 12(1) ... 176
reg 12(2) ... 176
reg 13(1) ... 176
reg 13(2) ... 176
Schedule 1 Part 1 ... 171
Schedule 1 Part 2 ... 171
Schedule 2 ... 171
Control of Noise at Work Regulations (Northern Ireland) 2006 (SR 2006 No 1) ... 170
Control of Noise (Code of Practice for Construction and Open Sites) Order 1987 (SI 1987/1730) ... 64–5

Environmental Assessment of Plans and Programmes Regulations 2004 (SI 2004/1633) ... 156
reg 2(1) ... 157
reg 3(2) ... 156
reg 4(1) ... 156
reg 4(3) ... 156
reg 5(1), (2) ... 157
reg 5(2) ... 157
reg 5(3) ... 157
reg 5(6) ... 157
reg 8(2), (3) ... 157
reg 9(1) ... 157
reg 9(2) ... 157
reg 9(3) ... 157
reg 10(3) ... 157
reg 11(2) ... 157
reg 12 ... 158
(1) ... 157
(2) ... 157
(3) ... 157
reg 13(1) ... 158
reg 13(2) ... 158
reg 13(3) ... 158
reg 13(4) ... 158
reg 16(1) ... 158
reg 16(2) ... 159
reg 16(3) ... 159
reg 16(4) ... 158, 159

Environmental Assessment of Plans and Programmes Regulations 2004 (SI 2004/1633) (*cont.*)
reg 17(1) ... 159
Schedule 1 ... 157
Environmental Noise (England) Regulations 2006 (SI 2006/2238) ... 131
reg 3(1) ... 132
reg 3(2) ... 132
reg 3(3) ... 132
reg 3(5) ... 132
reg 3(6) ... 132
reg 3(7) ... 132
reg 3(8) ... 132
reg 3(9) ... 132
reg 3(11) ... 132
reg 4 ... 137, 138
(1) ... 133
(2) ... 133
(3) ... 133
(3A) ... 133
(6) ... 133
reg 6 ... 133
reg 7 ... 136
(1) ... 133
(2) ... 133
(3) ... 133
reg 9(1) ... 134
reg 10 ... 133
reg 11 ... 136, 137
(2) ... 134
(3) ... 134
(4) ... 134
reg 12 ... 136, 137
(2) ... 134
(3) ... 134
(4) ... 134
(5) ... 134
(6) ... 134
reg 13(1) ... 135
reg 13(2) ... 135
reg 14(1) ... 135
reg 14(2) ... 135
reg 14A ... 135
reg 15 ... 138
(1) ... 135
(3) ... 136
reg 16 ... 136
reg 17(1) ... 136
reg 17(2) ... 136
reg 17(3), (4) ... 136
reg 18 ... 136
reg 19 ... 138
(1) ... 136
(2) ... 137
(3) ... 137
(4), (5) ... 137
(6) ... 137
reg 20(1) ... 137
reg 23 ... 134, 135, 136
(1) ... 137
(2) ... 137
(3) ... 137
(4) ... 137
(5) ... 137
(6) ... 138
reg 24 ... 136, 137
(1) ... 138
(2), (3) ... 138
(4) ... 138
(5) ... 138
(6) ... 138
(7) ... 138
reg 26(1) ... 138
reg 29(1) ... 138
reg 29(2) ... 138
reg 30(1) ... 139
reg 30(2) ... 139
Schedule 1 ... 133
Schedule 3 ... 133
Environmental Noise (Scotland) Regulations 2006 (SSI 2006/465) ... 139
reg 7 ... 139
reg 8 ... 139
reg 14 ... 139
reg 16 ... 139
reg 21 ... 139
Environmental Permitting (England and Wales) Regulations 2016 (SI 2016/1154) ... 50, 95
Explosives Regulations 2014 (SI 2014/1638) ... 90

Fireworks Regulations 2004 (SI 2004/1836) ... 89
reg 3 ... 89
reg 4(1) ... 89
reg 4(2) ... 89

reg 5 89
reg 6 89–90
reg 7(1) 90
reg 7(2) 90
reg 7(3) 90
reg 9(1) 90
reg 9(2) 90
reg 9(2A) 90
reg 9(3) 90
reg 9(4) 90
reg 9(5) 90
reg 9(8) 90
reg 10(1) 90
reg 10(2) 90
reg 10(3) 91
(a) 91
reg 11 91

Fireworks (Scotland) Regulations 2004 (SSI 2004/393) 91
reg 2 91
reg 3(1) 91
reg 3(2) 91
reg 3(3) 91
reg 3A(1) 91
reg 3A(2) 91
reg 3A(3) 91
reg 3B(1) 91
reg 3B(2) 91
reg 3B(3) 91
reg 4(1) 91
reg 4(2) 91
reg 4(3) 91
reg 4(6) 91–2
reg 5 92

Health and Safety (Safety Signs and Signals) Regulations 1996 (SI 1996/341) 173

Heathrow and Gatwick Airports – London Noise Insulation Grants (Revocations) Scheme 2014 (SI 2014/3233) 119

Household Appliances (Noise Emission) Regulations 1990 (SI 1990/161) 98

Landfill (Scotland) Regulations 2003 (SSI 2003/235) 95
reg 10(3) 95–6
Schedule 3 95–6

Management of Health and Safety at Work Regulations 1999 (SI 1999/3242)
Schedule 1 172

Motor Cycle Silencer and Exhaust Systems Regulations 1995 (SI 1995/2370)
reg 3 123

Noise Emission in the Environment by Equipment for use Outdoors Regulations 2001 (SI 2001/1701) 97
reg 2 98
reg 3 .... 97, 98
reg 4 98
reg 5 98
reg 6 .... 97–8, 98
reg 7 98
reg 8 98
reg 9 98
Schedules 1 and 2 97

Noise Insulation (Railways and Other Guided Transport Systems) Regulations 1996 (SI 1996/428) 26, 30, 126
reg 2(1) 127
reg 3(1) 127
reg 3(2) 127
reg 4 128
(1) 127
(2) 127
reg 5 128
(1) 127
(2) 127
reg 7(1) 127
reg 8 127
reg 9 128

Noise Insulation Regulations 1975 (SI 1973/1763) 21, 26, 30, 125
reg 2 125
reg 3 125
(1) 125
(2) 125
(3) 125
reg 4 125
reg 7 125
(1) 125
reg 9 125
Schedule 1 125

Noise Insulation (Scotland) Regulations 1975 (SI 1975/460) 125

Personal Protective Equipment Regulations 2002 (SI 2002/1144) 173
Pollution Prevention and Control (Scotland) Regulations 2012 (SSI 2012/360) 50, 95
Schedule 1 95
Pyrotechnic Articles (Safety) Regulations 2015 (SI 2015/1553)......... 92
reg 3... 92
reg 6... 92
reg 7... 92, 93
regs 11 and 12.................................. 93
reg 11(1) 93
reg 11(2) 93
reg 20(2) 93
reg 20(4) 93
reg 21(2) 93
reg 25... 93
reg 26... 93
reg 31... 93
reg 32... 93
reg 33... 93
reg 52(1) 93
reg 62(1) 93
reg 62(3) 93
Schedule 1 92
Schedule 2 92
Schedule 3 93

Road Vehicles (Approval) Regulations 2020 (SI 2020/818)
Schedules 1 and 2 122–3
Road Vehicles (Construction and Use) Regulations 1986 (1988 SI/1078) 122
reg 54... 122
regs 55–57 122
reg 97... 122
Rules of the Air Regulations 2015 (SI 2015/840) 112
Schedule 1, s 3 112–13

Statutory Nuisance (Appeals) Regulations 1995 (SI 1995/2644)......... 55
Statutory Nuisance (Appeals) (Scotland) Regulations 1996 (SI 1996/1076)......... 55

Town and Country Planning (Environmental Impact Assessment) Regulations 2017 (SI 2017/571) 143
reg 2(1) 144, 148
reg 3... 144
reg 4(1) 144
reg 4(2) 144
reg 4(5) 144
reg 5(4) 145
reg 5(5) 145
reg 5(6) 145
reg 6(1) 145
reg 6(2) 145
reg 6(4) 145
reg 6(6) 145
reg 6(9) 145
reg 6(10) 146
reg 7... 146
(5) 145
reg 15... 149
(1) 148
(2) 148
(4) 148
(6) 148
(7) 148
reg 16... 149
reg 18(1) 148
reg 18(3) 148–9
reg 18(4) 149
reg 20... 150
(1) 150
(2) 150
(7) 150
reg 23... 150
reg 26... 144
reg 30(1) 150
reg 30(2), (3) 150
Schedule 1 144
para 24............................ 144
Schedule 2 ....144, 145
Schedule 3 145
Schedule 4 149
Town and Country Planning (Environmental Impact Assessment) (Scotland) Regulations 2017 (SSI 2017/102) 151
Town and Country Planning (Section 62A Applications) Order 2013 (SI 2013/2140) 150

Waste Management (Scotland) Regulations 2011 (SSI 2011/228)
regs 11–13B 95

European Legislation

Directive 85/337/EEC (assessment of the effects of certain public and private projects on the environment) 142
Directive 86/594/EEC (airborne noise emitted by household appliances) 98
Directive 89/686/EEC (personal protective equipment) 173
Directive 92/43/EEC (Habitats Directive)
arts 6 and 7 .... 152, 157
Directive 96/61/EC (integrated pollution and control)
Annex I 6, 129
Directive 2000/14/EC (noise emission from outdoor equipment) 97
art 1 97
Directive 2001/42/EC (Strategic Environmental Assessment (SEA) Directive) 152, 154–5, 156, 159
art 1 152
art 2 .... 153, 155
art 3 152
art 4 153
art 5 155
Annex I 156
Annex II 153, 156
Directive 2002/49/EC (Environmental Noise Directive (END)) 6, 21, 129, 139
art 1 .... 6, 129
art 2 .... 6, 129
art 3 .... 6, 7, 129, 130
art 4 .... 6, 129
art 5 130
art 6 130
art 7 130
art 8 .... 6, 131
art 9 131
art 9(1) 7
Annex I 130, 133
Annex II 130, 133
Annex IV 130
para 7 133
Annex V 6
Directive 2003/4/EC (public access to environmental information) 131
Directive 2003/10/EC (exposure of workers to noise) 170
Directive 2007/2/EC (establishing an infrastructure for Spatial Information (INSPIRE)) 131
Directive 2008/98/EC (Waste Framework Directive) 95
Directive 2010/75/EU (Industrial Emissions Directive) 94, 95
art 3 94
art 4 94
art 5 94
art 11 94
art 14 94
Directive 2011/92/EU (Environmental Impact Assessment Directive) 142, 143
art 1 .... 142, 143
art 2 .... 142, 143
Annex I 144
Directive 2013/29/EU (free movement of pyrotechnic articles) 92
art 6 92
Directive 2014/58/EU (traceability of pyrotechnic articles) 92
Directive 2014/92/EU (Payment Accounts Directive) 142

Regulation (EC) 1702/2003 (airworthiness and environmental certification of aircraft) 114
Regulation (EC) 216/2008 (common rules on civil aviation) 114
Regulation (EU) 748/2012 (airworthiness and environmental certification of aircraft) 113
Regulation (EU) 923/2012 (common rules of the air) 113
Regulation (EU) 139/2014 (aerodromes) 114
Regulation (EU) 598/2014 (noise-related restrictions at airports) 165
Regulation (EU) 2016/425 (personal protective equipment) 173
Regulation (EU) 2018/1139 (common rules on civil aviation) 113–14
art 9 114
art 62 114

Regulation (EU) 2018/1139 (common rules on civil aviation) (*cont.*)
art 75 114

International Documents

Convention on International Civil Aviation (the Chicago Convention)
Volume 1 of Annex 16 113–14

European Convention of Human Rights (ECHR) 99
art 8 ..... 99–102, 103–10, 120
(1) 103
(2) 102, 103
First Protocol, art 1 99–101

US National Environmental Policy Act 1969 141

Chapter 1

Introduction

THE DEVELOPMENT OF NOISE LAW AND POLICY

Unwanted sound or noise is indeed unique, in that it has prompted individuals who have been affected to commit murder.[1] Noise also enjoys the dubious distinction of having been used as an instrument of torture.[2] Environmental noise has been perennial in the UK since the Industrial Revolution. However, unlike other forms of pollution, noise has not been an emotive subject in the eyes of the general public. Individuals tend only to take an active interest in noise if they are personally affected. However, the importance of noise pollution is clear and beyond dispute. The World Health Organisation (WHO) has recognised that noise seriously harms human health and also interferes with peoples' daily activities at work, at home and during leisure time.[3] Noise can disturb sleep, cause cardiovascular and psychophysiological effects, reduce performance and also provoke annoyance responses and changes in social behaviour. The WHO expressed the view that traffic noise alone was harmful to the health of every third person in the WHO European region. Finally, one in five Europeans was exposed to sound levels at night that could significantly damage health. However, notwithstanding its importance, in terms of the development of environmental regulation as a whole, noise ranks as the Cinderella.[4] The lowly status of noise is no doubt due to the nature of noise. Noise is, of course, invisible. It leaves no residue and, therefore, does not have a 'fallout' factor. There can never be a noise disaster of a similar nature to that which afflicted either Bhopal or Seveso. Noise almost seems to have been tacitly accepted by society as the inevitable consequence of modern life. Indeed, in the Court of Appeal case of *AG v Hastings Corp*,[5] Tucker LJ laconically observed that, 'we move in an age of noise'. However, before proceeding to discuss the modern substantive law relating to noise, it is useful to give a brief mention of its chronological development.

---

1 See e.g. *Mitchell v Glasgow City Council* [2009] 1 AC 874. See also *Glasgow City Council v Ferguson* 2009 SLT (Sh Ct) 47.

2 See e.g. *Al Nashiri v Romania* (2019) 68 EHRR 3; *R(McGuigan) v Chief Constable of the Police Service of Northern Ireland* [2017] NIQB 96 and *Al Nashiri v Poland* (2015) 60 EHRR 16.

3 *https://www.who.int/europe/health-topics/noise* (last accessed 1 October 2022).

4 M Adams and F McManus, *Noise and Noise Law* (Wiley Chancery, 1994) at 151.

5 *AG v Hastings Corp* (1950) 94 Sol Jo. 225 at 225.

The nineteenth century

During the nineteenth century there was no national legislation that dealt with the subject of noise. Documentary evidence relating to noise pollution in the UK is sparse. However, given that heavy machinery was often employed in factories, etc. coupled with the fact that, due to poor planning controls, factories were often situated close to dwelling houses, noise must have been a widespread problem. Certain local authorities did, however, have byelaws (some of which survive today) that proscribed certain types of noise, for example, the playing of musical instruments on the streets, etc. to the annoyance of the general public.[6] However, such byelaws really only succeeded in scratching the surface of the problem.

The twentieth century

As far as the twentieth century was concerned, until 1960 there was no national legislation which dealt with noise. However, an effective pressure group[7] managed to secure the passing (by way a private member's Bill) of the Noise Abatement Act 1960 (repealed). The Act was rather unadventurous in that it simply grafted noise pollution on to the list of statutory nuisances that could be dealt with by a local authority, either under the Public Health Act 1936 or, in Scotland, by the Public Health (Scotland) Act 1897 (repealed). Little thought seems to have been accorded as to whether the rather technical law of nuisance was the appropriate instrument to deal with environmental noise in the community. The fact that it had to take a pressure group to effect a change in the law was, quite possibly, indicative not only of the lowly status then enjoyed by noise but, arguably, by environmental pollution in general.

While central government seemed to accord fairly low priority to the subject of noise pollution, it was not completely ignored. Indeed, noise was deemed sufficiently important for the government to set up a special expert group to investigate the subject. The remit of the Wilson Committee, which was appointed in 1960, was 'to examine the nature, sources and effects of the problem of noise and to advise what further measures can be taken to mitigate it'. The report[8] was somewhat bland and made some recommendations about minor changes in the law. Of importance was the fact that the committee was sanguine about the retention of the concept of nuisance as the principal instrument of the control of noise. Whilst the cynic of the present day can indeed quite easily cast a jaundiced eye at the report for its conservatism, the report did make some important recommendations about the practical measures which could be adopted to combat noise, especially from industrial and commercial premises. Indeed, BS 4142, which is used as a guide to predict potential noise nuisance from such premises owes its origin to the Wilson Report.

[6] The celebrated case of *Kruse v Johnson* [1898] 2 QB 91 centred on the legality of a byelaw that forbade the playing of musical instruments, etc. in certain circumstances.

[7] The Noise Abatement Society.

[8] Cmnd. 2056 (1963) 'Final Report on the Problem of Noise' (London: HMSO, 1963). See B. W. Clapp, *An Environmental History of Britain* (Longman, 1994) at 144.

The 1970s witnessed a growing awareness of the effects of pollution, in general, on the environment. There seemed also to be a distinct awareness by central government that a more holistic approach to environmental control was required. This resulted in the passage of the passage of the Control of Pollution Act 1974 (COPA), which was, indeed, revolutionary in its approach to environmental control. As far as noise was concerned, COPA continued to employ the concept of nuisance as a means of supressing environmental noise. However, Part III of COPA, which dealt with noise abatement zones (NAZs),[9] offered something more innovatory by way of noise pollution control. The purpose of a NAZ was to prevent so-called 'creeping noise', that is to say, noise that gradually increased in volume over a period of time.[10] It is important to observe that the concept of nuisance was redundant in the NAZ regime. However, local authorities did not embrace NAZs with much enthusiasm. Indeed, in Scotland no NAZs were established. About eighty-six NAZs were established in England and Wales.[11] The reason (which is based on scanty anecdotal evidence) for such reticence on the part of local authorities, was that they feared that the expense of setting up and monitoring a NAZ would far outweigh any public benefit that would accrue from the existence of a NAZ. In short, the concept of the NAZ, while theoretically beneficial, was simply unsustainable.

The 1980s witnessed a growing awareness that environmental noise was becoming worse.[12] The government responded by setting up a working party,[13] whose remit was to consider aspects of noise controls with particular reference to COPA. The working party, in effect, examined the efficacy of the principal instruments which were being employed in the UK at the time to control noise. The working party was supportive about retaining nuisance as the main instrument of noise control, as far as local authority responsibility for noise was concerned.[14] However, the working party did recommend making the creation of a noise nuisance an offence of strict liability.[15] The crude response to the report of the working party (the Batho Report), which

[9] The sections of Part III of COPA dealing with noise abatement zones have now been repealed.

[10] Under Part III of COPA the relevant local authority would measure noise emanating from premises in the relevant noise abatement zone and then enter that figure in a noise register. After the relevant figure was entered, the occupier of the premises was placed under an obligation not to allow the noise from the premises to exceed that figure. It was an offence for the occupier to allow noise from the premises to do so. Whereas COPA permitted a local authority to include premises of any nature and size in a NAZ, the government intended that a NAZ be restricted to industrial/residential or commercial/residential areas.

[11] In 2012 only two NAZs were in active use: *Abolishing Noise Abatement Zones* (DEFRA, 7 December 2012).

[12] The Secretary of State for the Environment, in an answer to a parliamentary question, stated that complaints about noise had doubled during the 1980s: HC Deb,18 October 1990 Vol 177 cols 878–881.

[13] See Noise Review Working Party Report (1990). The working party was chaired by Batho, W. It included representatives of local government, industry and voluntary bodies.

[14] This finding was supported by the findings of a National Society for Clean Air (NSCA) survey where only 18 per cent of local authorities in England and Wales considered that nuisance was no longer an appropriate standard to use: see the NSCA survey 1998, p 14. The NSCA survey 1999 (p 12) revealed that only 13 per cent of local authorities considered that nuisance was no longer an appropriate standard.

[15] Under Part III of the Environmental Protection Act 1990 a local authority is obliged to serve an abatement notice on the author of a nuisance. However, an offence is committed only if the terms of the relevant notice are flouted.

had drawn attention to the problem, was the passing of the Noise and Statutory Nuisance Act 1993, which gave local authorities *inter alia* power to deal with noise from burglar alarms and loudspeakers in streets or roads.

The 1990s experienced a rapid increase in the number of noise complaints to local authorities in relation to neighbourhood noise. The main problem stemmed from noise from hi-fi equipment, house parties and the like.[16] The legislative response to this perceived problem was the passage of the Noise Act 1996, which, *inter alia*, made the creation of noise an offence if it exceeded a given limit at night.[17] The Act introduced for the first time an objective standard against which noise could be measured. The Act, for some reason, was confined to England and Wales. The outstanding feature of the statute was that it eschewed the concept of nuisance and relied, rather, on fixed standards.

The twenty-first century

The late 1990s and early twenty-first century witnessed neighbourhood noise being viewed as part of a wider problem of antisocial behaviour, in general, rather than as a stand-alone problem. The Crime and Disorder Act 1998 allowed a local authority to lodge a complaint before a magistrates' court if the former believed that any person had acted in an antisocial manner, that is to say, in a manner that caused, or was likely to cause, harassment, alarm or distress to one or more persons, not being of the same household as themselves. Noise was, therefore, clearly included in the definition of 'antisocial'. The Act also allowed, *inter alia*, the court to make antisocial behaviour orders (ASBOs).[18] As far as Scotland was concerned, in its *Partnership for a Better Scotland*[19] the Scottish Government committed itself to social justice to ensure that everyone in Scotland could enjoy a decent quality of life. In particular, the creation of excessive neighbourhood noise was to be regarded as antisocial and, therefore, was required to be dealt with, in conjunction with other forms of antisocial conduct. The Antisocial Behaviour etc. (Scotland) Act 2004 (ABSA) makes provision for various forms of antisocial behaviour, amongst which is noise. Part 2 of the ABSA allows a sheriff (on the application of a relevant local authority), if they are satisfied that certain conditions are met, to make an ASBO. The provisions of Part 5 of the ABSA, which are adoptive in nature (that is to say, that the provisions of ABSA applied only if the relevant local authority so resolves) are roughly similar to those which are contained in the Noise Act 1996.

The Anti-social Behaviour, Crime and Policing Act 2014[20] contains a variety of provisions which are aimed at surpressing various forms of antisocial behaviour, including the power of an authorised person to issue community protection notices on an individual aged sixteen or over, or a body, if the authorised person is satisfied that the conduct of the individual, or body, is having a detrimental effect of a

[16] In the 1999 NSCA noise survey amplified music was top of the list of causes of complaint, for 62 per cent of respondents to the NSCA study: see p 7.

[17] The Noise Act 1996 was originally introduced in the House of Commons as a private member's Bill by H. Greenway, MP.

[18] The ASBO provisions of the 1998 Act were repealed by the Anti-social Behaviour, Crime and Policing Act 2014.

[19] Scottish Government, May 2003.

[20] Anti-social Behaviour, Crime and Policing Act 2014 s 43.

persistent or continuing nature on the quality of life of those living in the locality and that the conduct is unreasonable.

Whereas neither the UK Government, nor any of the devolved nations, has prepared a noise strategy outlining the direction that noise policy should take in the respective jurisdiction, in 2010 the UK Government published a *Noise Policy Statement for England* (NPSE).[21] The purported object of the NPSE was to 'provide clarity regarding current policies and practices to enable noise management decisions to be made within the wider context'. The NPSE set out a long-term vision for UK noise policy. That was to promote good health and a good quality of life through the effective management of noise, within the context of government policy on sustainable development. The NPSE set out three aims. The first was to avoid significant adverse effects on health and the quality of life from environmental, neighbour and neighbourhood noise, within the context of government policy on sustainable development. The second was to mitigate the adverse effects of such noise; and the third was, where possible, to contribute to the improvement of health and the quality of life through the effective management and control of environmental, neighbour and neighbourhood noise, within the context of government policy on sustainable development.

EU NOISE POLICY

No discussion of the development of noise in the UK would be complete without reference to the contribution of the EU.[22] The development of European noise policy was slow and, indeed, unimaginative. The earliest measures that were used by the EU to deal with noise were harmonisation measures that were aimed at specific products, such as vehicles, in order to eliminate barriers to trade and also to facilitate the free movement of goods within the EU. Ostensibly, at least, there was no EU noise policy. However, a change in direction was seen in the EU's Fifth Environmental Action Programme,[23] which dealt with the problem of urban noise. It was recognised that noise had a negative impact on human health. Under this programme a general environmental objective was established, to the effect that no person should be exposed to noise levels that endangered life and the quality of life. The next major development in EU noise policy was contained in the EC Green Paper *Future Noise Policy*,[24] which was published in 1996. Importantly, a major driving force, as far as such policy was concerned, was the impact of noise on human health. The Commission accepted the view that whereas the impact of noise is, essentially, a local responsibility and, therefore, best dealt with by Member States themselves, the

[21] *Noise Policy Statement for England*, *http://www.defra.gov.uk*, March 2010 (last accessed 4 October 2022).

[22] For a general discussion of the development of EU law and policy in the from the 1960s until the 1990s, see F. McManus and T. Burns, 'The Impact of EC Law on Noise Law in the United Kingdom' in J Holder (ed), *The Impact of EC Law in the United Kingdom* (Wiley, 1997) at 183. For a general discussion of the development of EU law and its impact on the UK see F. McManus 'Noise Pollution', paras 5.64–5.82 in F. McManus (ed), *Environmental Law in Scotland* (SULI, W.Green, looseleaf).

[23] Fifth Environmental Action Programme [1993] OJ C138/1.

[24] Commission Green Paper on Future Noise Policy, COM (96) 540 of 4 November 1996. See F. McManus, 'The EC Green Paper on Future Noise Policy and its impact on the United Kingdom' (1995) 5 European Public Law 125.

sources of noise pollution were best dealt with at EU level. Importantly, the Green Paper recognised that the lack of available data on noise was having a detrimental effect on the formulation of a coherent noise policy. The proposal for a Sixth Environmental Action Programme, which was published in 2001,[25] recognised that noise pollution affected both the health and the quality of life of at least 25 per cent of the EU population. The Action Programme set targets for the systematic reduction of the numbers of those who were affected by noise. The policy, which was embedded in the Action Programme, found expression in the EU Environmental Noise Directive (the END) relating to the assessment and management of noise.[26] The END Directive represents the most important measure the EU has taken, thus far, in battle against ambient noise. Indeed, the END represents the flagship of the EU's efforts to reduce ambient noise.

The END's main objective is to establish a common EU framework for the assessment and management of exposure to environmental noise[27] by using common methods of noise measurement and, furthermore, and importantly, ensuring that such information is made available to the public.[28] The END focuses mainly on transportation noise (rail, traffic, aircraft) and industrial noise. However, the END does not set limit values (i.e. noise levels that must not be exceeded) in any area. This is left to the discretion of the Member State. Thus, the principal of subsidiarity, which is engrained in EU law, is upheld.

The scope of the END is wide-ranging and it applies to environmental noise to which humans are exposed, particularly in built-up areas, in public parks or other quiet areas in an agglomeration,[29] in quiet areas in open country, and near schools, hospitals and other noise-sensitive buildings and areas.[30] However, the END does not apply to noise that is caused by the exposed person themselves, noise from domestic activities, noise created by neighbours, noise at workplaces, noise inside means of transport or noise that is caused by military activities in military areas. Overall responsibility for implementing the END lay with Member States who were required to designate competent authorities and bodies responsible for implementing the END.[31] Member States were required[32] to ensure that action plans which are designed to manage within the relevant territory, noise issues and effects, including noise reduction, were drawn up by the relevant competent authorities.[33] The END lays down minimum requirements as far as action plans are concerned.[34]

[25] European Commission, COM (2001) 31 January 2001.

[26] Directive 2002/49/EC.

[27] 'Environmental noise' is defined as unwanted or harmful outdoor sound created by human activities, including noise emitted by means of transport, road traffic, air traffic and from sites of industrial activity such as those defined in Annex I to Council Directive 96/61/EC of 24 September 1996 concerning integrated pollution prevention and control.

[28] Directive 2002/49/EC art 1.

[29] An agglomeration is defined as 'part of a territory, delimited by the Member State having a population in excess of 100,000 persons and a population density such that the Member State considers it to be an urbanised area': Directive 2002/49/EC art 3.

[30] Directive 2002/49/EC art 2.

[31] Directive 2002/49/EC art 4.

[32] By 18 July 2008.

[33] Directive 2002/49/EC art 8.

[34] Directive 2002/49/EC Annex V.

A fundamental problem that has been associated with noise pollution, whether it takes the form either of ambient or neighbourhood noise, is that the public are generally unaware of both the nature and also the levels of noise that affect their locality. Such a general lack of insight into the problem has profoundly affected the accountability of local authorities who are charged with the responsibility of implementing the law relating to noise.[35] The END attempts to address at least some of the problem by requiring Member States to ensure that both strategic noise maps[36] and also action plans, are made available and also disseminated to members of the public.[37] Importantly, the information requires to be clear, comprehensible and accessible. Furthermore, a summary, which sets out the most important points, requires to be provided.

No introduction to noise law and policy would be complete without making brief reference to the implications of Brexit. The UK's leaving the EU, which has had a profound effect in the shaping of UK environmental law, especially in relation to water, air pollution and waste, certainly leaves a legislative gap. It would indeed take the foresight of a Hebrew prophet to predict the direction the law will take in the wake of Brexit. In this context, reference must, of course, be made to the Environment Act 2021 that has been recently passed by Parliament. The Act, *inter alia*, makes provision for targets, plans and policies for improving the natural environment. Under s 1(1) a duty is placed on the Secretary of State to set long-term targets for any matter which relates to the natural environment, or people's enjoyment of the natural environment. In turn, under s 8(1) the Secretary of State is required to prepare an environmental improvement plan, which is defined in s 8(2) as a plan for significantly improving the natural environment. Under s 44 the expression 'natural environment' includes 'air'. In turn, s 45 defines, 'environmental protection', *inter alia*, as protection of the natural environment from the effects of human activity. Such activity, of course, could include the generation of environmental noise, through the medium of air. Under s 17(1) and (2) the Secretary of State is under a duty to prepare a policy statement on environmental principles, that is to say, how such principles should be interpreted and proportionately applied by ministers of the Crown when making policy. Under s 17(5) the term 'environmental principles' means:

(a) the principle that environmental protection should be integrated into the making of environmental policies;
(b) the principle of preventative action to avert environmental damage;
(c) the precautionary principle so far as relating to the environment; and
(d) the principle that environmental damage should as a priority, be rectified at source; and
(e) the polluter pays principle.

It will be interesting to observe the extent, if any, to which noise will feature in any such targets or plans in the future. Will the Act elevate the importance of noise on the political agenda?

---

35 See F. McManus, 'Noise law in the United Kingdom – a very British solution' (2000) 20 LS 264 at 282.
36 A strategic noise map means a map that is designated for the global assessment of noise exposure in a given area due to noise sources or for overall predications of such an area: Directive 2002/49/EC art 3.
37 Directive 2002/49/EC art 9(1).

Chapters 2 and 3 of *Noise and Noise Law* provide the reader with an overview of the scientific background to noise, with special reference to the practitioner. The book then goes on to discuss both the common law and statutory controls over noise. Finally, as stated in the preface, the environment is a devolved function in the UK. The central authority of each nation is, therefore, responsible for formulating noise policy within its jurisdiction.

Chapter 2

Basic Acoustics and Human Sound Perception

INTRODUCTION

This chapter introduces some important factors in the understanding of sound, sound propagation and transmission, and sound perception without, as far as possible, any maths or complex scientific descriptions. There are plenty of text books available that do include this greater level of detail, but this chapter, and the one that follows it, are intended as a general introduction to those who may need a working knowledge of some of the concepts involved and, in particular, how they may affect legal arguments and the formulation of legal cases.

It outlines the objective concepts that are used to describe sound, together with a brief introduction to the way sound is perceived and how it can lead to annoyance and, possibly, nuisance.

It is important that any legal considerations are properly informed by reference to objective measurement and assessment, in order that any decision-makers can properly take them into consideration and that those presenting the arguments, on both sides, understand the work of the expert witnesses, on both sides, and their reports.

BASIC ACOUSTICS

Sound pressure level

Sound is, essentially, rapidly fluctuating pressure above and below the resting pressure of the atmosphere. The average atmospheric pressure at sea level is just over 100,000 Pascals; Pascals being the international standard (SI) unit of pressure. The lowest pressure fluctuations that can be detected by the ear are around five billion times less at 20 micro-Pascals. As the pressure fluctuations increase, the corresponding sound gets louder, up to the point where it becomes physically uncomfortable to listen to, which occurs at a fluctuation level of around 20 pascals where physical damage to the hearing mechanism can occur.

It can readily be seen that representing the magnitude of the sound using the physical attributes of the pressure signal, as it oscillates above and below atmospheric pressure, is unwieldy. It needs to be quantified in such a way that an unchanging level of sound can be quantified with a single unchanging number. Additionally, because the loudest sounds of interest are approximately one million times greater than the quietest, in the 1930s the magnitude of sound began to be expressed in terms of

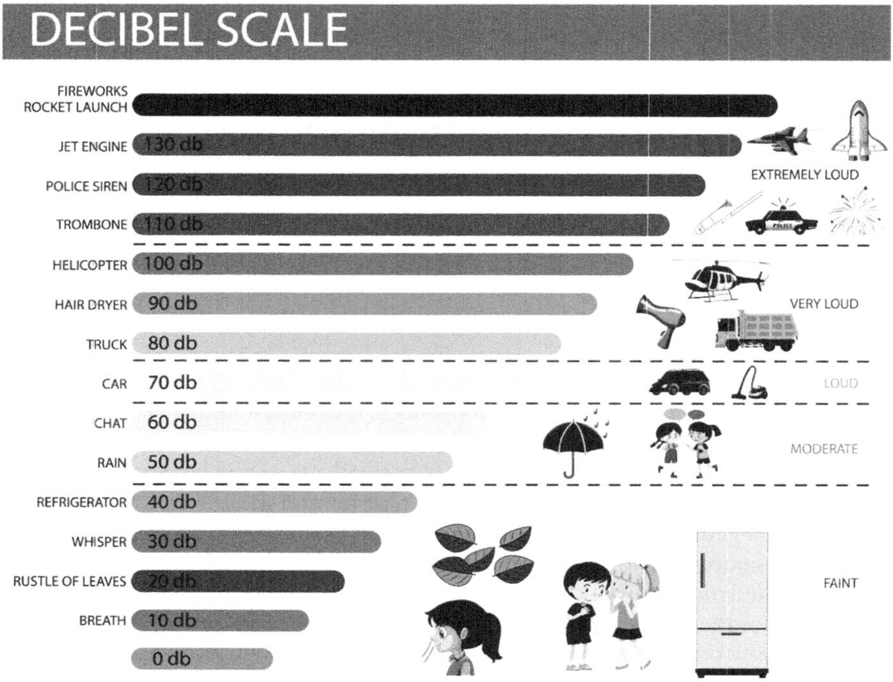

Figure 2.1 The Decibel Scale

the ratio of the average pressure level of the sound of interest over a very short period (see 'time weightings' in Chapter 2) to a reference level of 20 micro-pascals; the results of this ratio being expressed as a logarithmic value, multiplied by 20 to provide a convenient scale for use in measurements and assessments. This is the basis of the decibel (dB) scale which is used ubiquitously today to quantify '*sound pressure level*', which forms the basic unit of sound although, in practice, it is not a unit but a ratio.

The reference level used in the decibel calculation, of 20 micro-pascals, equates to 0 dB, with the corresponding threshold of pain occurring at a level of around 140 dB. This 0–140 dB is the approximate 'dynamic range' available to healthy human ears (i.e. between sounds that can only just be heard, to those which cause pain).

Sound power level

Sound pressure level should not be confused with *sound power level*, as they are entirely different concepts. It is almost inevitable that confusion arises because both are expressed in dB and both relate to sound. However, just as sound pressure level is the ratio of the *pressure* fluctuations received at the measurement point to a reference pressure, expressed as a logarithmic value as described above, sound power level is the ratio of the acoustic *power* of the source, in watts (the unit of power), to a reference power of 10^{-12} watts, also with the results expressed as a logarithmic value.

Broadly speaking, if a 'sound level' is quoted with no reference to the location, or the distance, at which it was measured, then, to have any meaning it must be assumed that it is a sound *power* level.

Frequency or pitch

The rate of fluctuation of the air pressure producing the sound gives the sound its apparent pitch. A slower rate of variation causes the perception of a lower pitched sound and, correspondingly, a faster rate of variation causes the perception of a higher pitched sound. This rate of variation is referred to as the *frequency* of the sound and it is measured in pressure cycles per second or Hertz (Hz). The human ear is less sensitive to sounds at high and low frequencies than to sounds in the middle of the hearing range, which results in low and high frequency sounds appearing to be quieter at the same sound pressure level. This change in sensitivity with frequency is referred to as the 'frequency response' of the ear, which is most sensitive to sounds at the frequencies corresponding to the weaker sounds of speech known as the 'unvoiced fricatives' ('f', 's' and 'th', for example), probably to do with the evolution of speech communication, This most sensitive part of the hearing range covers frequencies just above the middle of the audible range of frequencies where the hearing threshold (the quietest sounds that can be heard at that frequency) is actually lower than the 0 dB reference level, referred to above, at about -10 dB.

Apart from some musical sounds, sounds from various specific mechanical sources and those produced for scientific or analytical purposes, such as hearing tests, most sounds are made up of many different frequencies. Most sounds, particularly those in the general environment, are quantified in terms of their dB(A) or dBA value, which means that an 'A-weighting curve' is applied to the measurement device (usually a 'sound level meter'). This compensates for the frequency response of the ear, discussed above, by applying reduction in measured level to sounds of lower and higher frequency than those in the middle of the hearing range. This will be discussed in more detail in Chapter 3, which addresses the way sound is measured and assessed, rather than on the way it behaves and the way it is perceived, which is the purpose of this chapter.

Sound propagation

Sound is produced by anything that vibrates in the surrounding atmosphere, causing fluctuating air pressure in its immediate vicinity, which is then transmitted by, and through, the atmosphere to the receiver (normally the ear), rather akin to ripples on an otherwise still pond surface. For a single small sound source (a 'point source') in free space (i.e. with no reflections), the distance to the receiver causes the sound pressure level to reduce (or 'attenuate') by 6 dB every time the distance from the source doubles. Where the source of sound is large compared to the distance to the receiver, this rate of decrease no longer applies. A good example of this is for traffic on a busy road where distance causes the sound pressure level to decay at a reduced rate of 3 dB per doubling of distance from the road instead of the standard 6 dB discussed above.

In practice, there are other factors that need to be taken into account, including attenuation by the atmosphere, which is more significant for high frequency sound than low frequency sound, hence why low bass notes from a music venue may appear to travel further than other music noise. Other factors that can be significant are the effects of sound reflections, which can increase the received sound pressure level and physical barriers between the source and the receiver, which normally reduce it and which, as with atmospheric attenuation, reduce low frequency sound more than high frequency sound.

SOUND INSIDE A BUILDING AND SOUND TRANSMISSION

Sound inside a building behaves very differently to sound outside, and the effect of reflections become much more important. In fact, when we are inside, our ears tend to receive more reflected sound, due to the build-up of reflections from the room surfaces, than direct sound. In practice, this depends on how absorbent the surfaces of walls, ceilings and floors are, with harder surfaces causing stronger reflections. In a very big room or building, the first reflections are perceived as echoes due to the time it takes for the sounds to be reflected from more distant surfaces. The effect of the combined delay and strength of these echoes are referred to as the *reverberation time* of the space. A shorter reverberation time can be more conducive to understanding speech because of the lack of overlap of the individual elements thereof, whereas a longer reverberation time can make music sound fuller and more pleasant to listen to. It can even improve speech to a certain degree, because it has the effect of making it sound louder due to the combination of all the reflections, so a balance has to be found whereby acoustical engineers install different levels of absorption, depending on the purposes of the space.

The extent to which sound is transmitted between different rooms in the same building is crucial to residential amenity, especially where it occurs between different residential units, such as within blocks of flats. For a given sound source, the amount of sound that is transmitted depends on the reverberation time of the room containing it, that of the room in which the receiver is situated, and the construction of the building elements (walls and ceilings/floors) separating them. Generally speaking, the sound-reducing capability of such elements depends on their weight. Therefore, a brick wall will be much more effective in reducing sound than a plasterboard wall (a wooden structure faced with plasterboard on both sides). Although absorbent material, which has no sound reduction properties itself, is usually included between the two plasterboard 'skins', this is to prevent the build-up of reflections within the structure and improve its overall performance.

As well as travelling through the air, sound can also be transmitted by the solid elements of the structure. In addition to insulation, isolation in the form of 'flexible' joints, such as rubber, between building elements may also be necessary to prevent such structural transmission and to reduce airborne transmission between two spaces. This would apply to, say, footsteps in a first floor flat being transmitted by the building structure and re-radiated as sound within a ground floor flat. However, sound in a room, as well as direct vibration, can also be transmitted to another one by the structure.

As well as sound transmission between rooms, or other acoustic spaces, sound transmission from outside to inside a building, and vice versa, can be equally as important although, in this case, it is usually the windows that are the acoustically-weakest points. Sound transmission through a roof/ceiling can also be significant, as this tends to allow more sound transmission than standard cavity walls. The amount of sound reduction afforded by standard double glazing is quite significant, although the seals, particularly around opening windows are critical for optimising performance. Improved acoustic performance is achieved by increasing the weight of the glass in the panes and the separation distance between them. For critical applications, further improvements can be made by using different thickness of glass in two isolated panes that are slightly off-parallel.

As for barriers and atmospheric attenuation, sound transmission between rooms and from outside to inside, and vice versa, is greater for lower frequency sounds than for those of higher frequency, so the amount and type of insulation required will vary, depending on the nature of the sound.

THE HEARING MECHANISM

Sounds arriving at our ears, as pressure variations, travel down the external ear canal and cause the eardrum to vibrate. This section of the hearing mechanism is referred to as the 'outer ear'. The vibrations of the ear drum are then transmitted by the small bones of the 'middle ear' (the smallest bones in the human body) to the 'inner ear', which comprises the 'cochlea', the organ of hearing, and the 'semi-circular canals', the organ of balance.

The middle ear is connected to the back of the throat by the 'eustachian tube', which is normally closed to protect the middle ear from infection. It opens, however, when we yawn or swallow partly in order to ventilate the middle ear, which, apart from the bones, is an air-filled cavity, but also, and more importantly, to equalise the pressure in the cavity with that in the external ear canal. If the pressure is not equal, it results in slight temporary deafness or even pain due to difference in pressures pushing or pulling the eardrum outside its normal operating position. This pressure difference normally results from relatively sudden changes in height, such as when an aircraft takes off or lands, and the eustachian tube fails to open as required. The ability of the tube to open can be hampered by excessive secretions in the middle ear, which normally pass down the tube, such as might occur with a common cold. The resulting delay in pressure equalisation can cause extended pain and deafness. This is why children's eardrums are sometimes fitted with 'grommets', which are tiny tubes inserted into the ear drum to keep the pressure on either side permanently equalised, improving hearing and reducing pain during childhood and which fall out in due course. The three bones of the middle ear form a system of levers that transfer the relatively large but weak movements of the eardrum to the cochlea which requires smaller, higher strength, movements to stimulate the fluid system it contains. These levers are controlled to an extent by the brain such that, for sudden loud sounds, they change the way in which they operate to reduce the signals entering the inner ear. This is referred to as the '*acoustic reflex*'.

It is not proposed to discuss the functioning of the semi-circular canals, which constantly monitor our head's position and any movements it makes, enabling us to balance, except to note that they are connected to the cochlea, the other component of the inner ear, and shares the fluid with part of the cochlea. The cochlea itself is a spiral tube of about 30 mm in length that contains three separate fluid-filled

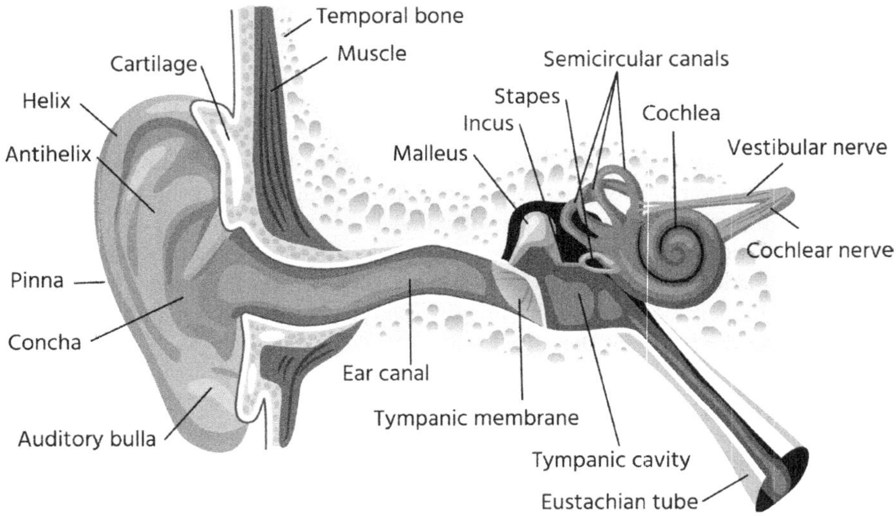

Figure 2.2 The Hearing Mechanism

tubes, or 'ducts'. One of these, the vestibular duct, has a small opening covered with a membrane (the '*oval window*') in which the third and smallest bone of the middle ear, the '*stapes*', is positioned to transmit the vibrations of the eardrum into the cochlea. These vibrations, which travel along the '*vestibular duct*' from the oval window and back down the '*tympanic duct*' to the '*round window*', a similar opening, cause hairs on cells in the middle duct, which separates the other two, to move. As they move, these cells (the '*hair* cells') transmit signals to the brain in line with the vibrations of the hairs of the cells that, in turn, depend on the vibration in the fluid as stimulated by the movement of the stapes. There are four rows of hair cells consisting of 3,500 hairs in an inner row, which send signals along the auditory nerve to the brain, and a further 12,000 in three outer rows which receive signals back from the brain, as part of an internal feedback system that improves on the cochlea's mechanical inherent electro-mechanical properties to enable it to respond more accurately to the very complex signals it receives, and to translate them into the electrical impulses the brain needs to process them.

When the hearing mechanism goes wrong, causing hearing loss, it can result from problems in either the outer and middle ear, referred to as '*conductive hearing loss*'; or in the inner ear or auditory nerve, referred to as '*sensori-neural hearing loss*'. Conductive hearing loss can result from a blockage, damage to the eardrum or damage to, or malfunction of, the middle ear bones. Sensori-neural hearing loss results from damage to the hair cells due to genetic issues, infection, high levels of noise exposure or from the ageing process. In the case of one-sided hearing loss, it could be indicative of a possible tumour on the auditory nerve. The big difference between the two types of hearing loss is that conductive hearing loss reduces the level of *all* sounds, albeit by different amounts, depending on frequency, whereas sensori-neural hearing loss means that quiet sounds are no longer audible. However, loud sounds are audible at normal levels, thus reducing the dynamic range of the ear.

In this respect, conductive hearing loss can be considered to be frequency-dependent attenuation whereas sensori-neural hearing loss is a malfunction of the mechanism that translates the sound into electrical signals going to the brain. This means that hearing aids can be quite effective for conductive hearing loss, which can be overcome by selective amplification at different frequencies. They are, however, much less useful for sensori-neural hearing loss, which requires the faulty processing mechanism to be compensated for in some way and this is not necessarily possible with a basic hearing aid. The situation can be improved to a certain extent, however, with various types of signal processing. which are increasingly available within commercially available hearing aids.

SOUND PERCEPTION

The way sounds are perceived depends on their nature, including how loud they appear; the relative sound pressure levels of sounds of different frequency contained within the overall sound; any specific 'acoustic features' which are present such as tones (sounds of specific pitch), impulses (sudden sounds or repetitive or intermittent sudden changes in level); or anything else that draws attention to the sound.

Non-acoustic factors can also be very significant in determining how we perceive and respond to what we hear. These factors can include the information content of the sound; the way we feel about the producer of the sound; the extent to which we have control over the sound; the time of day; the activity we are engaged in at the time the sound occurs; and many other social, economic and psychological considerations that may, in some cases, be more significant than the acoustical characteristics of the sound itself. The sound of road traffic noise, for instance, is generally accepted by people who live in urban environments but the sound of music from a neighbouring property, at the same sound pressure level, may well not be.

The human ear is commonly said to perceive sounds from low frequencies, from around 20 Hz, to high frequencies around 20,000 Hz (20 kHz) but, in fact, sounds outside this frequency range can also be perceived – although not necessarily as identifiable sound – but only if the sound pressure level is high enough. A more complete description is that the sensitivity of the ear gradually reduces from its most sensitive region around 1,000 to 4,000 Hz and this continues into the region below 20 Hz, which is referred to as infrasound. Similar effects occur at high frequencies extending into the ultrasound region above 20,000 Hz.

The threshold of pain does not change significantly with frequency, meaning that the ear has a much-reduced dynamic range at low and high frequencies, possibly as little as a few decibels at the highest and lowest ends of the frequency range, meaning that a sound can go from completely inaudible to very uncomfortable with a very small change in sound pressure level for these types of sounds.

EFFECTS OF UNWANTED SOUND

The reader will note that the term 'sound' has been used up to this point rather than 'noise' which, although integral to the title of this book, can be a highly emotive word albeit that it is widely used in legislative terminology. 'Sound' is the all-encompassing word for anything that we perceive in our brains as a result of pressure fluctuations at our ears. All noise is sound but not all sound is 'noise'. Noise is a purely subjective description and was defined in the final report by the Committee on the Problem of Noise,[1] sometimes called the Wilson Report, as 'sound which is undesired by the recipient'. This was one of the earliest reports on the effects of unwanted sound, or noise, in the environment, as opposed to in buildings, and it was published in 1963.

Both noise in the environment, and in buildings can, depending on its level, cause interference with communication; noise-induced hearing loss; sleep disturbance of various types; effects on performance and activities; and annoyance. Annoyance can, in turn, cause stress, which may lead to sleep disturbance and other adverse health effects. Any combination of the factors causing annoyance can lead to a noise being considered to be a 'nuisance' in the legal sense of the word, although noise-induced hearing loss is not normally considered as a nuisance issue. Unlike other forms of noise exposure, it occurs in the workplace and has ongoing physical consequences that persist after exposure to the noise has ceased.

The effects of different types of noise, as it varies with sound pressure level, is often quantified by 'dose response' curves which are based on research and show the way annoyance increases as sound pressure level increases. These are different for different sources of noise because of the difference in attitudes (the non-acoustic factors discussed above). This means that one source of noise may show as being more annoying than another at the same noise level. In addition, individual responses will vary significantly above and below the average response so average dose response curves, based on research, may be of limited value in individual cases. Such dose response curves can also depend on the way the noise is quantified, as this can be done in different ways. Specific ways of quantifying noise, over and above what can be done through instantaneous measurements of sound pressure level, are referred to as noise 'metrics' or 'indices' and are discussed further in Chapter 3.

It is very clear that noise which is generated by identifiable individuals, such as neighbours, or that generated by industrial premises, is much more annoying at the same level, than noise that is caused by sources that are anonymous in nature, such as that from road traffic, as discussed in the previous section. Noise from natural sources, such as wild bird song, rivers and streams, waves lapping, etc. is very rarely a cause of annoyance and it should also, of course, be noted that what is 'wanted sound' for some people may be unwanted sound for others. This is particularly so in the case of music sources, but even low sound pressure level sources such as garden wind chimes. A very important consideration in respect of annoyance, where it is generated by an individual, is whether or not the noise is seen to be preventable, or whether it represents lack of consideration by the generator of the noise towards the receiver. Conversely, where the source of the noise provides some benefit to the recipient, such as employment or other financial benefit, annoyance will be less for noise at the same sound pressure level.

[1] Final Report of the Committee on the Problem of Noise (HMSO 1963).

Chapter 3

The Measurement and Assessment of Noise

INTRODUCTION

The purpose of this chapter is to explain how noise is quantified using a 'sound level meter' with its basic function explained and the various options that are available for assessing the noise in various circumstances, in order to provide objective assessments of noise as it affects people. In this chapter the word 'noise' will be used rather than sound, bearing in mind the commentary in the previous chapter on the fact that noise is essentially unwanted sound and, for the most part, this is why it is being assessed. It should, however, be borne in mind that unwanted sound is often heard in the context of 'wanted' sound. However, for the purposes of brevity, noise will be used, in most cases, to cover the measurements and assessments described in this chapter.

THE SOUND LEVEL METER

It is rather ironic, perhaps, in the context of the above, that noise measurements are made using a device called a 'sound level meter', which is used to quantify 'sound pressure level'. But, of course, such an electronic device is incapable of making such a distinction! Sound pressure level is explained in Chapter 1 and is a way of quantifying a sound that is constant in level as a single number value expressed in decibels (dB).

Basic function

A sound level meter consists of a microphone, which converts the fluctuating sound pressure into a fluctuating electrical signal corresponding precisely, subject to certain tolerances, to the pressure signal it is being used to measure. This is converted by electronic circuitry to a fixed voltage corresponding to the voltage fluctuations over a specified very short time period referred to as the 'time-weighting', as discussed very briefly under the definition of sound pressure level in Chapter 1. The specifications for sound level meters are very precise in respect of microphone directivity, frequency response and linearity (changes in noise level being accurately matched by changes in reported sound pressure level) and are regulated by the provisions of BS EN 61672, *Electroacoustics – Sound Level Meters*. This document provides specifications for two 'classes' of meter: Class 1 and Class 2 with Class 1 meters normally being use for environmental noise measurements due to their superior performance.

Time-weightings and sound level meter displays

There are three time-weightings in use; slow, fast and impulse, corresponding to integration times of 1 second, 125 milliseconds and 35 milliseconds respectively. In the past, the sound level meter display consisted of a moving needle on a scale. The needle moved slower or faster depending on the time weighting and a degree of 'eyeball' averaging could be achieved by use of the slow weighting. With the current use of digital displays, the display changes too rapidly to allow such visual averaging.

Longer term averaging

In practice, sound in the environment is only very rarely constant. The measured sound pressure level is, therefore, constantly varying, to a greater or lesser extent, depending on the sound, or combination of sounds, reaching the sound level meter. Because of this, the most commonly used noise measurement index, the '*equivalent continuous sound level*' (dB $L_{eq,t}$), is the level of sound that, if continuous, would have the same acoustic energy as that fluctuating sound. This represents a way of quantifying the sound pressure level, as it varies with time, over a given measurement interval, 't'. Where an A-weighting, as discussed below and in Chapter 1, is applied by the sound level meter, the result is expressed as a dB $L_{Aeq,t}$ value. This is discussed further under noise measurement indices below.

Compensating for the frequency response of the ear

As discussed in Chapter 1, the threshold of hearing for the human ear varies with frequency, with the ear being less sensitive at low and high frequencies. This can be referred to as the 'frequency response' of the ear at threshold and is compensated for by setting the sound level meter to apply the 'A' weighting as part of its initial processing of the noise signal. This is rather akin to using a graphic equaliser or other tone controls on audio equipment.

The ear's frequency response changes, however, as sounds get louder, meaning that the apparent difference in volume between sounds at low frequency, e.g. 50 Hz, and mid-frequency, e.g. 1000Hz, at the same sound pressure level, becomes less as the sound pressure level increases. In this way, music listened to at low volume will appear to have less low frequency (bass) content than at medium or high listening levels. This is the purpose of a loudness switch on a hi-fi amplifier, which applies a high level of bass boost at low volume settings and progressively reduces as volume level is increased.

To accommodate this changing frequency response, sound level meters have also included other weighting settings, known as 'frequency weightings'; B-weighting to approximate the ears response to mid-range sound pressure levels and C-weighting to approximate its response to high sound pressure levels. An additional D-weighting, which added a substantial peak to the response at 3,000 and 4,000 Hz, was also made available to replicate the human subjective response to turbojet* aircraft noise but neither this, nor the B-weighting, is now included in specifications for sound level meters.[1] The C-weighting is, however, still used, mostly so that results using this

* As opposed to modern turbofan jet engines.

[1] BS EN 61672-1:2013, *Electroacoustics – Sound level meters – Part 1: Specifications* (BSI, 2013).

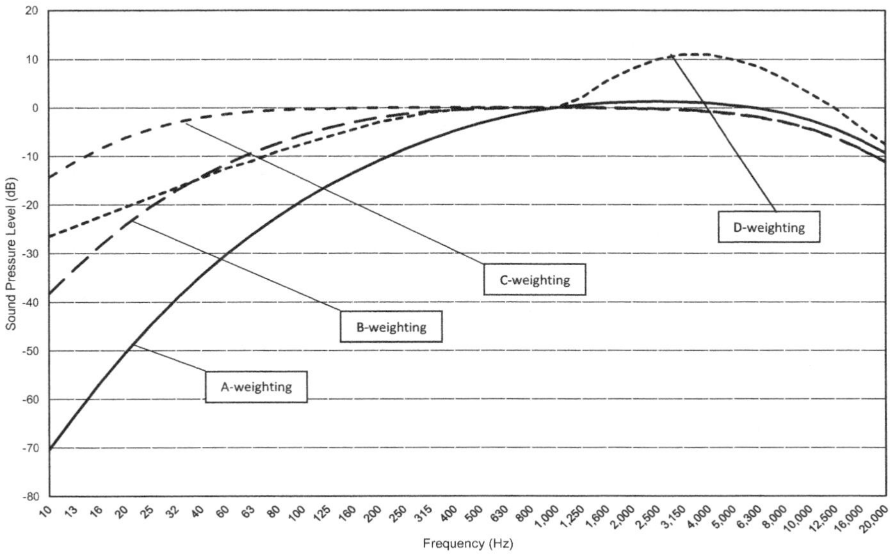

Figure 3.1 Sound Level Meter Weighting Curves

weighting can be compared with those obtained using the A-weighting in order to provide an indication of the relative amount of low frequency content in the noise in the absence of more detailed (frequency specific) measurements that will be covered later in this chapter. It can also be used as an approximation to a linear response (i.e. with no weighting) to evaluate 'peak' sound level, for example, for the purposes of the Noise at Work Regulations.[2] The peak sound level is the maximum sound pressure generated by a sound source over a given time period without any 'time-weighting' (see earlier) being applied. It is quite distinct from the maximum sound pressure level over the same time period, which would have a different value depending on the time-weighting applied to the integration process used to quantify it.

There are two further frequency weightings in use, consisting of the G-weighting and the Z-weighting. The G-weighting is intended to approximate the human ear's response to sound pressure levels below 20 Hz, which is sometimes, erroneously, considered to be the lower bound of human hearing (see Chapter 1). By using this weighting, the significance of noise in the sub-20 Hz region can be evaluated without reference to the specific frequency at which it occurs. The resultant G-weighted result will show the level of the noise in relation to the threshold of perception that is normally considered to be at a level of 85 dB(G). The Z-weighting approximates a linear weighting but allows for the fact that standard noise measurement instrumentation is unlikely to be able to provide a linear response below 10 Hz or above 20 kHz so instead it specifies a linear response between these two values.

[2] The Control of Noise at Work Regulations 2005 (SI 2005/1643).

QUANTIFICATION OF VARYING NOISE LEVEL

dB/dB(A) and maximum and minimum levels

As previously discussed, the basic noise measurement index is the decibel (dB), more usually the A-weighted decibel dB(A). However, for most purposes, as discussed above, this value is constantly changing in response to the changes in the noise environment being measured. This variation is obvious for passing traffic, trains and over-flying aircraft. But even noise sources that are relatively steady, for example from industry or construction; general noise in the environment (usually distant road traffic); other sound of human origin; or natural sounds, are constantly varying. This means that, in most cases, a simple dB or dB(A) reading of the instantaneous noise level every 125 milliseconds or 1 second (see time weightings (above)) cannot be used to quantify the noise environment except, possibly to indicate the range from the minimum (L_{min} or L_{Amin}) to the maximum noise level (L_{max} or L_{Amax}) over a given time period.

Equivalent continuous sound level (L_{eq})

Because of the limitations in assessing a rapidly varying noise level in overall terms, a number of other measurement indices are available and implemented on sound level meters in order to provide further quantification of the noise environment as it varies over a specified time period, 't'. The most commonly used of these is the equivalent continuous sound pressure level, measured in dB $L_{eq,t}$, or dB $L_{Aeq,t}$, dB $L_{Ceq,t}$, etc. where the signal is frequency weighted using the A or C weighting. A common time period for assessment would be one hour ($L_{Aeq,\,1hr}$), such as is used for construction noise (see BS 5228[3]) and daytime industrial/commercial noise,[4] although shorter or longer periods may be specified for other specific purposes. For instance, ten minutes is used for wind turbine noise, which varies with wind speed, with both of these being measured over the same time period. In this instance, however, it is the L_{A90} value, as discussed under statistical noise indices (below), which is used rather than L_{Aeq}. This is discussed further under ETSU-R-97[5] in the final section of this chapter. Noise in the workplace is evaluated over a whole working day[2] and aircraft noise over a sixteen hour day.*

For the purposes of sleep disturbance, the World Health Organisation (WHO) refers to the external night-time L_{Aeq} over a whole year quantified as L_{night},[6] although it is more likely such values would be derived through sampled noise level over shorter periods and/or predictions rather than through actual measurement over a whole year.

---

[3] BS5228-1:2009+A1:2014, *Code of Practice for Noise and Vibration Control on Construction and Open Sites, Part 1: Noise* (BSI, 2014).

[4] BS4142:2014+A1:2019, *Methods for Rating and Assessing Industrial and Commercial Sound* (BSI, 2019).

[5] ETSU-R-97, *The Assessment and Rating of Noise from Wind Farms* (DTI, 1996).

* See for instance, *Noise exposure contours around London airports*, *https://www.gov.uk/government/publications/noise-exposure-contours-around-london-airports* (last accessed 10 October 2022).

[6] WHO, *Night Noise Guidelines for Europe* (WHO, 2009).

Other indices based on L_{Aeq}

The *day-evening-night noise level* (L_{den}), as referred to in the European Environmental Noise Directive[7] is similar to the L_{night} as used in the WHO *Night Noise Guidelines for Europe*, insofar as it considers noise over a whole year, but the L_{den} considers noise from all periods of the day by calculating the daytime (7am–7pm) L_{Aeq}, the evening period (1900–2300) L_{Aeq} and the night-time (11pm–7am) L_{Aeq} over a whole year, adding 5 dB to the evening level and 10 dB to the night-time level. This allows for the increased sensitivity to noise during these periods. This should not be confused with the *day-night* noise level L_{dn}, used in the USA, which treats the evening period the same as for the daytime.

One further L_{Aeq}-based noise measurement index of note is the sound exposure level (SEL or sometimes LAE). This also used to be known as the single event level, which is a better description of what it is, which is an L_{Aeq} noise measurement over the duration of an event, normalised to a period of one second; effectively the sound energy level of an individual event. Where an L_{Aeq} measurement is made of a single event, the L_{Aeq} value will depend on how long the measurement is set to run on either side of the event taking place. By normalising the result to one second, the measurement duration is no longer significant as long as it captures the whole of the event and the results can be compared with similar measurements with different measurement durations.

Statistical indices (Ln)

An alternative to L_{eq} for assessing noise level, *L*, over a period of time, is to evaluate the noise level that is exceeded for a given percentage (N) of the measurement period (L_N, or L_{AN} when 'A' weighted). Common examples of this are the L_{A90}, which is used to quantify '*background noise level*' in British Standard BS 4142,[4] and L_{A10}, which is used for traffic noise predictions pertaining, *inter alia*, to the Noise Insulation Regulations. L_{A01} and L_{A99} can be used as surrogates for L_{Amax} and L_{Amin} with L_{A50} also substituting for L_{Aeq} because all of these have the advantage of giving less weight to atypical or unusual events or circumstances. One further index that is worth noting is the N_x index, used for aircraft noise assessment, which refers to the number of 'events' that exceed a specific (A-weighted) decibel level, X.

It should be noted that the indices referred to above do not comprise a complete list and other indices have been, and are currently, used for specific purposes and by different regulatory bodies as required.

ASSESSING THE SIGNIFICANCE OF TONES IN THE NOISE (FREQUENCY ANALYSIS)

It may be noted that all of the above deal with overall noise levels, albeit weighted according to the frequency response of the ear or other weighting. Far more precision, in terms of perceptibility, can be achieved by dividing the measured noise levels into different 'frequency bands' using electronic filters either in the sound level meter or,

[7] EU Directive 2002/49/EC, The Assessment and Management of Environmental Noise.

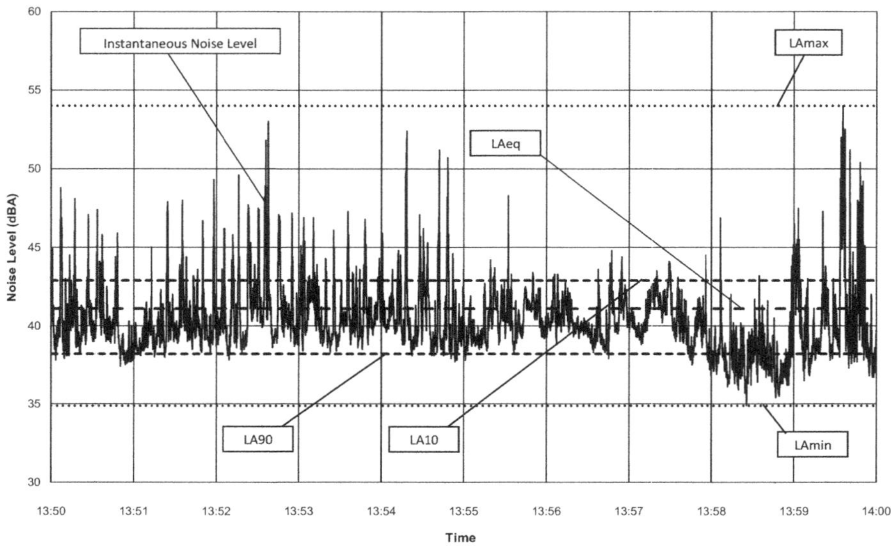

Figure 3.2 Noise Indices

for post-processing of audio data recorded by it, on a separate recording device. The simplest of these are low-pass, high-pass and band-pass filters wherein only sounds below a certain frequency, above a certain frequency or between two frequencies, are included in the results of measurements. Noise measurements can also be made using a series of band-pass filters operating in tandem. These can be 'octave' bands based in such a way that each band is centred on a frequency that is twice that of the one below; i.e. 125 Hz, 250 Hz, 500 Hz, etc. 1/3 octave bands where there are three bands to each octave; i.e. 100 Hz, 125 Hz, 160 Hz, 200 Hz, 250 Hz, 315 Hz, etc. or narrower bands (1/12 octave, 1/24 octave), which can give more precise information on specific features in the noise. These are referred to as 'constant percentage' filters where the high bands cover a greater number of frequencies than lower bands.

An alternative to band-pass filtering for frequency analysis is the use of a mathematical algorithm called a Fast Fourier Transform (FFT), implemented digitally within some sophisticated sound level meters, usually referred to as noise analysers or similar. This is referred to as 'constant bandwidth' filtering where higher bands and lower bands cover the same number of frequencies.

ASSESSING THE SIGNIFICANCE OF VARIATION IN THE NOISE LEVEL (TEMPORAL ANALYSIS)

Temporal analysis is what is required where the variation in noise level is of particular importance and provides much more detailed information than is available from an examination of the maximum, minimum, L_{Aeq} and the various statistical indices (see Figure 3.2). It can also be used to show when various noise 'events' start and stop, and their level. Noise levels can be shown as they vary over any particular period of interest and are often displayed in terms of the variation of 'short' L_{Aeq} values. These

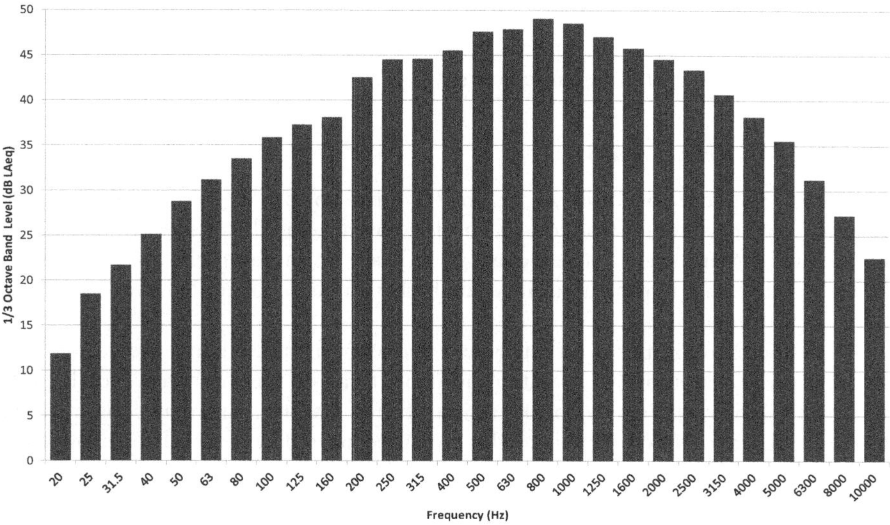

Figure 3.3 Example 1/3 Octave Band Chart

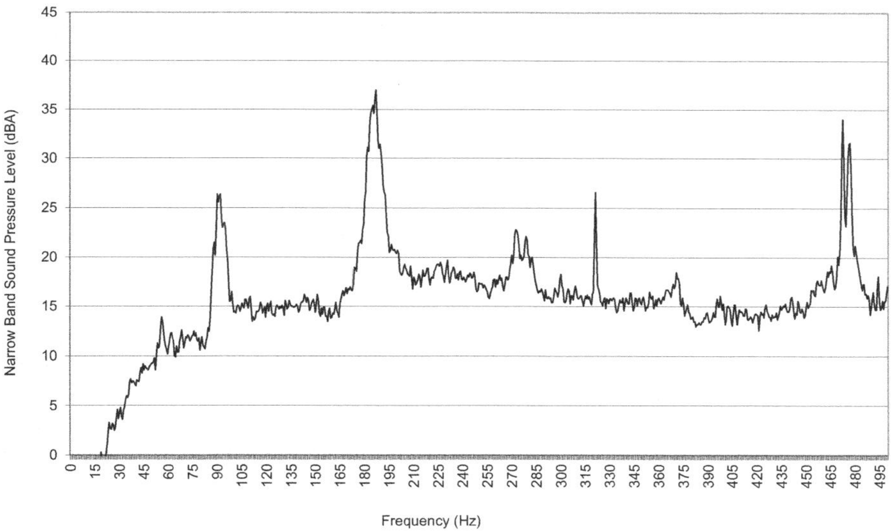

Figure 3.4 Example FFT chart

short L_{Aeq} values could each have a duration of as little as 100 milliseconds in order to show as precise detail as possible, although one 1 second values may be more practicable for most purposes and could be used, for instance, to show the variation in noise over an hour of operation of an industrial, commercial or construction site.

This kind of analysis can, if necessary, be combined with frequency analysis wherein the variation in noise level can be evaluated over a specific frequency range or over a series of frequency ranges. The two approaches can also be combined in a 'waterfall plot' showing the variation in noise level over time with different frequencies shown with different colours.

ACOUSTIC FEATURES

Subjective response to noise can be greater for a noise that has specific 'acoustic features', such as tones (sounds of specific pitch), impulses (sudden sounds or repetitive or intermittent sudden changes in level) or anything else that highlights it in the listener's attention, than it would be for a noise at a similar level with none of these features.

It is, therefore, important that, where necessary, measurements are carried out in such a way that appropriate data is available to allow the measured overall noise level to be supplemented, by consideration of such features. This may consist of the addition of a penalty/correction to the measured overall noise level to account for such features in subsequent assessment. The inclusion of an assessment of tonal noise would normally require, as a minimum, 1/3 octave band analysis to show whether a correction should be included in the measured noise level to account for this factor but, more usually, this would require narrow band analysis of either constant percentage or constant frequency bandwidth to allow the significance of any tones to be determined.

Likewise, impulsive noise, or even noise with a regular modulation or other such factor drawing attention to it, would require temporal analysis, showing the variation of noise, possibly band limited as necessary, with time, to determine its potential significance to a noise complaint or other investigation.

NOISE ASSESSMENT

Absolute or relative level assessment

The precise way a noise assessment is carried out will inevitably depend on the noise that is being assessed and any officially recognised guidance that is available to govern the way it is done. Broadly speaking, the impact of a noise can be assessed either in terms of its *absolute* level or as a *specific* level relative to the ambient or background noise in which it occurs, or as a combination of the two. A special case occurs for the second of these where an existing noise is increased in level, all other things staying the same, and it may be this change that is the most relevant factor in these circumstances.

An absolute level can be expressed in many different ways, as can be seen from the range of noise indices available, including the various noise 'dose' indices, such as L_{den}, which are only really applicable to predictive assessments, such as noise contour mapping, as they cannot be determined uniquely by measurement. Relative levels, in turn, are often difficult to quantify as both the specific noise (that which is being assessed) and the background or ambient noise (that which exists in the absence of the specific noise) are usually constantly varying. Assessment methodologies that utilise a comparison such as this require a way of processing the background/ambient noise in order to provide a statistically repeatable comparator to be defined. This may be achieved by averaging the data over specified times of the day/night and, in the case of wind turbine noise assessment, wind conditions. For clarity, 'ambient' noise in these circumstances usually refers to measurements using the L_{Aeq} measurement index and background noise usually refers to measurements using the L_{A90} index.

Acoustic character correction

For the purposes of assessment, it is often necessary to correct (or 'penalise') the specific noise where it has a distinctive character, or acoustic feature, that makes it more annoying than an equivalent noise of the same level without such features. This is not, however, ubiquitous across all noise assessment guidance and, for instance, is rarely applied to transportation noise or construction noise with the main focus of character correction being applied to industrial and commercial noise (see for instance BS 4142).

Where the noise character is an integral feature of the noise, such as that from music sources, or from predominantly low frequency noise sources, the assessment may be required for specific octave or 1/3rd octave bands (see frequency analysis (above)). This would certainly be required for any objective assessment of potential audibility.

Noise 'rating' (NR) curves are also used to assess the suitability of an acoustic environment for different purposes by comparing the ambient noise level in octave bands with a series of reference curves; the intention being that the rating is met if the ambient noise level is below the specified rating NR curve in all bands. Figure 3.5 shows a noise spectrum that just meets NR55.

The equivalent in the USA are noise criterion (NC) curves, which serve the same purpose. They are generally used in specifications for acoustic spaces such as concert halls and recording studios but have, on occasion, been used as the basis for planning

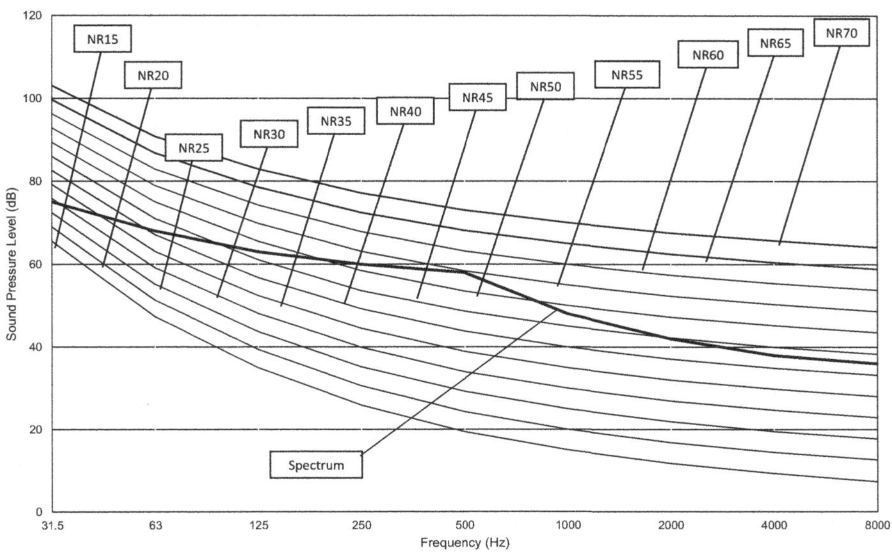

Figure 3.5 Noise rating curves

conditions imposed on industrial and/or commercial sources of noise. The example below shows a noise spectrum which just meets NC55.

Cumulative noise

It is far from clear whether cumulative noise from different sources is additive or whether a different noise source moderates the impact of a new noise or, indeed, whether the new noise moderates the impact of the existing noise. This varies according to the guidance available for the specific source. BS 4142, for instance, treats all background noise as a moderating factor in noise impact assessment. ETSU-R-97, for wind turbine noise, treats all wind turbine noise from any source as additive. Generally, this has to be reviewed on a case-by-case basis.

RELEVANT GUIDANCE AND STANDARDS

A brief overview is provided here of some of the guidance and standards available for the measurement and assessment of noise that affects members of the public. The methodologies covered here are by no means exhaustive and further documents, specifically those with legal status, are referred to in subsequent chapters, as well as reference being made in these chapters to some of the documents discussed here. It should be noted that none of the below have strictly legal status, except where they relate to the Noise Insulation Regulations (1975) or the Noise Insulation (Railways and Other Guided Transport Systems) Regulations (1996) as discussed in Chapter 8. They can, however, be considered as comprising current best practice and, as such, are likely to be given considerable weight in any legal proceedings.

In all cases, only a brief synopsis of each document is presented, and for more information reference must be made to the specific documents themselves and any revisions or other updates that are made available.

BS 4142 – *Methods for Rating and Assessing Industrial and Commercial Sound*

This standard[4] has been in existence, in various forms, since 1967, with a precursor to it appearing as an appendix in the 1963 Wilson Report (see Chapter 2). The current version, dated 2014, with an amendment made in 2019, represents the latest in an evolving series. As the title suggests, it is aimed at assessment of noise from industrial and commercial premises. It does this by comparing the noise that is being assessed, measured externally as an L_{Aeq}, with the noise that exists in its absence, measured as an L_{A90} (the 'background' noise). The noise that is being assessed is corrected or 'penalised' if it contains significant tones, impulses, intermittency or other features that are 'readily distinctive against the residual acoustic environment'. This corrected, or penalised, noise is referred to as the 'rating level'. In short, the greater the difference between the rating level and the background noise, the greater the magnitude of the impact of the noise being assessed. A difference of around +10 dB or more is 'likely to be an indication of a significant adverse impact'. A difference of around +5 dB is 'likely to be an indication of an adverse impact'. It is stated that 'the lower the rating level is, relative to the background noise, the less likely it is that the noise which is being assessed will have an adverse impact or a significant adverse impact'.

It is stated that these levels of impact are dependent on 'context'. This is, essentially a subjective element of the assessment wherein non-acoustic factors, such as likely attitude to the source, play a part. Reference is also made to the fact that, 'where background noise levels and rating levels are low, absolute levels might be as, or more, relevant than the margin by which the rating level exceeds the background, particularly at night'. In addition, it states that

> 'where residual sound levels are very high, the residual sound might itself result in adverse impacts or significant adverse impacts, and the margin by which the rating level exceeds the background might simply be an indication of the extent to which the specific sound source is likely to make those impacts worse' (see BS 4142 p 17).

It can be seen that despite this assessment methodology being a 'standard', the flexibility it allows is open to some considerable interpretation.

BS 8233 – *Guidance on Sound Insulation and Noise Reduction for Buildings*

This document[8] is particularly useful for noise assessment in that it contains details of appropriate noise levels for living rooms, dining rooms and bedroom during the day (sixteen hour average) and for bedrooms at night (eight hour average). It notes that the levels specified apply to noise without a specific character, generated externally, as it affects the internal acoustic environment. This reference to lack of acoustic character reflects the requirement in BS 4142 to correct measured or assessed noise levels for acoustic character (see above) although no such correction is specified by BS 8233. It notes that occupants are usually more tolerant of noise without a specific character and that non-acoustic characteristics, in the case of noise from neighbours, can trigger complex emotional reactions.

ISO 1996 – *Acoustics – Description, Measurement and Assessment of Environmental Noise*

This document[9] is divided into two parts: *Part 1: Basic Quantities and Assessment Procedures*; and *Part 2: Determination of Sound Pressure Levels*. This mirrors, in part, BS 7445, *Description and Measurement of Environmental Noise*, which has three parts, which correspond to the original version of ISO 1996. BS 7445 has not been updated as recently as ISO 1996, however.

The ISO 1996 document essentially describes the measurement procedures to be used in determining external noise levels and is similar to the corresponding parts of BS 4142 in this regard. Part 2 also contains a detailed tonal assessment methodology.

BS 5228 – *Code of Practice for Noise and Vibration Control on Construction and Open Sites – Noise*

This standard consists of two parts relating to noise and vibration respectively. It describes what is essentially good practice, but Part 1 also provides source noise

[8] BS8233:2014, *Guidance on Sound Insulation and Noise Reduction for Buildings* (BSI 2014).
[9] ISO 1996, *Acoustics – Description, Measurement and Assessment of Environmental Noise.*

data for an extensive range of plant and equipment used for construction purposes, together with noise prediction methodologies for static and mobile plant. It also includes suggested noise limits to apply to different times of the week in terms of L_{Aeq} noise levels.

UK Government guidance on noise from extraction of minerals

This guidance includes noise limits in terms of L_{Aeq} for daytime, evening and night-time.[10]

ETSU-R-97 – *The Assessment and Rating of Wind Farm Noise* and the IoA good practice guide

Wind farm noise is unique in that the source noise, and usually the background noise, particularly in rural areas where it is often dominated by wind in trees and foliage, both vary with wind speed. ETSU-R-97,[5] published in 1996, is essentially a refinement of BS 4142, adapting it for use in this case and introducing low noise limiting values to apply when background noise is low (see BS 4142, above, on this issue). It also specifies the use of L_{A90} for the source noise level, as well as for background noise, as the low levels of noise involved are easily contaminated by transient noises in the environment if quantified using L_{Aeq}.

A good practice guide to the use of ETSU-R-97 was published by the UK Institute of Acoustics in 2013,[11] which included recommendations on the prediction of noise from wind turbine developments that was not covered by ETSU-R-97.

Noise from pubs and clubs and other music noise

Noise from pubs and clubs is covered by the 2006 Contract report NANR163 for the UK government Department for Environment, Food and Rural Affairs (DEFRA),[12] which provided recommendations on controlling noise from such sources, including an applicable absolute noise level criterion, as well as other noise indices which can be used to assess potential effects.

The *Code of Practice on Environmental Noise Control at Concerts*, produced by the Noise Council in 1995,[13] made recommendations on controlling noise from concerts. The Noise Council was established by a group of professional bodies consisting of the Chartered Institute of Environmental Health, the UK Institute of Acoustics, the Royal Environmental Health Institute of Scotland and the Institute of Occupational Safety and Health. It is no longer active but its code of practice continues to be referred to by those seeking to regulate and control noise from concerts.

[10] UK Government, *Guidance: Minerals*, *https://www.gov.uk/guidance/minerals#Noise-emissions* (last accessed 10 October 2022).

[11] UK Institute of Acoustics, *A Good Practice Guide to the Application of ETSU-R-97 for the Assessment and Rating of Wind Turbine Noise* (2013).

[12] DEFRA Contract Report NANR 163, *Noise from Pubs and Clubs* (DEFRA, 2006).

[13] The Noise Council, *Code of Practice on Environmental Noise Control at Concerts* (1995).

Noise from clay target shooting

This is covered by the 2003 publication by the Chartered Institute of Environmental Health, *Clay Target Shooting – Guidance on the Control of Noise*,[14] which includes a methodology and noise index, the 'shooting noise level', for its assessment. Guideline values are suggested in terms of a level below which annoyance is less likely to occur (55 dBA) and level above which it is highly likely to occur (65 dBA). The shooting noise level is defined as the logarithmic average of the loudest twenty-five shots in a thirty minute measurement period.

DEFRA low frequency noise criteria

Contract report NANR 45 for DEFRA[15] described limits that could be applicable to internal noise that is specifically low frequency in character. These are specified as 1/3 octave band L_{Aeq} levels from 10 to 160 Hz.

Publications by the World Health Organisation

The WHO has published a number of documents on appropriate noise criteria for protecting members of the public from excessive noise. The first of these was in 1980[16] and recommends specific L_{Aeq} noise levels for the prevention of 'serious' annoyance during the day and sleep disturbance at night, externally and internally, respectively.

This was followed in 1999 by the more detailed *Guidelines for Community Noise*,[17] which also contained similar recommended noise guideline values, but which covered more environments and an additional guideline value for preventing 'moderate' annoyance externally, in addition to that for serious annoyance. It also included an external noise guideline value for preventing sleep disturbance at night.

In 2009 this was followed by the *Night Noise Guidelines for Europe*,[18] which introduced the concept of a yearly L_{Aeq} evaluated over the night-time hours and referred to as $L_{night,\ outside}$ and a criterion level of 40 dB $L_{night,\ outside}$ to prevent adverse health effects 'such as self-reported sleep disturbance, environmental insomnia', and increased use of sleep-inducing drugs and sedatives.

In 2018 the WHO published *Environmental Noise Guidelines for the European Region*,[19] which provided specific noise target values for protecting human health from transportation noise (road, rail and aircraft), wind turbine noise and leisure noise. Industrial and other commercial noise was not included. The criteria for the transportation sources are set in terms of L_{den} and L_{night} values provided. Only the L_{den} value is included for wind turbine noise and, for leisure noise, the criterion is set in term of the yearly twenty-four hour L_{Aeq} value and doesn't include any time of day corrections, as are used for the calculation of L_{den}.

---

[14] Chartered Institute of Environmental Health, *Clay Target Shooting – Guidance on the Control of Noise* (2003).

[15] DEFRA Contract Report NANR 45, *Proposed Criteria for the Assessment of Low Frequency Noise Disturbance* (DEFRA, 2005).

[16] WHO, *Environmental Health Criteria 12 – Noise* (1980).

[17] WHO, *Guidelines for Community Noise* (1999).

[18] WHO, *Night Noise Guidelines for Europe* (2009).

[19] WHO, *Environmental Noise Guidelines for the European Region* (2018).

Noise prediction methodologies

Noise predictions, particularly from industrial and commercial activities, where they are not inherent in the assessment methodologies described above, are commonly carried out with reference to ISO 9613 – *Acoustics – Attenuation of Sound During Propagation Outdoors*.[20] The standard comes in two parts with Part 1 being solely concerned with the provision of values for atmospheric attenuation for different meteorological conditions (temperature and relative humidity) and Part 2 being that providing the methodology used for the predictions that consists of the quantification of a number of 'attenuation factors', including that from the atmosphere, relevant to noise propagation. A number of alternative methodologies to that contained in ISO 9613 are also available.

Noise from road traffic is more usually covered by the Calculation of Road Traffic Noise, published by the then Department of Transport and Welsh Office in 1988.[21] This is used to quantify traffic noise for the purposes of the Noise Insulation Regulations,[22] as discussed in Chapter 8.

Noise from railways is, similarly, covered by the Calculation of Railway Noise, published by Department of Transport in 1995[23] and used to quantify railway noise for the purposes of the Noise Insulation (Railways and Other Guided Transport Systems) Regulations 1996,[24] as also discussed in Chapter 8.

---

[20] ISO 9613-2, *Acoustics – Attenuation of Sound During Propagation Outdoors, Part 2: General Method of Calculation* (1996).

[21] UK Department of Transport and the Welsh Office, *Calculation of Road Traffic Noise*, (HMSO, 1988).

[22] The Noise Insulation Regulations 1975 (SI 1975/1763).

[23] UK Department of Transport, *Calculation of Railway Noise* (HMSO, 1995).

[24] The Noise Insulation (Railways and Other Guided Transport Systems) Regulations 1996 (SI 1996/428).

Chapter 4

Common Law Nuisance

INTRODUCTION

In this chapter we look at how the common law has attempted to provide redress for a variety of adverse circumstances (including the creation of noise) that unreasonably affects an individual's enjoyment of the land which they occupy. The law recognises the fact that the occupier (for example, by virtue of being the owner, tenant or subtenant) of land has the right to enjoy the occupation of that land. However, such a right is circumscribed by the law imposing an obligation on that occupier not to use their land in such a manner as to unreasonably interfere with the enjoyment their neighbour's occupation of their land.[1] That is to say, that one's neighbour possesses a similar right to enjoy the occupation of their land. The rights of the respective occupiers can often conflict with each other. For example, I may choose to sit at home in the evening and read, whereas my musically-inclined neighbour may wish to practice with his drum kit, the upshot of which is that I am discomfited. Essentially, the function of the law of nuisance is to strike a reasonable balance between these conflicting rights.[2] In the Court of Appeal case of *Fearn v Tate Modern Modern Galleries*[3] it was held that the unifying principle in the law of nuisance was reasonableness between neighbours. In short, the governing principle is 'good neighbourliness' and this involves reciprocity between neighbours.[4] The law was neatly summarised by Lord President Cooper in *Watt v Jamieson*[5] when he stated:

> 'The balance in all cases has to be held between the freedom of a proprietor to use his property as he pleases, and the duty on a proprietor not to inflict material loss or inconvenience on adjoining proprietors, and in every case the answer depends on considerations of fact and degree. The critical question is whether what he was exposed to was *plus quam tolerabile*, when due weight has been given to all the circumstances of the offensive conduct, and its effects.'

Watt, therefore, is authority for the proposition that before an adverse state of affairs can be categorised as a nuisance, it must be *plus quam tolerabile* (i.e. more than can be reasonably endured) in the eyes of the law. However, the concept of reasonableness is,

---

[1] See e.g. *Hunter v Canary Wharf Ltd* [1997] Env LR 488.

[2] See *Baxter v Camden LBC (No 2)* [2001] 1 AC 1 at 20 (per Lord Millett).

[3] [2020] EWCA Civ 104 at [38]. For a discussion of *Fearn* see (2020) 153 Rep.B. 5; D Howarth [2020] CLJ 394 and D Nolan (2021) 137 LQR 1.

[4] *Baxter* (above, fn 2) at 20 (per Lord Millett).

[5] 154 SC 56 at 58.

some consider, vague, and at worst, a meaningless shibboleth that offers little guidance as to whether the adverse state of affairs, which is the subject matter of the action, ranks as a nuisance. Indeed, some have argued that the notion of reasonableness has now become redundant and misleading in many cases of private nuisance.[6] *Watt* also emphasises the point that whether any given state of affairs ranks as a nuisance is a matter of fact and degree.[7] For example, the louder the noise from my neighbour's television, the more likely the courts will be inclined to classify the adverse state of affairs as a nuisance in law. The outcome of any nuisance case is, indeed, fact-sensitive and will depend on the claimant being able to convince the court that they were unreasonably discomfited by the relevant adverse state of affairs.[8]

ELEMENTS OF THE LAW OF NUISANCE

We now discuss the various factors that the courts apply when considering whether any adverse state of affairs ranks as a nuisance in law. However, it is important to emphasise that only unreasonable conduct is capable of being categorised as a nuisance in law.[9] A leading case that illustrates this important point is *Baxter v Camden LBC (No 2)*.[10] In that case, the claimants were local authority tenants. They occupied flats that had been constructed, or adapted, for multiple occupation. However, the flats were inadequately soundproofed, the result being that the tenants could hear literally everything their neighbours were doing. The tenants, therefore, brought proceedings *inter alia*, in nuisance against their landlords. However, the House of Lords held that the relevant noise did not rank as a nuisance since the noise emanated from the normal and everyday use of the relevant flats. In short, the noise in question did not emanate from the unreasonable use of property.

What factors are taken into account?

We now consider the various factors that are taken into account in determining whether the adverse state of affairs does rank as a nuisance in law. However, it is important to note at the outset that the courts do not mechanically apply all these factors in every nuisance case. Rather, the courts have tended to emphasise certain factors, often to the exclusion of others.[11] Furthermore, it should be emphasised that the courts have refrained from constructing a hierarchy in terms of the relative

---

6 M Lee, 'What is a private nuisance' (2003) 119 LQR 298 at 298.

7 See also *Mutter v Fyffe* (1848) 11 D 303; *Haddon v Lynch* [1911] VLR 230 and *Howarth v Canadian Red Cross Society* [1943] 2 WWR 692.

8 See e.g. *MacBean v Scottish Water* [2020] CSOH 55 where it was held on the evidence presented before the court that the odours that emanated from the defender's waste water treatment plant, which was situated in the vicinity of the pursuer's property, did not rank as a nuisance.

9 *Watt v Jamieson* 1954 SC 56. See also *Western Silver Fox Ranch v Ross and Cromarty CC* 1940 SLT 144; See also *Pugliesi v National Capital* (1977) 3 CCLT 18 at 51 where Howland JA stated that in determining whether a nuisance exists it is not sufficient to ask whether an occupier has made reasonable use of his own property. Rather, one must ask whether his conduct is reasonable, considering the fact that he has a neighbour. See also *Baxter* (above) at 20 (per Lord Millett) and also *Fearn v Tate Modern Galleries* [2020] EWCA Civ 104. See (2020) 199 *SPEL* 58 and (2020) 153 Rep.B. 5.

10 [2001] 1 AC 1.

11 See e.g. *Fleming v Hislop* (1882) 10 R 426; (1886) 13 R (HL) 43 where the court simply focused on the smell from the offending mineral refuse situated on the defender's premises.

importance of each factor. It should be further emphasised that the factors that are discussed are probably not exhaustive. That is to say, that the list is not closed.

Social utility

The social utility of the activity, which generates the state of affairs that is the subject matter of the action, is taken into account in the court's deciding whether a nuisance exists. Essentially, the more socially useful the activity is, the less likely the court will be willing to castigate the activity as a nuisance in law.[12] The concept of social or public utility is not well-articulated in terms of the law of nuisance. However, the courts have been readily inclined to recognise the concept of social or public utility in relation to factories.[13] However, as far as other activities are concerned the courts have displayed more reticence, preferring simply to take this factor into account when considering whether to grant an interdict or an injunction.[14] *Dennis v Ministry of Defence*[15] illustrates this point. In that case, the claimants owned and lived in a large estate that was situated in close proximity to RAF Wittering, which was then the home of the Harrier jet, which was a noisy aircraft. Indeed, the witnesses who gave evidence before the court described the noise as sometimes intolerable. The claimants brought an action in nuisance against the MoD. Buckley J accepted the former's claim to the effect that that the noise in question amounted to a nuisance.[16] However, it was also beyond dispute that the flying of military aircraft was in the public interest.[17] Put simply, Britain needed its air force, including aircraft that, at times, created noise. However, to weigh this factor in the judicial scales when deciding if the noise in question ranked as a nuisance would deprive the claimants of a remedy at common law.[18] In the view of the judge, the growing *corpus* of human rights law dictated that the appropriate remedy under the law of nuisance should be that of damages, as opposed to, for example, a declaration or an injunction. However, in the Outer House case of *King v Advocate General for Scotland*[19] Lord Pentland refrained from expressing the view that *Dennis* represented the law of Scotland. It can be said that *Dennis* does not, on the grounds that the factors that the courts consider whether a nuisance exists should be kept quite separate from relevant remedies. To link the latter to the former would lead to confusion in the law of nuisance.

Motive of the defender

If the relevant adverse state of affairs (in the present context the creation of noise) is caused by the defender to simply punish, or annoy, the pursuer, the courts are readily prepared to accept the fact that the noise ranks as a nuisance in law. The leading case

12 *Harrison v Southwark Water Co Ltd* [1891] 2 Ch 409.
13 See e.g. *Bellew v Cement Ltd* [1948] IR 61.
14 See e.g. *Miller v Jackson* [1977] QB 966 and *Webster v Lord Advocate* 1984 SLT 13. The decision of the Outer House was reversed in terms of the interdict that was granted on appeal to the Inner House; 1985 SC 173.
15 [2003] EHLR 17.
16 [2003] EHLR 17 at [34].
17 [2003] EHLR 17 at [45].
18 [2003] EHLR 17 at [46].
19 2009 CSOH 169 at [17].

here is *Christie v Davy.*[20] In that case, the claimants were musically inclined. They frequently practised their instruments at home. This annoyed the defendant, who resided next door to the claimants. The former decided to retaliate by banging trays on the party wall. It was held that the noise that the defendant created ranked as a nuisance. Another example of the relevance of malice in terms of the law of nuisance is illustrated in *Hollywood Silver Fox Farm Ltd v Emmet.*[21] Here the claimant bred foxes on his land. The defendant, who was about to develop the land that adjoined that of the claimant, objected to the presence of foxes on grounds that the former feared that this would deter people from purchasing houses on the estate. The defendant, therefore, caused shots to be fired on the boundary that separated his premises from that of the claimant. It was held that the defendant's conduct ranked as a nuisance in law.

Locality

In deciding whether a state of affairs is a nuisance the courts take into account the nature of the relevant locality.[22] Essentially, the more typical in nature the state of affairs is, in relation to the relevant locality, the less likely the state of affairs will be categorised by the court as a nuisance. The rationale here is that if the state of affairs is typical of a given locality, a reasonable person who resides in that locality is presumed to be less likely to be annoyed, by having become habituated, at least to some extent, to the state of affairs in question.[23]

However, whilst the courts may be less inclined to castigate as a nuisance a state of affairs that is indigenous in an area, the courts are not prepared to accord *carte blanche* to create a nuisance there. For example, in *Rushmer v Polsue and Alfieri Ltd*[24] the claimant resided in an area that was especially devoted to the printing and allied trades. The defendants set up machinery that caused serious disturbance to the claimant and his family during night-time hours. At first instance, the court granted an injunction, restraining the defendants from causing a noise nuisance. The defendants appealed. The House of Lords dismissed the appeal. Lord Loreburn stated[25]:

> 'A dweller in towns cannot expect to have as pure air, as free from smoke, smell and noise, as if he lived in the country, and distant from other dwellings, and yet an excess of smoke, smell and noise may give a cause of action, but in each case it becomes a question of degree, and the question in each case is whether it gives rise to a nuisance which will give rise to an action. This is a question of fact.'

However, the nature of the locality is only relevant if it affects personal comfort. That is to say, that if the adverse state of affairs causes physical damage to property of the claimant, the locality principle is redundant. The leading case here is the House

[20] [1893] 1 Ch 316.
[21] [1936] 2 KB 468.
[22] See e.g. *Trotter v Farnie* (1830) 9S 144.
[23] See e.g. *Bamford v Turnley* (1862) 31 LJQB 286; *Inglis v Shotts Iron Co* (1881) 8 R 1006 and *Swinton v Pedie* (1837) 15 S 775.
[24] [1907] AC 121.
[25] [1907] AC 121 at 123.

of Lords case of *St Helens Smelting Co v Tipping*.[26] In that case, vapours from the defendant's copper-smelting works, which was situated in a heavily industrialised area, damaged trees on the claimant's estate. The House decided in favour of the claimant. The House held it irrelevant that the claimant lived in an industrial area. In short, the nature of the locality was irrelevant.[27]

Locality and the effect of planning law

To what extent, if any, does the grant of planning have on the application of the locality factor in relation to the law of nuisance? For example, if a planning authority were to designate an area (that was formerly designated as green belt) for industrial use in the development plan, and then the planning authority proceeded to grant planning permission for the erection of a factory on the land, to what extent, if any, would it be legitimate for the court to take this factor into account when it was making its decision as to whether or not effluvium from the factory ranked as a nuisance in law. In short, could the occupiers of the factory argue that whereas the land on which the factory stood was once green belt, it was now an industrial area, and that this factor should be taken into account by the court when it decides whether or not the effluvium ranks as a nuisance?

The leading case is the Supreme Court case of *Lawrence v Fen Tigers Ltd*.[28]

The facts of the case were simple. Planning permission was granted in 1979 to construct a sports complex and stadium. At first, speedway racing took place. Later, banger and stock car racing was introduced. Planning permission was subsequently granted for other motor-related sports. The claimants, who lived in close proximity to the stadium, became affected by noise from the stadium. They raised an action against the organisers of the motor sports, amongst others. At first instance, it was held that the noise that emanated from the stadium constituted a nuisance in law. On appeal, the Court of Appeal held that both the grant of planning permission, coupled with the implementation of that permission, had the effect of changing the character of the area in terms of the law of nuisance. For the court the key question was the effect of implementing the planning permission. The court held that the trial judge had been wrong in deciding that the character of the land had not been changed by both the grant and the subsequent implementation of the planning permission. In conclusion, the noise in question did not rank as a nuisance in law. The claimants successfully appealed to the Supreme Court.

As far as the significance of planning permission in terms of the law of nuisance was concerned, Lord Neuberger was of the view that the implementation of planning permission could give rise to a change of character of the locality.[29] However, simply because the relevant work had been given planning permission was no different from work that did not require planning permission. Furthermore, the mere fact that the activity that is said to give rise to the nuisance had the benefit of planning permission, would normally be of no assistance to the defendant in a

[26] (1865) 11 HL Cas 642.

[27] For an interesting discussion of *Tipping*, see A. Simpson, *Leading Cases in the Common Law* (OUP, 1997) Ch 7.

[28] [2014] AC 822.

[29] [2014] AC 822 at 846.

nuisance action.[30] In turn, Lord Carnwath, after stating that there should be a strong presumption against allowing private rights to be overridden by administrative decisions without compensation, stated that in exceptional cases (i.e. in relation to large-scale developments) a planning permission could be the result of a considered policy decision by the competent authority, which could not sensibly be ignored in assessing the character of the area, against which the acceptability of the defendant's activity was to be judged.[31]

By way of conclusion, whereas the Supreme Court had a splendid opportunity to clarify the law as to the effect of the town and country planning regime on the law of nuisance in relation to the former's ability to change the character of land for the purposes of the latter, some would say that that opportunity was missed. However, *Lawrence* does establish the fact that normally planning permission is an irrelevant factor in the equation and, therefore, should be accorded little import. In the last analysis, this issue remains a rather grey area of law.

Lawrence, however, is not binding on the Scottish courts and does not, in the view of the author, represent the law of Scotland, that is to say that planning permission has no relevance in a private nuisance action north of the border.[32]

Duration and intensity

Essentially, the length of time a state of affairs lasts, and its intensity, are taken into account by the court when it considers if a nuisance exists. In the leading case of *Bamford v Turnley*[33] Pollock CB stated:

> 'A clock striking the hour, or a bell ringing for some domestic purpose, may be a nuisance, if unreasonably loud or discordant, of which the jury must judge; but although not unreasonably loud, if the owner, from some whim or caprice made the clock strike every 10 minutes, or the bell ring continually, I think that the jury would be justified in considering it to be a very great nuisance.'

As far as noise nuisances are concerned, the nature of the noise is a relevant factor in determining whether the noise ranks as a nuisance in law. The more pleasant-sounding the noise is, the less likely will it be deemed a nuisance.[34]

Time of day

The time of day during which an adverse state of affairs exists is only relevant in relation to noise and, perhaps, light. The courts are more inclined to regard night-time noise as a nuisance than noise that takes place during the day.[35] The obvious reason for this is that noise that manifests itself during the night-time hours is more likely to disturb than noise that only takes place during the day.

---

[30] [2014] AC 822 at 849.

[31] [2014] AC 822 at 878.

[32] For a discussion of *Lawrence* see F. McManus, 'Noise Nuisance' (2014) 163 *SPEL* 64.

[33] (1862) 31 LJQB 286 at 292.

[34] *Webster v Lord Advocate* 1984 SLT 13 at 16. Decision overruled in the Inner House in relation to terms of the interdict that the Outer House made against the defender; 1985 SC 173.

[35] *Bamford v Turnley*; *De Keyser's Royal Hotel Ltd v Spicer Bros Ltd* (1914) 30 TLR 257.

Sensitivity of the claimant

It is a general rule in law that the courts are unwilling to assist the over-sensitive. As far as noise pollution is concerned, the leading case is *Heath v Brighton Corporation*.[36] In that case a priest complained about noise and vibrations that emanated from the defendants' electricity generating station. However, the court denied him a remedy in terms of the law of nuisance, since the only reason he was discomfited was that he possessed hypersensitive hearing.[37]

Social utility of thing interfered with

The question that is to be answered here is the extent, if any, to which the court takes into account the social utility of that which is interfered with by the conduct of the defendant. The leading cases have concerned the reception of television signals. In *Bridlington Relay Ltd v Yorkshire Electricity Board*,[38] which concerned liability for the reception of television signals, Buckley J took into account the fact that, in the main, television simply served a recreational function in society and he, therefore, accorded lowly status in deciding whether the interference ranked as a nuisance in law.

However, in the House of Lords case of *Hunter v Canary Wharf Ltd*,[39] which concerned the potential liability in nuisance, comprising the presence of a tall building that interfered with the reception of television signals, Lord Goff expressed the view that television transcended the mere function of entertainment and that interference with such amenity might, indeed, be protected by the law of nuisance.[40]

Could the adverse state of affairs have been avoided by the claimant?

To what extent, if any, can the court take into account the fact that the relevant adverse state of affairs (for example, the effects of noise) could have been avoided by the claimant? While there is little authority on this point, the general rule is that the courts are unwilling to place the claimant under an obligation to take preventative or remedial action to counter the noise, etc. This point is neatly illustrated in the leading case of *Webster v Lord Advocate*.[41] The pursuer, who lived in the vicinity of Edinburgh Castle esplanade, raised an action against the defender, alleging that both the noise from the performance of the Edinburgh Military Tattoo, and also the erection of the scaffolding to accommodate the seating on the castle esplanade, amounted to a nuisance. The Lord Ordinary rejected the contention that the pursuer would be unable to succeed if it could be shown that the provision of double glazing to the windows of the pursuer's flat would have reduced the ingress of noise to an acceptable level.[42]

---

36 (1908) 24 TLR 414.

37 See also *Morris v Curran* 2019 GWD 31-496; See (2020) 198 *SPEL* 42.

38 [1965] Ch 436.

39 [1997] Env LR 488.

40 Cf *Nor Video Services Ltd v Ontario Hydro* (1978) 84 (3d) 221 at 231.

41 1984 SLT 13. Decision of Outer House reversed by Inner House in relation to terms of interdict that had been made by the court; 1985 SC 173.

42 1984 SLT at 15.

Is the state of affairs typical of modern life?

In determining whether any given state of affairs ranks as a nuisance, to what extent, if any, is it relevant that the state of affairs that is complained of is typical of modern life? There is little authority on this point. However, in *Hunter v Canary Wharf Ltd*[43] (above) where the House of Lords held that the mere presence of a tall building that interfered with the reception of television signals, could not rank as an actionable nuisance, in the Court of Appeal, Pill LJ (in deciding that the building did not constitute a nuisance) was of the view that tall and bulky buildings had become a feature of urban landscapes and, therefore, less likely to rank as a nuisance. However, the judge seemed to suggest that that factor may not be relevant if the state of affairs comprised an activity as opposed to the mere presence of a building.

LIABILITY IN NUISANCE – WHO MAY BE SUED?

The author of the nuisance

The person who creates the nuisance, namely the author of the nuisance, is liable in law.[44] The author need not have any interest in the land from which the nuisance arises to be held liable.[45] For example, the organisers of a so-called 'rave' that is held on vacant land could be held liable in law for any noise nuisance that is caused, notwithstanding the fact that the organisers have no propriety interest in the land.

The occupier of land

The occupier of the land from which the nuisance emanates is normally liable in law.[46] The basis of liability is both the possession and also the control of the land from which the nuisance proceeds.[47] However, the occupier of land is not liable for an adverse state of affairs that has been created by a third party, for example, in relation to a noise nuisance, a trespasser, unless the occupier takes insufficient steps to abate the nuisance after they becomes aware of its presence, either actually or constructively, in which case the law will presume that they have adopted the nuisance. This principle was established in a trilogy of leading cases. It should be mentioned that whereas the facts of the respective cases do not relate to noise pollution, the legal principles that derive from the cases are of general applicability.

In *Sedleigh-Denfield v O'Callaghan*[48] local authority trespassed on the land of the defendant and then constructed a culvert on a ditch. One of the employees of the defendant knew of the existence of the culvert. Furthermore, the defendants used the culvert to get rid of water from their own property. However, the culvert was not properly constructed, the upshot of which was that it became blocked with detritus. A heavy thunderstorm caused the ditch to be flooded. The claimant's land became flooded. The House of Lords held the defendants liable in nuisance by virtue of both

[43] [1997] Env LR 488 at 493.
[44] *Watt v Jamieson* 1954 SC 56.
[45] *Slater v McLellan* 1924 SC 854; *Marcic v Thames Water Utilities* [2004] 2 AC 42.
[46] *Sedleigh-Denfield v O'Callaghan* [1940] AC 880; *Smith v Scott* [1973] Ch 314.
[47] [1940] AC 880 at 903 (per Lord Wright).
[48] As above (fn 46).

continuing and adopting the nuisance. The defendants had continued the nuisance by virtue of failing to take the necessary remedial action after the defendants had become aware (through their servant) of the existence of the nuisance. The nuisance had also been adopted by the defendants since they had used the nuisance for their own purposes.

The Privy Council had the opportunity to discuss liability in the law of nuisance in respect of a nuisance that had been created on the defendant's property not by the act of a third party but, rather, by nature in *Goldman v Hargrave*.[49] In that case, a tall gum tree that was situated on the defendant's land was struck by lightning and then caught fire. The defendant cut down the tree the following day. However, he did not take further steps to prevent the fire from spreading, preferring to simply allow the fire to burn itself out. Several days later the weather changed. The wind became stronger and the air temperature increased. This caused the fire to revive. It spread over the plaintiff's land, which was damaged.

The Privy Council held that the defendant was liable for the harm that had been caused to the plaintiff's land, on the grounds that the former had failed to remove the hazard from his land. In so deciding, the Board held that no distinction fell to be made between liability in terms of the law of negligence and liability in nuisance.[50] However, in deciding whether the defendant had reached the standard of care that the law demanded, one was required to take into account the defendant's knowledge of the hazard, as well as his ability to foresee the consequences of not checking or removing it, and also the ability to abate the nuisance.[51] However, in deciding whether the defendant had failed to attain the standard of care that the law demanded of him, one was required to adopt a subjective approach. One would, therefore, require to take into account the resources of the defendant. One would also expect less of the occupier of small premises than one would of the occupier of larger premises. Again, less would be demanded of the infirm than of the able bodied.

The Court of Appeal had the opportunity to apply the learning in *Sedleigh-Denfield* and *Goldman*, in *Leakey v National Trust for Places of Historic Interest or Natural Beauty*.[52] In that case, the claimants owned houses that were situated at the base of a steep conical hill. Part of the hill that adjoined the claimants' land had become unstable. The condition of the hill was made known to the defendants by the claimants. However, no remedial action was taken by the former. A few weeks later there was a substantial fall of earth and tree stumps from the hill on to the claimants' land. The claimants then brought an action against the defendant. The court held the defendant liable. In so doing, the court refused to draw a distinction between an adverse state of affairs that had been foist on the defendant by man-made activities and those which arose by the operation of nature. Megaw LJ, in endorsing the decisions in both *Sedleigh-Denfield* and *Goldman*, discussed[53] both the nature

[49] [1967] 1 AC 645.

[50] In *Delaware Mansions Ltd v Westminster City Council* [2001] 1 AC 321 at 323 Lord Cooke expressed the view that in circumstances that were similar to those in *Sedleigh-Denfield* and *Goldman*, the label 'nuisance' and 'negligence' were of no real significance.

[51] [1967] 1 AC 645 at 663 (per Lord Wilberforce). See also *Bybrook Barn Garden Centre Ltd v Kent County Council* [2000] Env LR 30.

[52] [1980] QB 485.

[53] [1980] QB 485 at 524.

and scope of the affirmative duty that the law imposes on the occupier of land in relation to nuisances that had been foist on them. In his Lordship's view, the extent of the harm to the claimant's premises should an accident occur, the practicability of preventative action, the cost of remedial works, and also the time that was available to take remedial action, were all relevant in determining the liability of the defendant.

The landlord

A landlord is not liable for every nuisance that emanates from premises that they have leased to a third party.[54] Therefore, if I lease my house to a third party who proceeds to regularly hold noisy house parties, and thereby causes a nuisance to the residents of adjoining property, I would not be liable in terms of the law of nuisance. A landlord is only liable in nuisance if the creation of noise by the tenant is either the certain, or a highly probable, result of the tenant's occupation of the relevant premises.[55]

The licensor of the nuisance

The person who authorises the creation of the relevant nuisance is liable,[56] especially if they make no attempt to either abate, or remove the nuisance, after they become aware of its existence. The leading case on this point is *Webster v Lord Advocate*.[57] In that case, the pursuer claimed that the noise from the performance of the Edinburgh Military Tattoo and also the erection of scaffolding to accommodate seating on the Edinburgh Castle esplanade, amounted to a nuisance in law. The Lord Ordinary accepted that the Secretary of State for Scotland, as occupier of the esplanade, was liable for the nuisance which had been created by the erection of the scaffolding, on the basis that he had authorised the creation of the nuisance. The judge held it irrelevant that the contract between the Secretary of State and the Tattoo policy committee (which was responsible for staging the Tattoo) contained a 'no nuisance' condition, since no attempt had been made by the latter to either monitor, or to inspect the activities of the licensee, or to enforce the condition.[58] Therefore, if a licensor was capable and, did take appropriate measures to enforce a 'no-nuisance' condition in the relevant contract, he could potentially, escape liability for having authorised a nuisance.

---

[54] *Smith v Scott* [1973] Ch 314. See also *Lawrence v Fen Tigers Ltd (No 2)* [2015] AC 106 at 113 (per Lord Neuberger).

[55] In *Smith v Scott* (above) at 321 Pennycuik V-C was of the view that the proper test was that of 'virtual certainty', which was another way of saying 'a high degree of probability'. In *Tetley v Chitty* [1986] 1 All ER 663 at 671 McNeill J was of the view that the proper test for establishing the liability of lessors, in terms of the law of nuisance, was whether the creation of the nuisance was the ordinary or necessary or the natural consequence of the operation of the lease. See also *Dunn v Hamilton* (1837) 15 S 853 and *Caledonian Railway Co v Baird* (1876) 3R 839.

[56] *Baxter v Camden LBC (No 2)* [2001] 1 AC 1 at 22 (per Lord Millett).

[57] 1984 SLT 13. The decision of the court was reversed, on appeal, by the Inner House in relation to the terms of interdict that the court had granted. See 1985 SC 173.

[58] 1984 SLT 13 at 16.

DEFENCES

The authors now consider defences that have specific application to the law of nuisance.

Statutory authority

The basis of this defence is that if Parliament has sanctioned or approved the creation of the nuisance, this deprives the claimant a remedy. However, the defence only applies to the direct sanction of the adverse state of affairs by an Act of Parliament. For example, if the state of affairs that generates (for example, noise) has been approved by the grant of planning permission, such approval would not have a similar effect in denying the pursuer a remedy.[59] The defence of statutory authority was commonly invoked during the course of the nineteenth century in nuisances cases, stemming from the operation of the railways.[60] Indeed, much of the authority on the defence of statutory authority derives from the so-called 'railway cases', which represent a rather untidy area of law. Fortunately, the law that was embodied in the railway cases was reviewed and clarified by the House of Lords in *Allen v Gulf Oil Refining Ltd*.[61]

In that case, a private Act of Parliament[62] authorised a multi-national company to acquire land that was situated in a rural area to construct an oil refinery. However, soon after the refinery commenced operations residents who lived in the vicinity began to complain about the smell, noise and vibration that emanated from the plant. The House held that the Act had, by necessary implication, authorised both the construction and operation of the oil refinery, the inevitable consequence of which was the creation of the nuisance in question. The claimants, therefore, failed in their action.

However, the defence of statutory authority does not apply if the relevant activities are being carried out negligently.[63] Finally, if the relevant statute authorises the activity to be carried out without causing a nuisance the defence of statutory authority is inapplicable if the activity is carried out in such a manner as to cause a nuisance.[64]

While there is no authority on this point, it is suggested that the defence of statutory authority would also be applicable to an activity that has been authorised by an order that has been made by the Scottish Ministers under s 1 of the Transport and Works (Scotland) Act 2007.

---

[59] *Lawrence v Fen Tigers Ltd* [2014] AC 822.

[60] See e.g. *Hammersmith and City Railway Co v Brand* (1869–1870) LR 4 HL 171.

[61] [1981] AC 1001.

[62] The Gulf Oil Refining Act 1965.

[63] *Vaughan v Taff Vale Railway* (1860) 5 H and N 679; *Geddis v Proprietors of Bann Reservoir* (1887–1888) LR 3 App. Cas. 430. See also *Tate and Lyle Industries Ltd v Greater London Council* [1983] 2 AC 509 and *Dobson v Thames Water Utilities Ltd* [2011] EWHC 3253.

[64] *Managers of the Metropolitan Asylum District v Hill* (1880–1881) LR 6 App Cas 193, HL; *Hammersmith and City Rly v Brand* (1869–1870) LR 4 HL 171.

Prescription

It is possible to acquire the right to create a noise nuisance by way of prescription.[65] In order for an individual to acquire such a right, the noise must have remained in uninterrupted existence for twenty years or more. Furthermore, in order that the defence can succeed, the noise must have remained substantially constant over the prescriptive period.[66] The noise must also have constituted an actionable nuisance over that period.[67] Furthermore, on the authority of both *Sturges* and *Webster* the nuisance need not have been in perpetual existence over the prescriptive period for the defence to succeed, that is to say, it is sufficient that the nuisance manifests itself on a regular basis. For the defence of prescription to succeed the claimant must have had either actual or constructive knowledge of the existence of the nuisance.[68] The relevant prescriptive period commences from the date on which the claimant could successfully have raised an action against the defendant.[69]

If the defendant does acquire the right to continue a nuisance, he does not thereby acquire the right either to create another nuisance or to increase the intensity of the nuisance, in respect of which the prescriptive right has been acquired.[70]

Acquiescence

As far as Scotland is concerned, an individual may lose their right to raise an action in nuisance if they acquiesce in the face of a nuisance. Whereas the defence of acquiescence has some similarity to that of prescription, the former is a quite separate defence.[71] The defence of acquiescence must be specifically pled.[72] For the defence to succeed there requires a clear unequivocal and positive act on the part of the pursuer that indicates that they have consented to the nuisance in question. The person who is alleged to have acquiesced is required to have had both full knowledge of, and also the power, to stop the nuisance.[73] Mere silence or passiveness in the face of the nuisance on the part of the pursuer is insufficient to ground the defence.[74] However, the occupation of the land affected by the nuisance, coupled with the knowledge of the existence of the nuisance, is capable of raising the presumption that the pursuer has acquiesced.[75] The longer the pursuer remains impassive in the face of the nuisance, the stronger is the presumption that they have acquiesced in its face. However, in *Colville v Middleton*[76] it was held that twenty-two years passive inaction

65 *Lawrence* (fn 59 above) at 838 (per Lord Neuberger).

66 *Webster v Lord Advocate* 1984 SLT 13, decision reversed on a different point by Inner House. See 1985 SC 173.

67 *Sturges v Bridgman* (1879) 11 Ch D 22. See also *Lawrence* (fn 59) at 839 (per Lord Neuberger).

68 *Liverpool Corp v Coghill and Son Ltd* [1918] 1 Ch 307.

69 *Liverpool Corp* above.

70 *Baxendale v MacMurray* (1867) LR 2 Ch 790; *MacIntyre Bros v McGavin* [1893] AC 268; *Lawrence* (fn 59) at 839 (per Lord Neuberger) and *Webster v Lord Advocate* 1984 SLT 13. Reversed on appeal by Inner House in relation to terms of interdict granted; see 1985 SC 173.

71 *Collins v Hamilton* (1837) 15 S 902.

72 *Duke of Buccleuch v Cowan* (1866) 5M 214.

73 *Earl of Kintore v Pirie* (1903) 5 F 818.

74 *Cowan v Kinaird* (1865) 4 M 236.

75 *Colville v Middleton* 27 May 1817, FC.

76 Above.

was insufficient to ground the defence. Since the defence is based on implied consent, the defence is redundant if the pursuer objects timeously to the relevant state of affairs.[77] Furthermore, the pursuer can only acquiesce in the face of the nuisance, in contradistinction to the creation of the state of affairs from which the nuisance arises.[78] For example, an occupier of premises could only be held to have acquiesced in relation to noise that emanates from a newly established factory that is situated in the vicinity of their premises, in contrast to the mere presence of the factory before it commences to operate. The act or acts of acquiescence can be implied from the circumstances of the case.[79] The defence does not apply if the nuisance differs either in nature or intensity from that which has been consented to.[80]

However, the courts are unwilling to infer acceptance or acquiescence of a given state of affairs from the mere fact that the pursuer has 'come to' the nuisance. The leading case is now *Webster v Lord Advocate*[81] where the court refused to accept the proposition that simply because the pursuer, by choosing to live in the vicinity of the Castle esplanade, in full knowledge that she would thereby expose her to the noise that was generated by the Edinburgh Military Tattoo, had consented to the nuisance. Again, in *Miller v Jackson*[82] the majority of the Court of Appeal held that it was no defence in a nuisance action that the claimants, by deciding to live in close proximity to a cricket pitch in the knowledge that by so doing would expose themselves to the risk of being hit by cricket balls, had thereby consented to the risk. The principle that coming to a nuisance was not a defence that was recognised by the English courts was endorsed by the Supreme Court in *Lawrence*[83] where it was held that the fact that the claimants had decided to live in close proximity to a stadium and race track where motor sports took place, did not provide the defendant occupiers of the premises with a defence in a nuisance action that the claimants brought against them in relation to the noise that emanated from the premises.

REMEDIES

In order to raise an action in nuisance, the claimant requires possessing a proprietary interest in the land that is affected by the nuisance. Therefore, someone who simply resides in the premises affected by the nuisance cannot successfully raise an action against the author of the nuisance.[84]

The remedies of damages, declaration/declarator (Scot) and injunction/interdict (Scot), which are of general applicability in the law of tort/delict (Scot), apply, of course, to actions which are brought in nuisance. However, a discussion of these remedies is outwith the scope of this book.[85]

---

[77] *Hill v Wood* (1863) 1 M 360.
[78] *Earl of Kintore v Pirie* (1903) 5 F 818.
[79] *Hill v Wood* (1863) 1 M 360; *Houldsworth v Wishaw Magistrates* (1887) 14 R 920.
[80] *Colville* (fn 75).
[81] See fn 70.
[82] [1977] QB 966.
[83] Fn 59 at (840) per Lord Neuberger.
[84] *Hunter v Canary Wharf Ltd* [1997] Env LR 488.
[85] For a discussion of these remedies see e.g. *Clerk and Lindsell on Torts*, 23rd edn (Sweet and Maxwell, 2020) and F. McManus and R. Conway, *Delict – A Comprehensive Guide to the Law*, 3rd edn (EUP, 2021).

Chapter 5

Statutory Nuisance

INTRODUCTION

In the last chapter we discussed how an individual, who is adversely affected *inter alia*, by noise can invoke the law of nuisance in order to secure redress. However, common law nuisance as a means of securing the abatement of an alleged nuisance has pronounced limitations. First, in order to successfully raise an action in nuisance the claimant is required to have a proprietary interest in the land that is adversely affected.[1] Furthermore, the cost of an individual taking action at common law has the obvious effect of discouraging recourse by way of such an action.

In this chapter we look at the subject of statutory nuisance, which represents the oldest branch of modern environmental law. Statutory nuisance has its origins in the mid-nineteenth century, when it was widely believed that cholera was spread amongst the population by foul odours, or miasms, that emanated from foul matter.[2] Cholera was a shocking disease. Victims of the disease suffered from high temperature, severe abdominal pain, vomiting and explosive diarrhoea that left the patient severely dehydrated. The upshot of this was that those who had recently died of cholera were skeletal in appearance.

The opposing theory as to the transmission of disease was the contagion theory. However, until germs were discovered by Pasteur and Lister, the contagionist's theory lacked credibility, simply because there was no scientific foundation to which their theory could attach.

However, the miasmatists were in the majority in the government. The views of this majority, therefore, shaped the content of the legislation that was intended to strike against the cholera threat. The statutes that were passed were, therefore, 'nuisance-based', that is to say that the main purport of the legislation was to eradicate the perceived causes of the environmental threat.[3] Public health legislation continued to employ the law of nuisance as a remedial device. For example, the Public Health Acts 1875 and 1936 employed the concept of statutory nuisance to deal with a range of adverse environmental circumstances. In Scotland the Public Health (Scotland) Act 1867 and 1897 (both repealed) contained similar provisions. The statutory nuisance provisions contained in these statutes are now contained, in a more expanded form,

---

[1] *Hunter v Canary Wharf Ltd* [1997] AC 655.

[2] See E. Ackernecht, 'Anticontagionism between 1821 and 1864' (1948) 22 Journal of the History of Medicine 562; N. Longmate, *King Cholera* (Hamish Hamilton, 1966) and R. Morris, *Cholera 1832* (Croom Helm, 1976).

[3] See e.g. the Public Health Act 1848 and the Nuisance Removal Acts 1846–1855.

in s 79(1) of the Environmental Protection Act 1990 (the EPA),[4] which we now discuss with particular relevance to noise.

STATUTORY NUISANCES

Section 79(1) of the EPA designates a variety of adverse environmental circumstances a nuisance.

Premises

As we have already observed, the origins of the provisions of the EPA derive from the mid-Victorian era. An outstanding problem during that period was poor, insanitary housing conditions. Perforce, public health legislation had to strike at this problem by making such premises a statutory nuisance.

Under s 79(1)(a) of the EPA 'any premises[5] in such a state as to be prejudicial to health or a nuisance' rank as a statutory nuisance and, therefore, fall to be dealt with in terms of the EPA. The subsection comprises two quite separate limbs, namely:

(a) premises which are prejudicial to health, and
(b) premises which are a nuisance.[6]

Therefore, in order to rank as a statutory nuisance, the relevant premises must either be prejudicial to health, or a nuisance, or both.[7]

'Prejudicial to health'

As far as premises that are prejudicial to health are concerned, it is the state of the premises as opposed to the user (or use) to which the premises are put that constitutes the relevant proscribed state of affairs.[8] In order that the relevant premises is prejudicial to health, in terms of s 79(1)(a), there must be some intrinsic feature or attribute of the premises that renders it prejudicial to health. That is, it is insufficient that the layout of the premises is unsatisfactory. The leading case is the House of Lords case of *Oakley v Birmingham City Council.*[9] In that case the ground floor of a house included a bathroom with a washbasin, which was situated next to a kitchen that had a sink. On the side of the kitchen that was opposite the bathroom was a door that led to a lavatory. There was no washbasin in the lavatory. Furthermore, there was no space to install a washbasin. Therefore, anyone using the toilet who wished to wash their hands would require to do so in the kitchen sink or, alternatively, would require to go through the kitchen into the bathroom. The House

[4] The EPA applies to England, Scotland and Wales. The Clean Neighbourhoods and Environment Act (Northern Ireland) 2011 provides for a statutory nuisance regime similar to that applying to the rest of the UK.

[5] 'Premises' includes land and any vessel (with the exception of a steam vessel) (s 79(7)).

[6] *Salford City Council v McNally* [1976] AC 379 at 388–389 (per Lord Wilberforce). See also *Vella v Lambeth* [2006] Env LR 33, *NCB v Thorne* [1976] 1 WLR 543, *Robb v Dundee City Council* 2002 SC 301 and *Milne v Stuartfield Windpower Ltd* [2019] SC ABE 25; [2018] 5 WLUK 717.

[7] For a general discussion of statutory nuisance see F. McManus, 'Statutory Nuisance: Success or Failure out of a Myth?' (2003) 24 *Statute Law Review* 77.

[8] *R v Parlby* (1889) 22 QBD 520; See also *Pike v Sefton MBC* [2000] Env LR D31.

[9] [2001] 1 AC 617.

held that the premises were not prejudicial to health in terms of s 79(1)(a). It was not sufficient that the premises were conducive to unhygienic practices on the part of persons who resided in the house. The risk to health had to derive from some source of possible infection or disease or illness, such as dampness, mould, dirt or evil smelling accumulations or the presence of rats.[10] The state of the house itself required to be prejudicial to health. In order to rank as premises that are prejudicial to health it is not sufficient that the relevant state of affairs interferes with personal comfort. Rather, the premises must cause injury to health.[11] The state of the premises may be prejudicial to the health of both occupiers of the premises, as well as that of the general public.[12]

The substantive issue that was required to be addressed in the divisional court case of *Vella v London Borough of Lambeth*[13] was whether noise that was created outwith a house, and adversely affected the health of an occupant, could rank as a statutory nuisance in terms of the EPA. In that case, the occupant of a house ('V') that was situated in a block of local authority flats brought an action under s 82 of the EPA against the local authority, on the basis that the sound insulation of the premises was so poor that V was adversely affected by the noise his neighbour, who lived in the flat above, was making simply by the conduct of the neighbour's everyday activities. V also claimed that he was further affected by noise made in the communal hallway and stairs. V's mental health had suffered as a result of being exposed to such noise. V claimed that the premises in question (that is to say, either the flat above or his own flat) were prejudicial to health in terms of s 79(1)(a) of the EPA. However, the court held that the premises were not a statutory nuisance, in terms of the section, on the grounds that the statutory nuisance provisions that were contained in the predecessors to the EPA, including the various Nuisance Removal Acts, were aimed at suppressing disease from insanitary, filthy or verminous premises. In short, s 79(1)(a) was not aimed at the state of affairs that was the subject matter of the action, namely noise caused by premises that were poorly insulated.

Vella should be contrasted with *Southwark LBC v Ince*.[14] In that case, tenants of a local authority brought an action against their local authority landlords under s 99 of the Public Health Act 1936, on the grounds that the premises were prejudicial to health, in terms of s 92,[15] by virtue of having poor sound insulation, as a result of which the tenants were exposed to noise from road and rail traffic running near the building. The divisional court held that the premises were prejudicial to health on those grounds. However, *Ince* was decided before both *Oakley* and *Vella* and in the author's' opinion, *Ince* no longer represents good law. In short, lack of adequate sound insulation in premises does not render the premises prejudicial to health in terms of s 79(1)(a).

---

10 [2001] 1 AC 617 at 627 per Lord Slynn of Hadley. See also *R v Bristol City Council ex p Everett* [1999] 1 WLR 1170 where the Court of Appeal held that premises that contained a steep staircase and therefore posed a risk of accident was not 'prejudicial to health' in terms of s 79(1)(a).

11 *Salford City Council v McNally* [1976] AC 379 at 389 per Lord Wilberforce.

12 [1976] AC 379 at 389.

13 [2006] Env LR 33.

14 (1989) 21 HLR 504.

15 Both sections repealed.

Whether the premises are prejudicial to health is assessed objectively. That is to say, one is required to assess whether the premises would pose a risk to the health of an ordinary person, in contrast to the health of the residents of the relevant premises.[16]

'Nuisance'

As far as the meaning of 'nuisance' in terms of s 79(1)(a) of the EPA, unlike the position at common law the state of affairs that gives rise to the nuisance may exist within the premises that is adversely affected.[17] However, the impact of the relevant state of affairs must be similar to that which ranks as a common law nuisance in order to rank as a 'nuisance' in terms of s 79(1)(a).[18]

'Noise'

Under s 79(1)(g) of the EPA noise[19] emitted from premises so as to be prejudicial to health or a nuisance, ranks as a statutory nuisance that falls to be dealt with under the provisions of the EPA.[20]

However, the general utility of the paragraph, as far as the suppression of noise is concerned, is circumscribed by the fact that the relevant noise is required to emanate from premises.[21] Noise that emanates from the streets and other public places would not, therefore, normally fall within the meaning of the section. It is not necessary for the relevant local authority to prove that a specific individual is affected by the relevant noise.[22] Furthermore, it is sufficient for the prosecution to rely solely on evidence submitted by those who are affected by the noise, including expert evidence, to prove the existence of the nuisance.[23] There is also no requirement that scientific evidence is presented to the court.[24] Indeed, it is open to the court to lay greater store by the non-technical evidence of witnesses to that presented by experts.[25] However, the court is not bound to uncritically accept the opinion of a witnesses, including an expert witness.[26] The court must decide on the whole of the evidence whether a noise nuisance exists. A subjective judgement is involved in that determination. Furthermore, the judgement is that of the court.

---

[16] *Robb v Dundee City Council* 2002 SC 301. For a discussion of *Robb* see (2002) 93 *SPEL* 118. See also *Cunningham v Birmingham City Council* [1998] Env LR 1. For a discussion see also *Anderson v City of Dundee Council* 2000 SLT (Sh Ct) 134 and *R (Anne) v Test Valley BC* [2002] Env LR 22.

[17] *Robb v Dundee City Council* 2002 SC 301.

[18] 2002 SC 301. The majority of the Inner House were of that opinion. See also *Newham LBC v White* (12 March 2015, unreported); *Dennis Rye Ltd v Bolsover DC* [2013] EWHC 1041. For a discussion of *Dennis Rye* see (2013) 160 *SPEL* 142. See further *Milne v Stuartfield Windpower Ltd* [2018] WLUK 717. For a discussion of *Milne* see (2019) 193 *SPEL* 67.

[19] 'Noise' includes vibration: s 79(7).

[20] Subsection 79(1)(g) does not apply to premises: (a) occupied on behalf of the Crown for naval, military or air force purposes or for the purposes of the department of the Secretary of State having responsibility for defence; or (b) occupied for the purposes of a visiting force: s 79(2).

[21] *Tower Hamlets LBC v Manzoni and Walder* [1984] JPL 436.

[22] *Westminster City Council v McDonald* [2005] Env LR; *Wellingborough BC v Gordon* [1993] Env LR 218.

[23] *Cooke v Adatia* (1989) 153 JP 129.

[24] *Wellingborough BC v Gordon* (above). See also *R (Hackney LBC) v Rottenberg* [2007] Env LR 24.

[25] *Milne v Stuartfield Windpower Ltd* [2019] SC ABE 25.

[26] *R (Hackney LBC) v Rottenberg* [2007] Env LR 24.

The courts give the expression 'nuisance', as used in the subsection, its ordinary common law meaning.[27] In other words, when a court has to determine if a given state of affairs constitutes a nuisance, in terms of s 79(1)(g), the court takes into account the same factors as those which were discussed above.[28] It is not necessary that a particular noise level requires to be exceeded before a nuisance in terms of s 79(1)(g) can be said to exist.[29] It is also sufficient that the noise in question derives from a one-off event.[30] While locality is an important factor to be taken into account[31] in determining whether a nuisance exists, if the noise in question has the capacity to annoy a reasonable person, the noise can rank as a statutory nuisance, notwithstanding the fact that the noise is no louder than other noises in the locality.[32]

In order to constitute a nuisance under s 79(1)(g) the noise requires to be of such intensity, duration, etc. as to constitute a nuisance at common law.[33]

We have already observed, in our discussion on the impact of planning law on the development common law nuisance, that in the Supreme Court case of *Lawrence v Fen Tigers Ltd*[34] (where the court was required to decide whether noise from the defendants' premises ranked as a nuisance at common law) the court was of the opinion that whereas the grant of planning permission could not sanction a nuisance and, furthermore, was normally of no relevance when one was deciding if a nuisance existed, in certain circumstances the fact that the relevant planning authority had granted planning permission could be accorded some importance in determining whether the noise in question was unreasonably loud and, therefore, constituted a nuisance.

In the sheriff court case of *Milne v Stuartfield Windpower Ltd*,[35] the sheriff was of the opinion that the fact that the defender's wind turbine had been granted planning permission was of some relevance in determining whether the noise in question ranked as statutory nuisance in terms of s 79(1)(g).[36]

Vehicle noise

Under s 79(1)(ga) noise that is prejudicial to health, or a nuisance, and is emitted from or caused by a vehicle, machinery or equipment[37] in a street (or, in Scotland, a road) ranks as a statutory nuisance. It is important to note that subsection s 79(1)(ga) simply relates to noise from individual vehicles, machinery or equipment. The subsection does not apply to noise made by traffic; by any naval or military or

---

[27] *A Lambert Flat Management Ltd v Lomas* [1981] 1 WLR 898; *East Northamptonshire DC v Fossett* [1994] Env R 388; *Godfrey v Conwy CBC* [2001] Env LR 38 and *Milne v Stuartfield Windpower Ltd* [2018] WLUK 717. See also *R (Hackney LBC) v Rottenberg* [2007] Env LR 24 at [26] (per Scott Baker LJ).

[28] See pp. 32–8, incl.

[29] *Godfrey v Conwy* (above).

[30] *East Northamptonshire DC v Fossett* (above).

[31] *Roper v Tussauds Theme Parks Ltd* [2007] Env LR 31.

[32] *Godfrey v Conwy* (above).

[33] *Robb v Dundee City Council* (above); *Milne v Stuartfield Windpower Ltd* (above).

[34] [2014] AC 822.

[35] As above, fn 25.

[36] [2019] SC ABE 25 at [176]. See also *R (Hackney LBC) v Rottenberg* [2007] Env LR 24 at [11].

[37] 'Equipment' includes a musical instrument: s 79(7).

air force of the Crown; or by a visiting force; or by a political demonstration or a demonstration supporting or opposing a cause or campaign.[38]

The subsection would cover a variety of different noise sources, including noise from car radios, diesel generators and parked refrigerator vehicles in the street.

Statutory nuisances and the Pollution Prevention and Control Act 1999

A local authority may not institute summary nuisance proceedings under Part III of the EPA, in relation to a nuisance falling *inter alia* under s 79(1)(g) and, in Scotland, also under s 79(1)(ga), without the consent of the Secretary of State (or, in Scotland, the Scottish Ministers) if proceedings in respect of that nuisance might have been instituted under s 2 of the Pollution Prevention and Control Act 1999.[39] The rationale for this provision is to avoid regulatory duplication, in that the Environment Agency (and, in Scotland, the Scottish Environment Protection Agency) regulate the range of installations that fall to be regulated in terms of the regulations that have been made under s 2.[40]

Duty of local authority to inspect area

A local authority is under a duty to inspect its area, from time to time, to detect any statutory nuisances which ought to be dealt with under ss 80 and 80A of the EPA.[41] Where a complaint of a statutory nuisance is made to it by a person living within its area, the local authority is placed under a duty to take such steps as are reasonably practicable to investigate the complaint. However, in actual practice, a local authority does not systematically inspect its area to ascertain the presence of nuisances. Rather, local authorities simply react to complaints from members of the public. In short, the statutory nuisance regime is one that is largely, if not entirely, complaints-driven. In this context, it is pertinent to note that the EPA does not specify precisely what steps a local authority requires to take in order to investigate a complaint. There is no obligation on part of the local authority to either visit the relevant *locus* or communicate in any way with the complainant, or any person (if any) who is alleged to be responsible for the reputed nuisance. Furthermore, the EPA does not specify the form that the complaint should take. It would seem, therefore, that a complaint could be made to by means of email, phone call, fax, letter or verbal.

Summary proceedings for statutory nuisances

The procedure for the abatement of statutory nuisances has hardly changed since the inception of the statutory nuisance regime in the 1840s. We now discuss the procedure under the EPA.

---

[38] EPA s 79(6A).

[39] EPA s 79(10).

[40] See the Environmental Permitting (England and Wales) Regulations 2016 (SI 2016/1154) (as amended) or in Scotland the Pollution Prevention and Control (Scotland) Regulations 2012 (SSI 2012/360) (as amended).

[41] EPA s 79(1).

Where a local authority is satisfied that a statutory nuisance exists, or is likely to occur or recur, in the area of the local authority, it is required to serve an abatement notice, which imposes all or any of the following requirements:

(a) requiring the abatement of the nuisance or prohibiting or restricting its occurrence or recurrence; and
(b) requiring the execution of such works, and the taking of such other steps, as may be necessary for any of those purposes.[42]

The notice is required to specify the time, or times, within which there must be compliance with the notice.

Once the local authority has decided that a nuisance exists, the local authority must serve an abatement notice. In other words, the local authority has no discretion. It has a mandatory duty to do so.[43] Furthermore, there is no requirement that the local authority should consult with the person who is responsible for the nuisance, prior to serving the notice.[44]

Person on whom the notice is to be served

The abatement notice is required to be served on the person who is responsible for the nuisance, unless the nuisance arises from a defect of a structural character, in which case the notice requires to be served on the owner of the premises.[45] The abatement notice must be served on the owner or occupier of the premises if either the person responsible cannot be found or the nuisance has not yet occurred. The EPA defines the expression 'person responsible' as the person through whose act, default or sufferance the nuisance is attributable.[46] The words 'act,' 'default' and 'sufferance' have tended to be construed conjunctively by the courts. That is, the words have been given a similar meaning.[47] However, the words, 'act' 'default' and 'sufferance' have separate and distinct meanings. The word 'act' bears its everyday meaning. The words 'default' and 'sufferance' are now briefly discussed.

'Default'

The word 'default' simply means not doing what it is reasonable to do under the circumstances.[48] One can be in default in terms of the EPA, notwithstanding the fact that the relevant adverse state of affairs has arisen wholly, or partly, by a third

[42] EPA s 80(1).
[43] *R v Carrick DC ex p Shelley* [1996] Env LR 273.
[44] *R v Falmouth and Truro Port Health Authority ex p South West Water Services* [2001] QB 445.
[45] EPA s 80(2) The expression 'owner' is not defined in the EPA. However, in *Camden LBC v Gunby* it was held that the expression 'owner' of the premises, in terms of s 80(2) was the person who received the rack rent of the premises, regardless of whether that person was acting as an agent or a trustee for any person.
[46] EPA s 79(7). In relation to a vehicle, includes the person whose name the vehicle is for the time being registered under the Vehicle Excise and Registration Act 1994 and any other person who is for the time being the driver of the vehicle. In relation to machinery or equipment, includes any person who is for the time being operator of the machinery or equipment.
[47] See e.g. *Robb v Dundee City Council* 2002 SC 301; *Network Housing Association v Westminster City Council* [1995] Env 176;
[48] *Re Young & Harston's Contract* (1885) 31 Ch D 168 at 174 (per Bowen LJ).

party being wholly or partly in default of their legal obligations, including statutory obligations.[49]

'Sufferance'

One suffers an adverse state of affairs if one is in a position in which one can both physically, and legally, put an end to the state of affairs that constitutes a nuisance but, nonetheless, one fails to do so.[50] Furthermore, for one to suffer a nuisance, one is required to either have had either actual or constructive knowledge of its existence.[51]

Defect of a structural character

We have already observed above, that if the nuisance arises from a defect of a structural character, the abatement notice is required to be served on the owner of the relevant premises.

In the sheriff court case of *Pettigrew v Inverclyde Council*[52] it was held that defects in the sound insulation of a house could rank as defects of a structural character in terms of s 80(2). In the sheriff court case of *Anderson v City of Dundee Council*[53] it was held that the expression 'defect of a structural character' implied that the existing state of the building should be different from what was originally designed. However, the fact that the building, in its present form, did not suit its purpose in the way it did thirty years ago, did not mean that it was structurally defective. Furthermore, in deciding the building's original purpose, the court took into account the relevant building standards of the time.

The Inner House had the opportunity to discuss the meaning of 'defect of a structural character' in *Robb v Dundee City Council*[54] Lord Johnson was of the opinion that, whereas lack of insulation was part of the structure of a building it did not rank as a structural defect in terms of the EPA.[55] In her dissenting judgement, Lady Paton[56] was of the opinion that the expression 'defect of a structural character' could cover situations where there existed a defect that did not threaten the structural integrity of the building but, nonetheless, arose from the manner in which, or the materials from which, the premises were built.

Noise nuisances

In England, where a local authority is satisfied that a statutory nuisance falling within s 79(1)(g) exists or is likely to occur or recur in the area of the authority, it is either required to serve an abatement notice in accordance with s 80(1), (2) or take such other steps as it thinks appropriate for the purpose of persuading the appropriate person to abate the nuisance, or prohibit or restrict its occurrence or recurrence.[57] If

[49] *Wincanton Rural District Council v Parsons* [1905] 2 KB 34.
[50] *Rochford Rural DC v Port of London Authority* [1914] 2 KB 916.
[51] *Network Housing Association v Westminster City Council* (above).
[52] 1999 Hous. L.R. 31.
[53] 2000 SLT (Sh Ct) 134.
[54] 2002 SLT 853.
[55] 2002 SLT 853 at 865.
[56] 2002 SLT 853 at 867.
[57] EPA s 80(2A). The relationship between the statutory nuisance abatement procedure under the EPA

the local authority has taken such other steps and either of the following conditions are satisfied, the local authority is required to serve an abatement notice in respect of the nuisance.[58] The conditions are:

(a) that the authority is satisfied that before the end of the relevant period the steps taken will not be successful in persuading the appropriate person[59] to abate the nuisance or prohibit or restrict its occurrence or recurrence;
(b) that the authority is satisfied that at the end of the relevant period[60] the nuisance continues to exist, or continues to occur or recur in the area of the authority.[61]

Street noise

In the case of a statutory nuisance that falls within s 79(1)(ga) which; (a) has not yet occurred; or (b) arises from noise emitted or caused by an unattended vehicle or unattended machinery or equipment, the abatement notice requires to be served in the following manner[62]: where the person responsible for the vehicle machinery or equipment can be found, on that person[63]; where that person cannot be found, or where the local authority so determines, by fixing the notice to the vehicle, equipment or machinery. In such circumstances, if the person responsible for the vehicle, machinery or equipment can be found, and served with a notice within an hour of the notice being fixed to the vehicle, machinery or equipment, a copy requires to be served on that person accordingly.[64] Where an abatement notice is served under s 80A(2)(b) by virtue of a determination of the relevant local authority, the notice is required to state that if a copy is served under s 80A(3) the time specified in the notice within which the requirements are to be complied with is extended by such further period as is specified in the notice.[65] Where an abatement notice is served in accordance with s 80A(2)(b) the person responsible for the vehicle, machinery or equipment may appeal against the notice under s 80(3) as if they had been served with the notice on the day on which it was fixed to the vehicle, machinery or equipment.[66] Section 80A(4) applies in relation to a person on whom a notice is served under s 80A(3) as if the copy of the notice was the notice itself.[67] A person who removes or interferes with a notice that is fixed to a vehicle, machinery or equipment in accordance with s 80A(2)(b) commits an offence, unless they are the person responsible for the vehicle machinery or equipment, or they do so with the

---

and the provisions of the Equality Act 2010 and also Human Rights Act 1998 were discussed in *R (Fisher) v Durham CC* [2020] Env LR 28. For a discussion on *Fisher* see (2020) 202 *SPEL* 141.

[58] EPA s 80(2B).

[59] The appropriate person is the person on whom the authority would otherwise be required under s 80(2A)(a) to serve an abatement notice in respect of the nuisance: s 80(2E).

[60] The relevant period is seven days starting with the day on which the authority was first satisfied that the nuisance existed or was likely to occur or recur: s 80(2D).

[61] EPA s 80(2C).

[62] EPA s 80A(1).

[63] EPA s 80A(2).

[64] EPA s 80A(3).

[65] EPA s 80A(4).

[66] EPA s 80A(5).

[67] EPA s 80A(6).

consent of that person.[68] Such a person is liable, on summary conviction, to a fine not exceeding level 3 on the standard scale.[69]

Content of abatement notice

The EPA does not prescribe the precise content of the abatement notice. However, where an appeal against a notice, which has been served under s 80, lies to a magistrates' court or, in Scotland, to the sheriff, the notice is required to contain a statement that such an appeal lies and also specify the time within which it must be brought.[70] Furthermore, the terms of the notice must be clear, precise, practical, reasonable and certain.[71] The notice must also be proportionate in terms of the ends that are to be achieved, and also enforceable.[72] The abatement notice can be worded to take immediate effect.[73] Furthermore, the notice must make clear to the person on whom the notice is served what is wrong.[74] However, in determining whether the notice is sufficiently clear, one can take into account certain external factors into account. For example, the content of an accompanying letter can be taken into account.[75] Furthermore, the abatement notice need not specify whether that which is the subject matter of the notice is either prejudicial to health or a nuisance.[76] Rather, it suffices that the person on whom the notice is served knows what is required to be done in order to abate the nuisance.

The local authority can simply require the recipient of the notice to abate the nuisance. That is to say that the authority need not specify the measures that are required to be taken in order to abate the nuisance.[77] The local authority can simply leave it up to the perpetrator of the nuisance to choose the mode of abatement of the nuisance. However, in *Budd v Colchester BC*[78] Swinton Thomas LJ stated *obiter* that there could be certain cases where a duty lay on the authority to specify the works or steps that were required to be taken in the abatement notice. If the relevant notice requires works or other steps to be carried out, the relevant measures must be specified.[79]

If the abatement notice concerns noise nuisance, the local authority need not specify an acceptable maximum noise level that is to be achieved. That is, the notice can simply impose a requirement for the perpetrator of the noise nuisance to abate

---

68 EPA s 80A(7).

69 EPA s 80A(8).

70 EPA Schedule 3, para 6.

71 *Strathclyde RC v Tudhope* 1983 SLT 22; *Network Housing Association v Westminster City Council* [1995] Env LR 176.

72 *Roper v Tussauds Theme Parks Ltd* [2007] Env LR 31.

73 *Strathclyde RC v Tudhope* 1983 SLT 22.

74 *Myatt v Teignbridge DC* [1995] Env LR 78.

75 *Camden LBC v London Underground* [2000] Env LR 369; *Camden LBC v Easynet Ltd* [2002] EWHC 2929.

76 *Lowe Watson v South Somerset DC* [1998] Env LR 143.

77 *Budd v Colchester BC* [1999] Env LR 739; *R v Crown Court at Canterbury* [2001] Env LR 36 and *North Lincolnshire County Council v Act Fast North Lincolnshire CC* (CIC) [2014] Env LR 7; [2014] JPL 371.

78 [1999] Env LR at 739 at 749.

79 *Surrey Free Inns v Gosport BC* [1999] Env LR 750; *R v Falmouth and Truro Port Health Authority ex p South West Water Services Ltd* [2001] QB 445 and *Elvington Park Ltd v City of York Council* [2010] Env LR 10.

the noise.[80] Nor is there a requirement that the notice should specify the activities that are the subject matter of the notice.[81] However, the person on whom the notice is served must be made aware of the nature of the relevant nuisance, for example, smell or noise.[82]

However, if the abatement notice specifies the levels of noise that must not be exceeded, the method of ascertaining (or measuring) whether such levels are being exceeded, and where the relevant noise readings should be taken, must be specified.[83]

Finally, in order to ascertain the validity of an abatement notice, one is required to look objectively at its substance.[84]

The relevant date by means of which one determines whether the relevant state of affairs is a statutory nuisance is on the date of the relevant trial, as opposed to the date on which court proceedings were begun.[85]

Time for compliance

The abatement notice can be framed in such a way that it has immediate effect.[86] Furthermore, if the abatement notice simply prohibits the recurrence the nuisance, it is not required to specify the period of time at the end of which the notice expires. That is to say that the notice continues indefinitely.[87]

Appeals against notice

A person on whom a notice is served may appeal against the notice to a magistrates' court or, in Scotland, to the sheriff within a period of twenty-one days, beginning with the date on which they were served with the notice.[88] The Statutory Nuisance (Appeals) Regulations 1995[89] and, as far as Scotland is concerned, the Statutory Nuisance (Appeals) (Scotland) Regulations 1996[90] specify, *inter alia*, the grounds on which an appeal may be made.

Failure to comply with abatement notice

It is an offence for the person on whom an abatement notice is served to fail, without reasonable excuse, to comply with any requirement or prohibition that is imposed by the notice.[91] In *Wellingborough BC v Gordon*[92] it was held that having a birthday party did not provide the defendant with a reasonable excuse for the

[80] *R v Fenny Stratford Justices* [1976] 1 WLR 1101. See also *R (Elvington Park Ltd) v York Crown Court* [2011] EWHC 2213. For a discussion of *Elvington Park Ltd* see (2012) 152 *SPEL* 93.
[81] *Elvington Park Ltd* above.
[82] *Elvington Park Ltd* above.
[83] *R v Fenny Stratford Justices* above.
[84] *McGillivray v Stephenson* [1950] 1 All ER 942.
[85] *Coventry CC v Doyle* [1981] 1 WLR 1325. Overruled in part by *Sandwell MBC v Bujok* [1990] 1 WLR 1350.
[86] *Strathclyde Regional Council v Tudhope* 1983 SLT 22.
[87] *R v Birmingham Justices ex p Guppy* (1988) JP 159; *R v Tunbridge Wells Justices* [1996] Env LR 88.
[88] EPA s 80(3).
[89] SI 1995/2644.
[90] SI 1996/1076.
[91] EPA s 80(4).
[92] [1993] Env LR 218.

defendant's breach of a noise nuisance notice, in terms of s 58(4) of the Control of Pollution Act 1974.[93] However, in *Hope Butuyuyu v Hammersmith and Fulham LBC*[94] it was held that it was not possible to provide a comprehensive definition of what matters either were, or were not, capable of amounting to a reasonable excuse for failing to comply with an abatement notice. The relevant circumstances would vary from case to case. In *Hope* the court considered it relevant to take into account the illnesses of both the defendant and her son. *Hope*, therefore, is authority for the proposition that the court can take subjective factors into account when determining what circumstances constitute a reasonable excuse in terms of s 80(4) of the EPA. In the divisional court case of *Waltham Forest LBC v Mitoo*[95] it was held that the playing of loud music by the person on whom an abatement notice had been served, in order to drown out noise from construction works, did not rank as a reasonable excuse.

Penalties, etc.

Other than in a case concerning industrial or trade premises, a person who commits an offence under s 80(4) is liable on summary conviction to a fine not exceeding level 5 on the standard scale, together with a further fine of an amount of a tenth of the greater of £5,000 or level 4 on the standard scale, for each day on which the offence continues after the conviction.[96] A person who commits an offence under s 80(4) on industrial, trade or business premises is liable, on summary conviction, to a fine.[97]

In Scotland, where a local authority has reason to believe that a person has committed an offence under s 80(4) the local authority may give that person a fixed penalty notice under s 80ZA, offering the person the opportunity of discharging any liability to conviction for that offence, by payment of a fixed penalty.[98] A person who commits an offence under s 80(4) on industrial, trade or business premises is liable, on summary conviction, to a fine not exceeding £40,000.[99]

Defence of best practicable means

The EPA makes provision for the defence of best practicable means[100] in relation to proceedings by a local authority for failure to comply with an abatement notice. Subject to certain exceptions, in any proceedings for an offence under s 80(4) in respect of a statutory nuisance it is a defence to prove that the best practicable means were used to prevent or to counteract the effects of a nuisance.[101] However, the defence is not available *inter alia* under s 79(1)(g) except where the nuisance arises on industrial, trade or business premises.[102] Nor is the defence available in relation

[93] Repealed.
[94] [1997] Env LR D 13.
[95] [2017] Env LR 9.
[96] EPA s 80(5).
[97] EPA s 80(6).
[98] EPA s 80(4A).
[99] EPA s 80(6).
[100] The expression 'best practicable means' is defined in s 79(9).
[101] EPA s 80(7). *See R (St Albans City and District Council) v Patel* [2009] Env LR 22.
[102] EPA s 80(8).

to noise that is emitted from, or caused by a vehicle, machinery or equipment, unless used for industrial, trade or business purposes.[103]

Noise nuisance – construction sites, etc.

In proceedings for an offence under s 80(4) in relation to a statutory nuisance falling within s 79(1)(g) or (ga), where the offence consists of contravening the requirements imposed by s 80(1)(a) (that is, the requirement imposed by an abatement notice, requiring the abatement of a nuisance, or prohibiting its occurrence or recurrence) it is a defence to prove that the alleged offence was covered by a notice served under s 60 or a consent given under s 61 or s 65 (construction sites) of the Control of Pollution Act 1974 (COPA).[104] The EPA also provides a defence[105] in relation to an alleged offence that was committed at a time when the premises were subject to a notice under s 66[106] (noise reduction notice) of COPA if it can be proved that the level of noise emitted from the premises, at that time, was not such as to constitute a contravention of the notice under that section. The EPA provides a further defence[107] where the alleged offence occurred at a time when the premises were not subject to a notice under s 66 of COPA, and when a level fixed under s 67[108] of COPA (new buildings liable to an abatement order) was applied to the premises, if it can be proved that the level of noise emitted from the premises, at that time, did not exceed that level. The defences under s 80(9) relating to ss 66 and 67 of COPA apply, irrespective of whether or not the relevant notice was subject to an appeal at the time when the offence was alleged to have been committed.[109]

More than one person responsible

Under s 81(1) of the EPA where more than one person is responsible for a statutory nuisance, summary proceedings under s 80 can be taken against any such person, whether or not what any one of them is responsible for would, by itself, amount to a nuisance. In effect, this replicates a common law principle that if one creates an adverse state of affairs (e.g. noise) that of itself would not constitute a nuisance but in combination with another source of noise would rank as a nuisance, that person would be liable.

In relation to a statutory nuisance falling within s 79(1)(ga) (i.e. noise from vehicles, machinery, equipment) for which more than one person is responsible (whether or not what any one of those persons is responsible for would in itself amount to a nuisance) the relevant abatement notice can be served on any such person.[110]

Similarly, as far as a statutory nuisance falling within s 79(1)(ga) that is caused by, or emitted from, an unattended vehicle, or unattended machinery or equipment,

[103] EPA s 80(8)(aa).
[104] EPA s 80(9).
[105] EPA s 80(9), this defence does not apply in Scotland.
[106] Repealed.
[107] This defence does not apply in Scotland.
[108] Repealed.
[109] EPA s 80(10).
[110] EPA s 81(1A).

for which more than one person is responsible, the relevant notice can be served on any such person.[111]

Non-compliance with an abatement notice

Where an abatement notice has not been complied with the local authority may, whether or not they take proceedings under s 80(4),[112] abate the nuisance and do whatever may be necessary in execution of the notice.[113] In Scotland the local authority can also abate the nuisance and take any necessary action, in circumstances where a fixed penalty notice has been given under s 80(4A) regardless of whether or not the fixed penalty notice is accepted. Furthermore, where the matter to be abated is a statutory nuisance under s 79(1)(g) the local authority has the power to seize and remove any equipment that it appears to the local authority is being used, or has been used, in the emission of the noise in question.[114] A person who wilfully obstructs a person who is acting in terms of s 81(3A), commits an offence and is liable to a fine on summary conviction.[115]

Expenses

Any expenses that are incurred by a local authority in abating or preventing the recurrence of a nuisance under s 81(3) may be recovered by it from the person by whose act or default the nuisance was caused.[116] If the relevant person is the owner of the premises, expenses can be recovered from any person who is for the time being the owner. In such circumstances, the court[117] may apportion expenses between persons whose acts or defaults the nuisance is caused, in such a manner as the court or sheriff considers fair or reasonable.[118]

Proceedings by local authorities

If a local authority is of the opinion that proceedings for an offence under s 80(4) would provide an inadequate remedy in the case of any statutory nuisance, the local authority may take proceedings in the High Court or, in Scotland, a court of competent jurisdiction, for the purposes of securing the abatement, prohibition or restriction of the nuisance.[119] In such circumstances, the local authority need not have suffered any damage from the nuisance.

In any proceedings that relate to a statutory nuisance under s 79(1)(g) or (1)(ga) it is a defence to prove that the noise was authorised by a notice under s 60 or a consent under s 61 (construction sites) of COPA.[120]

---

111 EPA s 81(1B).
112 Or, in Scotland, whether or not proceedings have been taken for an offence.
113 EPA s 81(3).
114 EPA s 81(3A).
115 EPA s 81(3B) Schedule 1 to the Antisocial Behaviour (Scotland) Act 2004 has effect, in relation to equipment seized under s 81(3)(A) of the EPA as it does in relation to equipment that is seized under s 47(2) of the 2004 Act: s 81(3C).
116 EPA s 81(4).
117 In Scotland, the sheriff.
118 EPA s 81(4).
119 EPA s 81(5).
120 EPA s 81(6).

Further supplementary proceedings under Schedule 3 of the EPA apply to any such proceedings.[121]

Before taking such proceedings, the local authority is required to conclude that the statutory nuisance proceedings would afford an inadequate, as opposed to a less convenient remedy, in the circumstances.[122] Furthermore, in reaching that conclusion, the local authority is required to address the statutory procedure for dealing with a statutory nuisance, which comprises both consecutive and distinct steps.[123] That is to say, first, the service of an abatement notice by the local authority is required. Second, if there is no compliance with the notice, either enforcement by way of prosecution in the magistrates' court or the use of self-help and cost recovery must be attempted by the local authority to secure redress. Third, only as a last resort, may the local authority take proceedings in the High Court or a court of competent jurisdiction.

SUMMARY PROCEEDINGS BY PRIVATE INDIVIDUALS

The EPA allows a person who is aggrieved by the existence of a statutory nuisance to take proceedings in a magistrates' court, by way of a complaint or, in Scotland, before the sheriff, on a summary application.[124] In *Watkins v Aged Merchant Seaman's Homes*[125] it was held that a complainant in actual occupation of premises would normally, though not necessarily, be a person aggrieved, regardless of whether the occupation was lawful. Furthermore, whether the complainant was a 'person aggrieved' was always a question of fact and degree.

If the magistrates' court or, in Scotland, the sheriff, is satisfied that the alleged nuisance exists, or that although abated it is likely to recur on the same premises, or in the case of a nuisance within s 79(1)(ga) in the same street, or, in Scotland, road, the court or the sheriff is required to make an order for either or both of the following purposes:

(a) requiring the defendant or, in Scotland, the defender, to abate the nuisance, within the time specified in the order, and to execute any works necessary for that purpose; and
(b) prohibiting a recurrence of the nuisance, and requiring the defendant, or defender, within the time specified in the order, to execute any works necessary to prevent the recurrence.[126]

In England and Wales, a fine, not exceeding level 5 on the standard scale, may be imposed on the defendant.

If the magistrates' court or the sheriff is satisfied that the alleged nuisance exists and is such as, in the opinion of the court or the sheriff, to render the premises unfit for human habitation an order under s 82(2) may prohibit the use of the premises for

[121] EPA s 81(7).
[122] *Vale of White Horse DC v Allen* [1997] Env LR 212.
[123] *The Barns (NE) Ltd v Newcastle upon Tyne City Council* [2006] Env LR 25.
[124] EPA s 82(1).
[125] [2019] Env LR 2. See (2019) 192 *SPEL* 44.
[126] EPA s 82(2).

human habitation until the premises are to the satisfaction of the court or the sheriff, rendered fit for that purpose.[127]

Proceedings require to be brought against the party who is responsible for the nuisance.[128] However, where the nuisance arises from any defect of a structural character, proceedings require to be brought against the owner of the premises. If the person responsible for the nuisance cannot be found, proceedings must be brought against the owner or occupier of the premises. In the case of a statutory nuisance falling within s 79(1)(ga) that is caused by noise emitted from or caused by an unattended vehicle, or unattended machinery or equipment, proceedings must be brought against the person responsible for the vehicle or equipment. Where more than one person is responsible for a statutory nuisance, s 82(1)–(4) inclusive of the EPA applies to each of those persons, whether or not what any one of them is responsible for would by itself amount to a nuisance.[129]

In relation to a statutory nuisance falling within s 79(1)(ga) for which more than one person is responsible (whether or not what any one of those persons is responsible for would not amount to a nuisance) proceedings require to be brought against each person responsible for the nuisance who can be found.[130] As far as a statutory nuisance falling within s 79(1)(ga) that is caused by noise emitted from or caused by an unattended vehicle or unattended machinery or equipment for which more than one person is responsible, proceedings require to be brought against each person responsible for the vehicle.

Prior to instituting proceedings under s 82(2) the person who is aggrieved by the nuisance is required to give the person responsible for the nuisance notice in writing of their intention to bring the relevant proceedings.[131] The notice is required to state the subject matter of the complaint. At least three days' notice of bringing the proceedings must be given in relation to statutory nuisances that fall within s 79(1)(g) and s 79(1)(ga).[132] In the case of other nuisances, not less than twenty one days' notice must be given.

A person who, without reasonable excuse, contravenes any provision that is imposed by an order under s 82(2) is guilty of an offence and liable on summary conviction to a fine not exceeding level 5 on the standard scale, together with a further fine of an amount equal to a tenth of the greater of £5,000 or level 4 on the standard scale, for each day on which the offence continues after the conviction.[133] In Scotland a person guilty of the offence is liable on summary conviction, to a fine not exceeding level 5 on the standard scale, together with a further fine of an amount equal to one tenth of that level for each day on which the offence continues after the conviction.

As is the case in respect of an abatement notice that is served by a local authority, subject to certain exceptions, the defence of best practicable means applies in relation

127 EPA s 82(3).
128 EPA s 82(4).
129 EPA s 82(5).
130 EPA s 82(5A).
131 EPA s 82(6).
132 EPA s 82(7).
133 EPA s 82(8).

to proceedings that are brought by a private individual.[134] As far as noise nuisance is concerned, the defence is not available in relation to s 79(1)(g) except where the noise arises on industrial trade or business premises.[135] Nor is the defence available in relation to s 79(1)(ga) except where the noise is emitted from or caused by a vehicle machinery or equipment being used for industrial, trade or business purposes.

If a person is convicted of an offence under s 82(8), a magistrates' court or the sheriff may, after giving the local authority in whose area the nuisance has occurred an opportunity of being heard, direct the local authority to do anything the person convicted was required to do by the order to which the conviction relates.[136] Where it is proved that the alleged nuisance existed at the date of the making of the complaint, or summary application, then whether or not at the date of the hearing it still exists, or is likely to recur, the court or the sheriff is required to order the defendant or defender (or defendants or defenders in such proportions as appears fair and reasonable) to pay the person bringing the proceedings such amount as the court or the sheriff considers reasonably sufficient to compensate the person for any expenses that were properly incurred by them in the proceedings.[137] However, if it appears to the magistrates' court or the sheriff that neither the person responsible for the nuisance, nor the owner or occupier of the premises or (as the case may be) the person responsible for the vehicle, machinery or equipment, can be found, the court or the sheriff may, after giving the local authority in whose area the nuisance has occurred an opportunity of being heard, direct the authority to anything which the court or the sheriff would have ordered that person to do.[138]

---

[134] EPA s 82(9).
[135] EPA s 82(10).
[136] EPA s 82(11).
[137] EPA s 82(12).
[138] EPA s 82(13).

Chapter 6

Neighbourhood Noise

INTRODUCTION

In this chapter we look at how noise from a wide range of sources and activities, which impact on the community, is controlled. This represents a fragmented area of the law indeed. The legislation relating to neighbourhood noise is piecemeal and is illustrative, perhaps, of the very nature of noise.

CONSTRUCTION SITE NOISE

Noise from construction sites presents a potential problem for those living in close proximity to the site in question. The noise from construction sites is normally generated by the carrying out of building operations (ranging from pile driving to demolition work) or by site traffic. Construction site noise in general may justifiably prompt complaints from those living in close proximity to the site for two main reasons. First, those living in close proximity to the site are not habituated to the noise in question, by virtue of the fact that duration of a construction project is normally comparatively quite short. Second, individuals tend to be more easily annoyed by intermittent noise, which is associated with building sites, than noise that emanates from a long-established source such as a factory. Noise from construction sites, therefore, warrants special legislative attention.

Section 60 of the Control of Pollution Act 1974 (COPA) gives local authorities extensive power to deal with noise from construction sites. The section applies to:

(a) the erection, construction, alteration, repair or maintenance of buildings, structures or roads;
(b) breaking up, opening or boring under any road or adjacent land, in connection with the construction, inspection, maintenance or removal of works;
(c) demolition or dredging work; and
(d) (whether or not also comprised in paragraph (a), (b) or (c) above) any work of engineering construction.[1]

Section 60(2) empowers a local authority to serve a notice that imposes requirements as to the way in which the relevant works are either being carried out or are going to be carried out on any premises.[2] The local authority may also publish notice of the

---

[1] COPA s 60(1).
[2] COPA s 60(2).

requirements in such a way as it appears to the authority to be appropriate. The terms that the local authority can stipulate are required to be both practicable and precise.[3] If the notice simply relates to works that are taking place when the notice is served, the notice is ineffective in relation to noise that emanates from work that, at that time, is not within the contemplation of the local authority.[4] In short, subsequent work would not be covered by the notice. However, there is no requirement that the local authority be in possession of definitive information as to the precise nature of the operations taking place on the site before the authority can lawfully serve a notice under s 60.[5] Furthermore, it must be made clear to the person on whom the notice is served that it relates to a specific area of land.[6]

Section 60(3) provides that the local authority may, in particular, specify the plant or machinery that is, or is not, to be used, and also specify the hours during which the works may be carried out and the level of noise that may be emitted from the premises in question, or at any specified point on those premises, or that may be so emitted during specified hours. The notice may also provide for any change of circumstances.

In *Adam (Scotland) Ltd v Bearsden and Milngavie District Council*[7] it was held by the sheriff that it was legitimate for a local authority to specify a requirement in the appropriate notice that all works that were audible at the site boundary should only be carried out between certain hours. There was no justification for the view that the 'audibility test' was objectionable on the basis that it was subjective.[8]

Under s 60(4) when a local authority acts under the provisions of s 60, the authority is required to have regard to both the relevant provisions of any code of practice that is issued under Part III of COPA[9] and also to the need to ensure that the best practicable means are employed to minimise noise. Before specifying any particular methods, or plant or machinery the local authority is required to address its mind to the desirability, in the interests of any recipients of the notice in question, of specifying other methods or plant or machinery that would be substantially as effective in minimising noise and more acceptable to them. Finally, the local authority is required to have regard to need to protect persons in the locality in which the premises in question are situated from the effects of the noise. The terms of the notice require to be both site-specific, reasonable and necessary.[10]

Under s 65(5) the relevant notice is required to be served on the person who appears to the local authority to be carrying out, or going to carry out the works, and on any other persons who appear to the local authority to be responsible for, or to have control over, the carrying out of the works, as the local authority thinks fit. The notice could, therefore, be served on the relevant building contractor as well as the

---

3 *Strathclyde Regional Council v Tudhope* 1983 SLT 22.
4 *Walter Lilley and Co Ltd v Westminster CC* [1994] Env LR 380.
5 *Wiltshire Construction (London) Ltd v Westminster City Council* [1997] Env LR 321.
6 [1997] Env LR 321 at 325 (per Schiemann LJ).
7 1996 SLT (Sh. Ct) 21.
8 1996 SLT (Sh. Ct) 21 at 27.
9 See the Control of Noise (Code of Practice for Construction and Open Sites) Order 1987 (SI 1987/1730).
10 *Brentwood BC v City and Country (Warley) Ltd* [2010] JPL 1443.

person who commissioned the works (if they are different persons) such as the owner or occupier of the relevant land.

The notice may specify the time within which the notice is to be complied with and may require the person on whom the notice is to be served, to execute such works and also take such other steps as may be necessary for the purpose of the notice, or as may be specified in the notice.[11]

The person served with a notice under s 60 may appeal against the notice to the magistrates' court or, in Scotland, to the sheriff, within twenty-one days from the service of the notice.[12] If a person on whom a notice is served under s 60 contravenes, without reasonable excuse, any requirements of the notice, that person commits an offence under COPA.[13]

One can readily see that the prospect of the relevant local authority serving notice under s 60 could present a constant threat to a building contractor who requires to know, at the outset of the construction operations, how long the building operations will last as well as the type of machinery and plant that will be used on the site. Section 61(1) therefore, allows a person who intends to carry out building operations to apply for consent to carry out the works. If, as normally will be the case, the building works require approval or, in Scotland, a warrant in terms of the Building (Scotland) Act 2003, the application for consent is required to be made at the same time or later than the request for approval under the building regulations or, as the case may be, the application for a building warrant under the 2003 Act.[14] The application must contain particulars of the works, the method by which they are to be carried out and also the steps that are proposed to be taken in order to minimise noise that results from the works.[15] The local authority is required to give its approval to the application if it considers that the application contains sufficient information for the purpose and that if the works are carried out in accordance with the application, the local authority would not serve notice under s 60.[16] When considering whether to grant consent, the local authority must address its mind to the provisions of s 60 of COPA.[17] The local authority have power to attach conditions to a consent; limit or qualify a consent; to allow for any change of circumstances; and also, limit the duration of the consent. It is made an offence for any person to either knowingly carry out works, or permit the works to be carried out, in contravention of any conditions that are attached to a consent.

The local authority is required to inform the applicant of its decision within twenty-eight days of the receipt of the application.[18] The applicant can appeal to the magistrates' court or, in Scotland, the sheriff, against the refusal of a local authority to grant consent or against any condition or any qualification that is attached to a

[11] COPA s 60(6).

[12] COPA s 60(7). See the Control of Noise (Appeals) Regulations 1975 (SI 1975/2116) reg 5 and the Control of Appeals (Scotland) Regulations 1983 (SI 1983/1455) reg 5.

[13] COPA s 60(8).

[14] COPA s 61(2).

[15] COPA s 61(3).

[16] COPA s 61(4).

[17] COPA s 61(5).

[18] COPA s 61(6).

consent.[19] In any proceedings for an offence under s 60(8) it is a defence to prove that the alleged contravention amounted to the carrying out of works that were in accordance with a consent given under s 61.[20] A consent that is given under s 61 is required to contain a statement to the effect that such a consent does not, of itself, constitute any ground of defence against proceedings that are instituted under s 82 of the Environmental Protection Act 1990 (EPA).[21] Finally, where a consent has been given under s 61 and the works are carried out by a person (for example, a subcontractor) other than the applicant, a duty is imposed on the applicant to take all reasonable steps to bring the consent to the notice of that other person.[22] A penalty is imposed for failure to comply with this requirement.

British Standard 5228[23] gives recommendations for basic methods of noise control relating to construction sites, including sites where demolition remediation and ground treatment or related civil engineering work are being carried out, and also open sites, where work activities/operations generate significant noise levels, including industry-specific guidance. The legislative background to noise control is described and recommendations are given regarding procedures for the establishment of effective liaison between developers, site operators and local authorities.

LOUDSPEAKERS IN STREETS AND ROADS

Loudspeakers in vehicles have been a problem for a number of years. More recently, the problem has worsened by virtue of certain antisocial individuals using powerful sound systems in their cars, which are capable of generating great volumes of noise, to the discomfort of members of the public. However, Parliament did not consider the problem sufficiently serious to warrant legislative attention until 1960, when the Noise Abatement Act 1960 (repealed) made special provision for loudspeaker street noise. The problem is now dealt with by the Control of Pollution Act 1974. Section 62(1)(a) makes it an offence to use a loudspeaker in a street[24] or, in Scotland, a road, between 9pm and 8am the following morning, for any purpose. It is also made an offence, under s 62(1)(b) to use a loudspeaker in a street, or road, at any other time for the purpose of advertising any trade or business. Power is given to the Secretary of State, or in Scotland, the Scottish Ministers, to amend the times specified in s 62(1)(a) by order.[25] However, such an order may not amend the times so as to permit the operation of a loudspeaker in a street or road at any time between the hours of 9pm in the evening and 8pm in the following morning.[26] Section 62(2) exempts from the

---

19 COPA s 61(7).

20 COPA s 61(8).

21 COPA s 61(9).

22 COPA s 61(10).

23 British Standard 5228, *Code of Practice for noise and vibration control on construction and open sites – Part 1: Noise* (2009).

24 A street is defined in s 62(1) as a highway and any other road, footway, square or court that is for the time being, open to the public. In *Westminster City Council v French Connection Retail Ltd* [2005] Env LR 42 it was held that the outer face of a shop window formed part of a street. Therefore, the window, which was being used by the defendant to amplify sound, could rank as a loudspeaker in the relevant street.

25 COPA s 62(1A).

26 COPA s 62(1B).

provisions of s 62(1) certain types of loudspeaker, including those which are used by the police, fire and ambulance services. Also exempt is the use of a loudspeaker, which is either in or fixed to a vehicle (for example, a loudspeaker that is part of a car radio system) and is used solely to entertain or communicate with the driver or passenger of the vehicle, or where the loudspeaker either is, or forms part of the horn, or similar warning instrument of the vehicle, solely for giving warning to other traffic, and is operated as not to give reasonable cause for annoyance to persons in the vicinity. Another important exemption, in practical terms, is made in respect of the operation of a loudspeaker between noon and pm of the same day, provided that the loudspeaker is fixed to a vehicle that is used for the purpose of a sale of a perishable commodity (for example, ice cream) for human consumption and is operated so as not to give cause for annoyance to persons who are in the vicinity.[27] Under s 62(3A) power is given to the relevant local authority to give consent to the operation of a loudspeaker, in terms of Schedule 2 to the Noise and Statutory Nuisance Act 1993, in which case the provisions of s 62(1) do not apply. However, the provisions of that schedule only come into effect if the local authority passes a resolution to that effect.[28]

NOISE FROM PLANT AND MACHINERY

Under s 68(1) of COPA the Secretary of State, or the Scottish Ministers, have power to make regulations to require the use, either on or in connection with plant or machinery, of devices or arrangements for reducing the noise caused by plant or machinery. Regulations may also limit the level of noise that may be caused by any plant or machinery, when used for works to which s 60 applies, or that may be caused outside a factory, within the meaning of the Factories Act 1961, by the use of the plant or machinery in the factory. It is made an offence to contravene the regulations.[29]

OTHER STATUTORY CONTROLS OVER NEIGHBOURHOOD NOISE

Civic Government (Scotland) Act 1982

Noise from musical instruments, etc.: dogs

Noise from televisions, radios, music systems and other amplified sound is a perennial problem in the UK. Excessive noise from such devices can rank either as a nuisance or a statutory nuisance as covered in Chapters 3 and 4 respectively.[30] In Scotland, the Civic Government (Scotland) Act 1982 gives police the power to deal with specific types of noise. Under s 54(1) of the Act any person who sounds or plays a musical instrument, sings, performs or operates any radio or television receiver, record player, tape recorder, or other sound-producing device so as to give any other

[27] COPA s 62(3).
[28] Noise and Statutory Nuisance Act 1993 s 8.
[29] COPA s 68(3).
[30] See Chs. 4 and 5, resp.

person reasonable cause for annoyance, and fails to desist on being required to do so by a constable in uniform, commits an offence under the Act.[31] Where a constable reasonably suspects that an offence has been committed in relation to a musical instrument, or in relation to a radio, television receiver, record player or other sound-producing device, the constable may enter the premises on which they reasonably suspect the instrument or device to be and seize any such instrument or device that they there.[32] The constable may use reasonable force in entering the premises and seizing the equipment.[33]

As far as noise being caused by dogs is concerned, s 49(1) provides that any person who suffers or permits any person in their charge to cause danger or injury to any other person who is in a public place, or to give such creature reasonable cause for alarm or annoyance, commits an offence and is liable to a penalty. Therefore, animals such as dogs that cause annoyance to neighbours, by barking, would fall within the scope of the section.

Noise Act 1996

Night-time noise has been a perennial problem. The Noise Act 1996 (the 1996 Act), which relates to the UK excluding Scotland, makes specific provision for night-time noise.

Investigation of complaints of noise at night

A local authority in England and Wales may, if it receives a complaint, falling within the scope of the Act, arrange for an officer of the authority to take reasonable steps to investigate the complaint.[34] The kind of complaint referred to is one that is made by an individual who is present in a dwelling[35] during night hours[36] (referred to in the Act as the 'complainant's dwelling'), that excessive noise is being emitted from another dwelling, (referred to as the 'offending dwelling') or any premises in respect of which a premises licence[37] or a temporary event notice[38] has effect (referred to as the 'offending premises').[39] A complaint may be made by any means.[40] If an officer of the authority is satisfied, in consequence of an investigation, that noise is being emitted from the offending dwelling or the offending premises, during night hours and the noise, if it were measured from within the complainant's dwelling, would or might exceed the permitted level (as defined in s 5) they may serve a notice under

---

31 Section 54(1) of the 1982 Act is without prejudice to any offence committed under s 62 of COPA (operation of loudspeakers in streets): s 54(2). See above.

32 Civic Government (Scotland) Act 1982 s 54(2A).

33 Civic Government (Scotland) Act 1982 s 54(2B).

34 Noise Act 1996 s 2(1).

35 A 'dwelling' means any building or part of a building, used or intended to be used, as a dwelling. References to noise emitted from a dwelling include noise emitted from any garden, yard or outhouse or other appurtenance belonging to or enjoyed with the dwelling: s 11(2).

36 'Night hours' means the period beginning with 11pm and ending with the following 7am: s 2(6).

37 'Premises licence' has the same meaning as in the Licensing Act 2003: s 2(7A).

38 'Temporary event notice' has the same meaning as in the Licensing Act 2003.

39 1996 Act s 2(2).

40 1996 Act s 2(3).

s 3.[41] The officer has power to decide whether any noise, if it were measured from within the complainant's dwelling, would or might exceed the permitted level.[42] The officer also has the power to decide whether to assess the noise either from within or outside the complainant's dwelling, and also whether or not to use any device for measuring the noise.

Warning notices

The Act makes provision for the service of warning notices. A warning notice is required to state that an officer of the authority considers that noise is being emitted from the offending dwelling or offending premises during night hours and that the noise either exceeds, or may exceed, the permitted level as measured from within the complainant's dwelling.[43] If the complaint is in respect of a dwelling, the notice must give warning that any person who is responsible for noise that is emitted from an offending dwelling, in the period specified in the notice, and that exceeds the permitted level as measured from within the complainant's dwelling, may be guilty of an offence. Where the complaint is in respect of other premises the warning notice is required to state that the responsible person, in relation to the offending premises, may be guilty of an offence if noise that exceeds the permitted level, as measured from within the complainant's dwelling, is emitted from the premises in the period specified in the notice. The period specified in the warning notice must be a period beginning not earlier than ten minutes after the time when the notice is served and ending with the following 7am.[44] Where the complaint is in respect of a dwelling, a warning notice must be served by delivering it to any person present at, or near, the offending dwelling and appearing to the officer to be responsible for the noise.[45] However, if it is not reasonably practical to identify any person present, at or near the dwelling as being the person responsible for the noise on whom the notice may reasonably be served, the warning notice requires to be served by leaving it at the offending dwelling. Where the relevant complaint relates to other premises, a warning notice must be served by delivering it to the person who appears to the officer of the authority to be the responsible person, in relation to the offending premises, at the time when the notice is served.[46] A warning notice requires to state the time at which it is served.[47]

Responsible person

A person is responsible for noise emitted from a dwelling if they are a person to whose act, default or sufferance the emission of the noise is wholly, or partly, attributable.[48] The responsible person in relation to offending premises at a particular time is:

---

[41] 1996 Act s 2(4).
[42] 1996 Act s 2(5).
[43] 1996 Act s 3(1).
[44] 1996 Act s 3(2).
[45] 1996 Act s 3(3).
[46] 1996 Act s 3(3A).
[47] 1996 Act s 3(4).
[48] 1996 Act s 3(5).

(a) where a premises licence has effect in respect of the premises,
  (i) the person who holds the premises licence (or a temporary event notice has effect) if he is present at the premises at that time,
  (ii) where that person is not present at the premises at that time, the designated premises supervisor under the licence, if he is present at the premises at that time, or
  (iii) where neither of the persons mentioned in sub-paragraphs (i) and (ii) is present at the premises at that time, any other person who is present at the premises at that time, and who is in charge of the premises,

(b) where a temporary event notice has effect in respect of the premises-
  (i) the premises user in relation to that notice, if he is present at the premises at that time, or
  (ii) where the premises user is not present at the premises at that time, any other person present at the premises at that time, who is in charge of the premises.[49]

Offences

If a warning notice has been served in respect of noise emitted from a dwelling, any person who is responsible for noise that is emitted from the dwelling in the period specified in the notice and exceeds the permitted level, as measured from the complainant's dwelling, commits an offence.[50] It is a defence for a person charged to show that there was reasonable excuse for the act, default or sufferance in question.[51] A person who commits an offence is liable to a fine.[52]

If a warning notice has been served under s 3 in respect of noise emitted from premises and that the noise is emitted in the period specified in the notice with such noise exceeding the permitted level, as measured from within the complainant's dwelling, the responsible person in relation to the offending premises at the time at which that noise is emitted commits an offence.[53] Any person who commits an offence is liable to a fine.[54]

Permitted level of noise

The appropriate person[55] is given the power, by directions, to determine in writing the maximum level of noise (i.e. the 'permitted level') that may be emitted during night time hours from any dwelling or other premises.[56] The permitted level is to be a level applicable to noise, as measured from within any other dwelling in the vicinity, by an approved device used in accordance with any conditions subject to which approval was given.[57] Different permitted levels may be determined for different circumstances and the permitted level may be determined partly by reference to

[49] 1996 Act s 3(6).
[50] 1996 Act s 4(1).
[51] 1996 Act s 4(2).
[52] 1996 Act s 4(3).
[53] 1996 Act s 4A(1).
[54] 1996 Act s 4A(2).
[55] The appropriate person is the Secretary of State for England and the National Assembly for Wales for Wales: s 11(2).
[56] 1996 Act s 5(1).
[57] 1996 Act s 5(2).

other levels of noise.[58] The appropriate person may vary the directions by further directions in writing.[59]

Approval of measuring devices

Power is given to the appropriate person to approve, in writing, any type of device that is used in the measurement of noise for the purposes of ss 2–9 inclusive.[60] Any such approval may be given subject to conditions as to the purposes for which, and the manner and other circumstances in which, devices of the type concerned may be used.[61] In any proceedings for an offence under ss 4 or 4A, a measurement of noise made by a device is not admissible as evidence of the level of noise unless it is an approved device and any conditions subject to which the approval was given are satisfied.[62]

Fixed penalty notices

The 1996 Act makes provision for the service of fixed penalty notices. Where an officer of a local authority, who is authorised for the purposes of s 8 of the Act, has reason to believe that a person is either committing, or has just committed an offence under ss 4 or 4A, the officer is empowered to give that person a fixed penalty notice, offering them the opportunity of discharging any liability to conviction for that offence by payment of a fixed penalty.[63] A fixed penalty notice may be given to a person either: (a) by delivering it to them; or (b) if it is not reasonably possible to deliver it to them, by leaving the notice addressed to them at the offending dwelling or offending premises, as the case may be.[64]

Where a person is given a fixed penalty notice in respect of such an offence, proceedings for that offence must not be instituted within fourteen days from the date of the notice.[65] The relevant person cannot be convicted of that offence if they pay the fixed penalty before the end of that period. The notice must give particulars of the circumstances that are alleged to constitute the offence, as are necessary for giving reasonable information of the offence.[66] The fixed penalty notice is required to state: (a) that proceedings cannot be taken against them within fourteen days from the date of the service of the notice; (b) the amount of fixed penalty; and (c) the person to whom, and the address at which, the fixed penalty may be paid.[67] The 1996 Act makes provision for the amount of fixed penalty.[68]

If a fixed penalty notice is given to a person in respect of noise emitted from any dwelling in any period specified in a warning notice, then no further fixed penalty notice may be given to that person in respect of noise emitted from that dwelling

58 1996 Act s 5(3).
59 1996 Act s 5(4).
60 1996 Act s 6(1).
61 1996 Act s 6(2).
62 1996 Act s 6(3).
63 1996 Act s 8(1).
64 1996 Act s 8(2).
65 1996 Act s 8(3).
66 1996 Act s 8(4).
67 1996 Act s 8(5).
68 1996 Act s 8A.

during that period.[69] However, that person may be convicted of a further offence under s 4,[70] in respect of noise emitted from the dwelling after the fixed penalty notice is given and before the end of that period.

If a fixed penalty notice is given to a person in respect of noise from other premises in any period that is specified in a warning notice, no further fixed penalty notice may be given to that person in respect of noise emitted from the premises during that period.[71] However, that person may be convicted of a further offence under s 4A, in respect of noise emitted from the premises after the fixed penalty notice is given and before the end of that period.

Powers of entry and seizure

The 1996 Act makes provision for powers of entry and seizure. An officer of a local authority, or a person authorised by the authority for the purpose, has the power to enter the relevant dwelling, or other premises, from which the noise in question either is being or has been emitted and may seize and remove any equipment that appears to them as being, or has been used in, the emission of the noise.[72] The power of entry may be exercised where an officer of the authority has reason to believe that: (a) a warning notice has been served in respect of noise emitted from a dwelling, or other premises; and (b) at any time in the period specified in the notice noise emitted from the dwelling or other premises, has exceeded the permitted level as measured from within the complainant's dwelling.[73] A person exercising the power of entry is required to produce their authority if they are required to do so.[74]

The 1996 Act empowers a justice of the peace to authorise entry to relevant premises. If it is shown to a justice of the peace, on sworn information in writing, that:

- (a) a warning notice has been served in respect of noise emitted from a dwelling or other premises,
- (b) at any time in the period specified in the notice, noise emitted from the dwelling, or other premises, has exceeded the permitted level as measured from the complainant's dwelling, and
- (c) entry of an officer of the local authority or a person authorised by the local authority for the purpose, to the dwelling or other premises, has been refused, or such refusal is apprehended, or a request by an officer, or of such a person, for admission, would defeat the object of the entry,

the justice of the peace may, by warrant under their hand, authorise the local authority, by any of their officers or any person authorised by them for the purpose to enter the dwelling or other premises, if need be by force.[75] The person who enters any dwelling or other premises, or by virtue of a warrant issued by a justice of the peace,

[69] 1996 Act s 9(2).
[70] Above.
[71] 1996 Act s 9(2A).
[72] 1996 Act s 10(2).
[73] 1996 Act s 10(1).
[74] 1996 Act s 10(3).
[75] 1996 Act s 10(4).

may take with him such other persons and such equipment as may be necessary.[76] If the dwelling, or other premises, is unoccupied when the person who enters leaves, they are required to leave it, or them, as effectively secured against trespassers as they found it, or them. A warrant issued under s 10(4) continues in force until the purpose for which the entry is required has been satisfied.[77] Any person who wilfully obstructs any person exercising any powers under s 10(2) or (7) is liable to a fine on summary conviction.[78]

ANTISOCIAL BEHAVIOUR

We now consider, chronologically, statutes that address the problem of antisocial behaviour, which can manifest itself in many ways, including conduct that generates noise to the annoyance of others.

Antisocial Behaviour etc. (Scotland) Act 2004

In *A Partnership for a Better Scotland: Partnership Agreement*[79] the Scottish Government committed itself to social justice, in particular to ensure that everyone in Scotland could enjoy a decent quality of life. It pledged to tackle antisocial behaviour. The Antisocial Behaviour etc. (Scotland) Act 2004 (ABSA) makes provision for various forms of antisocial behaviour, amongst which is the generation of noise.

Antisocial behaviour orders

Part 2 of ABSA makes provision for antisocial behaviour orders. Under s 4(1) a sheriff, on the application of a relevant authority,[80] if satisfied that the following conditions are met, can make an antisocial behaviour order. The conditions are:

(a) that the specified person is at least twelve years of age;
(b) that the specified person has engaged in antisocial behaviour towards a relevant person, and
(c) that an antisocial behaviour order is necessary for the purpose of protecting relevant persons from further antisocial behaviour by the specified person.[81]

The expression 'antisocial behaviour' is defined as such if the relevant person:

(a) acts in a manner that causes or is likely to cause alarm or distress; or
(b) pursues a course of conduct[82] that causes or is likely to cause alarm or distress to at least one person who is not of the same household as that person.[83]

---

[76] 1996 Act s 10(5).
[77] 1996 Act s 10(6).
[78] 1996 Act s 10(8).
[79] May 2003.
[80] 'Relevant authority' means: (a) a local authority; or (b) a registered social landlord: ABSA s 18.
[81] ABSA s 4(2).
[82] 'Conduct' includes speech, and a course of conduct must involve conduct on at least two occasions: s 143(2).
[83] ABSA s 143(1).

Antisocial behaviour can, therefore, include conduct that generates noise. The expression 'distress' as used in ABSA is not defined. It should, therefore, be given its everyday meaning. Any form of noise annoyance or anxiety on the part of the receiver, could, therefore, fall within the scope of ABSA. It would be a question of fact whether the conduct in question had caused distress.

Noise nuisance

Part 5 of ABSA makes special provision for neighbourhood noise. The provisions of Part 5 are similar to those contained in the Noise Act 1996, which have been discussed above.[84]

The provisions of ABSA that relate to the control of noise[85] apply to the area of a local authority only if the local authority has so resolved.[86] A local authority that has resolved to adopt ABSA has some flexibility as to the periods of the week (i.e. noise control periods) the noise control periods should apply.[87] The noise control provisions could be confined to night-time hours. The noise control provisions may be made to apply to the whole week.[88] The local authority may specify different noise control periods for different areas and also to different times of the year. The authority may also specify that different noise control periods apply for different circumstances. ABSA also makes provision for publicity. If a local authority resolves to apply the noise control provisions in its area, the local authority is required to have a notice published in a local newspaper that circulates in the area.[89] At least one month before the relevant commencement date (i.e. the date on which the noise control period commences) the local authority is required to give a copy of the resolution to the Scottish Ministers, and also to each local authority whose area adjoins its area. The relevant notice requires to state that the resolution has been passed.[90] The notice also requires to contain its commencement date, and *inter alia*, set out the general effect of the noise control provisions of ABSA, as well as the noise control periods specified in the resolution. ABSA also makes provision for the resolution to be either revoked or varied.[91]

Investigations of excessive noise

ABSA makes provision for the investigation of noise by the relevant local authority. Where a local authority receives a complaint from an individual that excessive noise is being emitted from relevant property[92] during a noise control period, the local

[84] See above.
[85] ABSA ss 43–47.
[86] ABSA s 41(1).
[87] ABSA s 41(2).
[88] ABSA s 41(3).
[89] ABSA s 41(5).
[90] ABSA s 41(6).
[91] ABSA s 42(1).
[92] 'Relevant property' means: (a) any accommodation; (b) any land belonging exclusively to; or enjoyed or enjoyed exclusively with any accommodation; (c) any land not falling within paragraph (b)(i) to which at least two people have rights in common; and (ii) which is used by those persons as a private garden; (d) any common passage, close, court, stair, lift or yard pertinent to any tenement or group of separately owned houses; or (e) such other place as may be prescribed (i.e. by the Scottish Ministers): ABSA s 53(1).

authority must ensure that an officer of the authority investigates the matter.[93] However, the expression 'investigates' is not defined in ABSA. Therefore, there is no statutory requirement, for example, that any officer of the local authority should visit the alleged offender's premises, or that of the complainant. The relevant complaint can be investigated by any means.[94] If, in consequence of such an investigation, an officer is satisfied that noise is being emitted from a relevant property (the 'offending property') and the noise, if it was measured from the relevant place,[95] would or might exceed the permitted level,[96] the officer may serve a notice about the noise under s 44.[97] It is a matter for the discretion of the officer concerned, first, whether any noise might exceed the permitted level, and second, to decide from which place to assess the noise and whether to use a device for measuring noise.[98] Where a local authority (the 'first local authority') receives a complaint that concerns offending property that is situated within the area of another local authority, the first authority is empowered to deal with that property under ABSA as if that property was situated in the area of the first local authority, whether or not the noise control provisions of ABSA apply to the latter area.[99]

Warning notices

ABSA makes provision for the service of warning notices. A warning notice requires to state that the officer of the authority considers that noise is being emitted from the offending property during a noise control period and that the noise either exceeds, or may exceed, the permitted level, as measured from a relevant place.[100] The notice must also state that any person who is responsible for noise emitted from the offending property in the period specified in the notice and exceeds the permitted level, as measured from a relevant place, may be guilty of an offence. The period that is specified in a warning notice is the period that begins not earlier than ten minutes after the time when the notice is served and ends at the relevant time.[101] The expression 'relevant time' is defined as the earlier of the end of the noise control period during which the warning notice is served and the point (if any) at which the permitted level at the time the notice is served ceases to be applicable.[102] The warning notice requires to be served, by delivering it to any person present at, or near, the

[93] ABSA s 43(1).
[94] ABSA s 43(2).
[95] 'Relevant place' means: (a) any place within accommodation (except in the case of measurement of noise emitted from relevant property which is accommodation, that accommodation); and (b) such other place as may be prescribed; ABSA s 53(1).
[96] Under s 48 the Scottish Ministers are empowered to prescribe the maximum level of noise by regulations. The permitted level of noise is the level of noise as measured from any relevant place by an approved device that is used in accordance with any conditions subject to which approval was given. Different permitted levels may be prescribed for different periods of the week, areas or description of areas, times of the year or other circumstances. The Antisocial Behaviour (Noise Control) (Scotland) Regulations 2005 (SSI 2005/43) reg 3 prescribe relevant noise levels for purposes of ABSA.
[97] ABSA s 43(3).
[98] ABSA s 43(4).
[99] ABSA s 43(5).
[100] ABSA s 44(1).
[101] ABSA s 44(2).
[102] ABSA s 44(3).

offending property, and appearing to the officer of the authority to be responsible for the noise.[103] If it is not reasonably practical to identify any person who is present either at, or near, the offending property as being a person responsible for the noise on whom the notice can reasonably be served, the warning notice requires to be served by leaving it at the offending property.[104] The warning notice requires to state the time at which it is served.[105]

Offences

If a noise notice has been served in respect of noise that is emitted from a relevant property, any person who is responsible for noise emitted from the relevant property in the period specified in the notice, and exceeds the permitted level, as measured from a relevant place, commits an offence.[106] Liability for the offence is strict. Therefore, there is no need for the prosecution to establish intention, or fault, on the part of the accused. A person who is guilty of such an offence is liable, on summary conviction, to a fine not exceeding level 3 on the standard scale.[107] However, in common with statutes that make provision for offences of strict liability, ABSA makes provision for statutory defence. It is a defence for a person who is charged with an offence under s 45(1) to show that there was reasonable excuse for the act, failure, or sufferance by reference to which the person was charged.[108] In proceedings for an offence under s 45, a measurement of noise by a device is not admissible as evidence of a level of noise unless the device is an approved device and any conditions subject to which the approval was given are satisfied.[109] The Scottish Ministers have power to approve by regulations any type of device that is used in the measurement of noise.[110] Approval may be given subject to such conditions as to the purposes for which, or the manner or circumstances in which, devices of the type approved are to used, as may be prescribed in the regulations.[111]

Fixed penalty notices

Traditionally, one of the main failings of noise control legislation has been the inability of local authorities to immediately compel an individual who is making excessive noise to refrain from so doing. ABSA addresses this problem. Where a relevant officer[112] has reason to believe that a person is either committing, or has just committed, an offence under s 45 the officer may give that person a fixed penalty notice, which offers the relevant individual the opportunity of discharging any

[103] ABSA s 44(4).
[104] ABSA s 44(5).
[105] ABSA s 44(6).
[106] ABSA s 45(1).
[107] ABSA s 45(2).
[108] ABSA s 45(3).
[109] ABSA s 45(5).
[110] ABSA s 49(1). The Antisocial Behaviour (Noise Control) (Scotland) Regulations 2005 reg 5 prescribes noise measuring devices that are approved in terms of ABSA.
[111] ABSA s 49(2).
[112] A relevant officer means an officer of the local authority who is authorised for the purposes of s 46 or a constable: ABSA s 46(2).

liability to conviction for that offence by payment of a fixed penalty.[113] If a fixed penalty notice is given to a person in respect of noise that is emitted from a relevant property in the period that is specified in a warning notice, no further fixed penalty notice may be given to that person in respect of the noise emitted from the relevant property during that period.[114] A fixed penalty notice may be given to a person by delivering the notice to the person.[115] However, if it is not reasonably practical to deliver the notice to the person, a fixed penalty notice is required to be given by leaving the notice addressed to the person at the offending property.[116] The notice requires to give sufficient particulars of the circumstances that are alleged to constitute the offence.[117] The fixed penalty notice is also required to state the period during which proceedings may not be taken for the offence, the amount of fixed penalty, and the address at which the fixed penalty can be paid.[118] Proceedings may not be instituted during a period of twenty-one days from the date of the service of the notice.[119] A person may not be convicted of the offence if the appropriate fixed penalty is paid before the expiration of that period.

Power of seizure of equipment

In practical terms and, indeed, in the mind of the public, one of the most important features of ABSA are the provisions that relate to the seizure of equipment used to create noise. An officer of the local authority, or a person who is authorised by the local authority for the purpose, may seize and remove any equipment that appears to either being, or has been used, in the emission of noise.[120] The equipment can be seized and removed if a warning notice has been served in respect of the noise that has been emitted from the relevant property and an officer of the local authority, in whose area the relevant property is situated, has reason to believe that at any time in the period specified in the notice, noise that was emitted from the relevant property exceeded the permitted level, as measured from a relevant place.[121] If required to do so, a person who is exercising the power of seizure, etc. must produce their authority.[122] If a sheriff, or justice of the peace, is satisfied by evidence on oath that a warning notice has been served in respect of noise emitted from relevant property and that at any time in the period that has been specified in the notice, noise that is emitted from the relevant property has exceeded the permitted level (as measured from a relevant place) and that entry of an officer of the local authority, or of a person who is authorised by the authority for the purpose, to a relevant property has been refused or refusal is apprehended (or, alternatively, a request by an officer of the authority would defeat the object of entry), the sheriff or justice may grant a warrant.[123] The

[113] ABSA s 46(1).
[114] ABSA s 46(3).
[115] ABSA s 46(4).
[116] ABSA s 46(5).
[117] ABSA s 46(6).
[118] ABSA s 46(7).
[119] ABSA s 51(2).
[120] ABSA s 47(2).
[121] ABSA s 47(1).
[122] ABSA s 47(3).
[123] ABSA s 47(4).

relevant warrant authorises the local authority, by any of its officers or any person authorised by it for the purpose, to enter the relevant property for the purpose of seizing and removing any equipment that appears to be being used, or to have been used, in the emission of noise and in order to do so, to open lockfast places on the relevant property.[124] The person who enters premises by virtue of a warrant that is granted under s 47 may be accompanied by such persons and take such equipment as may be necessary.[125] Where the relevant property is unoccupied, on the person's departure it must be left as effectively secure against trespassers as it was when the person entered it. It is made an offence for a person to wilfully obstruct a person in the exercise of their powers of seizure and removal of equipment under s 47(2), or in exercising the power that is conferred by warrant under s 47(2).[126]

Power to fund local authorities

A unique feature of ABSA is that in order to ensure that the provisions of the Act are properly enforced, ABSA empowers the Scottish Ministers to make payment to a local authority in respect of the whole, or any part, of the expenditure of the authority in carrying out its noise control functions under ABSA.[127]

General overview of ABSA Part 5 and the Noise Act 1996

We have seen that ABSA employs noise standards that are based on fixed noise levels, in contrast to the nuisance-based regime that has traditionally played such a prominent role in noise law in Scotland and, indeed, the UK thus far. One of the main practical disadvantages with a regime that is nuisance-based is that it is often difficult to ascertain whether a given state of affairs ranks as a noise nuisance in law. A regime that employs fixed standards is, in theory at least, simpler and easier to understand by the creator of the noise and, importantly, by the general public.[128]

Anti-social Behaviour, Crime and Policing Act 2014

In May 2012 the UK government published a White Paper, *Putting victims first: more effective responses to anti-social behaviour*.[129] The White Paper set out how the Government would support local areas to focus the response to antisocial behaviour on the needs of victims; empower communities to get involved in tackling antisocial behaviour; ensure that professionals were able to protect the public quickly and focus on long-term solutions. The proposed reforms were intended to provide better

124 ABSA s 47(5).
125 ABSA s 47(6).
126 ABSA s 47(7).
127 ABSA s 50(1).
128 Rowan-Robinson and Watchman argue that the use of general environmental standards such as nuisance make it difficult for traders, etc. to know with any degree of certainty whether or not they are complying with the law. Such standards also make enforcement problematic and lead to disagreement as to whether an offence has been committed: J. Rowan-Robinson and P. Watchman, *Crime and Regulation* (T. and T. Clark, 1990) at 191.
129 Cm 8367 (2012), available at *https://assets.publishing.service.gov.uk/government/uploads/system/uploads/attachment_data/file/228863/8367.pdf* (last accessed 20 October 2022).

protection for victims and communities and ensure that professionals had effective powers that were quick, practical and easy to use and acted as real deterrents to perpetrators. The policy, which was embodied in the White Paper, formed the basis of the Anti-social Behaviour, Crime and Policing Act 2014, which makes provision for a wide array of behaviour that can be included under the rubric 'antisocial'. However, we simply focus on the provisions that can include conduct that generates noise. The provisions dealt with relate to England and Wales.

Power to grant injunctions

Under the Anti-social Behaviour, Crime and Policing Act 2014 (the 2014 Act) a court has the power to grant an injunction against a person aged ten or over if two conditions are met.[130]

The first condition is that the court is satisfied, on the balance of probabilities, that that person either has engaged, or threatens to engage, in antisocial behaviour.[131] The second condition is that the court considers it just and convenient to grant the injunction for the purpose of preventing the respondent engaging in antisocial behaviour.[132] Antisocial behaviour is defined as conduct that has caused, or is likely to cause, harassment, alarm or distress to any person; conduct capable of causing nuisance, or annoyance, to a person in relation to that person's occupation of residential premises[133]; or conduct capable of causing housing-related nuisance, or annoyance, to any person.[134] The creation of noise would, therefore, clearly be included in the definition of 'antisocial'.

The injunction may, for the purpose of preventing the respondent from engaging in antisocial behaviour, prohibit the respondent from doing anything described in the injunction, and also require the respondent to do anything described in the injunction.[135] The prohibitions and requirements in any injunction must, so far is reasonably practical, be such as to avoid: (a) any interference with the times, if any, at which the respondent normally works, or attends school, or any other educational establishment; and (b) any conflict with the requirements of any other court order, or injunction, to which the respondent may be subject.[136] An injunction must: (a) specify the period for which it has effect; or (b) state that it has effect until further order.[137] In the case of an injunction granted before the respondent has reached the age of eighteen, a period must be specified. That period must be no longer than twelve months. The injunction may specify particular periods for which particular prohibitions, or requirements, have effect.[138] An application for an injunction requires

[130] Anti-social Behaviour, Crime and Policing Act 2014 s 1(1).
[131] 2014 Act s 1(2).
[132] 2014 s 1(3).
[133] Only a housing provider, local authority or chief officer of police may apply for an injunction in relation to conduct that is capable of causing nuisance or annoyance to a person in relation to that person's occupation of residential premises: 2014 Act s 2(2).
[134] 2014 Act s 2(1).
[135] 2014 Act s 1(4).
[136] 2014 Act s 1(5).
[137] 2014 Act s 1(6).
[138] 2014 Act s 1(7).

to be made to a youth court, in the case of a respondent aged under eighteen, or the High Court in any other case.[139]

Closure of premises

Whilst noise from licensed premises, including nightclubs, which ranks as a nuisance would fall within the scope of ss 79(1)(g) and 82 of the EPA, an important additional means of controlling noise from such premises is the closure of the premises.

Closure notices

Under s 76 of the Anti-social Behaviour, Crime and Policing Act 2014 a police officer of at least the rank of inspector, or the local authority, may issue a closure notice if satisfied on reasonable grounds: (a) that the use of particular premises has resulted or (if the notice is not issued) is likely soon to result in nuisance to the general public; or, (b) that there has been (or if the notice is not issued) is likely soon to be disorder near those premises associated with the use of those premises, and that the notice is necessary to prevent the nuisance or disorder from continuing, recurring or occurring.[140] A closure notice is a notice that prohibits access to the premises for a period specified in the notice.[141] A closure notice may prohibit access: (a) by all persons, except those specified, or by all persons, except those of a specified description; (b) at all times, or at all times except those except those specified; (c) in all circumstances, or in all circumstances except those specified.[142] However, a closure notice may not prohibit access by people who habitually live on the premises, or the owner of the premises.[143] Those persons must be specified under s 76(3)(a).

A closure notice is required to contain a variety of information, including: the identity of the premises; the effect of the notice; a statement to the effect that failure to comply with the notice is an offence; a statement that an application will be made under s 80 for a closure order[144]; specify where and when the application will be heard; and explain the effect of a closure order.[145] The notice must also give information of the names of and the means of contacting persons and organisations in the area that provide advice about housing and legal matters. A closure order can only be made if reasonable efforts have been made to inform people who live on the premises (whether habitually or not) and any person who has control of or responsibility for the premises, or who has an interest in them, that the notice is going to be issued.[146] Before issuing a closure notice the police officer, or the local authority, must ensure that any body or individual that the officer or the authority thinks appropriate, has been consulted.[147] The maximum period that may be specified

[139] 2014 Act s 1(8).
[140] 2014 Act s 76(1).
[141] 2014 Act s 76(2).
[142] 2014 Act s 76(3).
[143] 2014 Act s 76(4).
[144] See p. 81 below.
[145] 2014 Act s 76(5).
[146] 2014 Act s 76(6).
[147] 2014 Act s 76(7).

in a closure notice is twenty-four hours.[148] However, this period is extended to forty-eight hours if in the case of a notice issued by a police officer, the officer is of at least the rank of superintendent, or in the case of a notice issued by a local authority, the notice is signed by the chief executive officer of the authority, or a person designated by them for the purposes of s 77(2).[149] The period specified in the notice to which s 77(2) does not apply may be extended by up to twenty-four hours if: (a) in the case of a notice issued by a police officer an extension notice is issued by an officer of at least the rank of superintendent; or (b) if, in the case of a notice issued by a local authority, the authority issues an extension notice[150] signed by the chief executive officer of the authority, or a person designated by the chief executive officer for the purposes of s 77(2).[151]

The 2014 Act makes provision for the cancellation, or variation, of closure notices.[152] The Act also makes provision for the service of such notices.[153]

Closure orders

Wherever a closure notice is issued, an application must be made to a magistrates' court for a closure order, unless the notice has been cancelled under s 78.[154] An application for a closure order must be made by a constable if the closure notice was issued by a police officer.[155] If the notice was issued by an authority, the application for a closure order must be made by the relevant authority.

The application must be heard by the magistrates' court not later than forty-eight hours after the service of the closure notice.[156] The court has the power to make a closure order if it is satisfied that:

(a) the person has engaged or (or if the order is not made) is likely to engage, in disorderly offensive or criminal behaviour on the premises; or
(b) that the use of the premises has resulted or (if the order is not made) is likely to result, in serious nuisance to members of the public; or
(c) that there has been or (if the order is not made) is likely to be, disorder near those premises, associated with the use of those premises,

and that the order is necessary to prevent the behaviour, nuisance or disorder from continuing, recurring or occurring.[157]

A closure order is an order prohibiting access to the premises for a period specified in the order.[158] The relevant period must not exceed three months. A closure order may prohibit access: (a) by all persons, or by all persons except those specified; (b) in

[148] 2014 Act s 77(1).
[149] 2014 Act s 77(2).
[150] An extension notice is a notice that identifies the closure notice to which it relates and also specifies the period of the extension: 2014 Act s 77(5).
[151] 2014 Act s 77(4).
[152] 2014 Act s 78.
[153] 2014 Act s 79.
[154] 2014 Act s 80(1).
[155] 2014 Act s 80(2).
[156] 2014 Act s 80(3).
[157] 2014 Act s 80(5).
[158] 2014 Act s 80(6).

all circumstances, or in all circumstances except those specified.[159] A closure order may be made in respect of the whole or part of the premises and may also include provision about access to a part of the building, or structure, of which the premises forms part.[160]

Temporary orders

The 2014 Act makes provision for temporary orders. Section 81 of the Act applies where an application has been made under s 80 to a magistrates' court for a closure order.[161] If the court does not make a closure order it may, nevertheless, order that the closure notice continues in force for a specified further period of not more than forty-eight hours, if satisfied that: (a) that the use of particular premises has resulted (or if the notice is not continued) is likely soon to result in nuisance to the general public; or (b) that there has been (or if the notice is not continued) is likely soon to be disorder near those premises, associated with the use of those premises, and that the continuation of the notice is necessary to prevent the nuisance, or disorder, from continuing, recurring or occurring.[162]

Extension of closure orders

The 2014 Act makes provision for the extension of closure orders. At any time before the expiry of a closure order an application may be made to the justice of the peace, by complaint, for an extension (or further extension) of the period for which the order is in force.[163] Those entitled to make the order are: (a) where the closure order was made on the application of a constable, a police officer of at least the rank of an inspector; (b) where the closure order was made on the application of a local authority, that authority.[164] Either a police officer, or local authority, may make an application only if satisfied on reasonable grounds that it is necessary for the period of the order to be extended to prevent the occurrence, recurrence or continuance of:

(a) disorderly, offensive or criminal behaviour on the premises;
(b) serious nuisance to members of the public resulting from the use of the premises; or
(c) disorder near the premises associated with the use of the premises, and also satisfied that the appropriate consultee[165] has been consulted about the intention to make the application.[166]

---

159 2014 Act s 80(7).
160 2014 Act s 80(8).
161 2014 Act s 81(1).
162 2014 Act s 81(2).
163 2014 Act s 82(1).
164 2014 Act s 82(2).
165 'Appropriate consultee' means: (a) the local authority, in the case of an application by a police officer; (b) the chief officer of police for the area in which the premises are situated in the case of an application by a local authority: s 82(4).
166 2014 Act s 82(3).

If the magistrates' court is satisfied that the above requirements are satisfied, it may make an order either extending (or further extending) the period of the closure order by a period not exceeding three months.[167]

The 2014 Act makes provision for the discharge of a closing order.[168] The Act also provides for appeals to the crown court against a decision to make or extend a closure order.[169]

Enforcement of closure orders

An authorised person[170] has the power: (a) to enter premises in respect of which a closure order is in force; and (b) do anything necessary to secure the premises against entry.[171] The person entering the premises may use reasonable force.[172] The person seeking to enter the premises must, if required to do so by, or on behalf of the owner, occupier, or other person in charge of the premises, produce evidence of their identity and authority before entering the premises.[173]

Offences

It is made an offence for any person, without a reasonable excuse, to either remain on, or enter premises, in contravention of a closure notice (including a notice continued in force under s 81).[174] It is also made an offence for a person, without reasonable excuse, to remain on, or enter premises, in contravention of a closure order.[175] Furthermore, it is made an offence for any person, without reasonable excuse, to obstruct a person acting under ss 79 or 85(1).[176] Section 86 also makes provision for relevant penalties for offences that have been committed under the section.[177]

LICENSING OF PREMISES THAT SELL ALCOHOL

Licensing Act 2003

In recent years, in order to attract custom licensed premises have increasingly provided entertainment in the form of live music, karaoke and discotheques for their customers. Such activities can, of course, generate noise. Noise can also be generated by patrons entering or leaving premises. Premises that sell alcohol have been regulated for many years in the UK in order to ensure that they are properly managed. Other forms of public entertainment and activities can also generate noise, to the annoyance

---

[167] 2014 Act s 82(7).
[168] 2014 Act s 83.
[169] 2014 Act s 84.
[170] 'Authorised person' means: (a) in relation to a closure order made on the application of a constable means a constable or a person authorised by the chief officer of police for the area in which the premises are situated; (b) in relation to a closure order made on the application of a local authority means a person authorised by that authority: s 85(2).
[171] 2014 Act s 85(1).
[172] 2014 Act s 85(3).
[173] 2014 Act s 85(4).
[174] 2014 Act s 86(1).
[175] 2014 Act s 86(2).
[176] 2014 Act s 86(3).
[177] 2014 Act s 86(4)–(6).

of the neighbourhood. The Licensing Act 2003 (the 2003 Act)[178] provides a unified system in England and Wales for the licensing of the sale and supply of alcohol, the provision of regulated entertainment,[179] and the provision of late-night refreshments. The purpose of the system for licensing for licensable activities is to promote four fundamental objectives, namely 'licensing objectives'. Those objectives are: (a) the prevention of crime and disorder; (b) public safety; (c) the prevention of public nuisance; and (d) the protection of children from harm.[180]

The expression 'public nuisance' as used in the Act has never been judicially determined. The leading modern authority on public nuisance is *Attorney General v PYA Quarries Ltd*.[181] That case concerned a civil action that was brought by the attorney general on the relation of Glamorgan County Council and the Pontardawe Rural District Council to restrain a nuisance that had been caused by quarrying activities that were said to project stones and splinters into the neighbourhood, and cause dust and vibrations. Romer LJ was of the view that a public nuisance was a nuisance that materially affected the reasonable comfort of life of a class of Her Majesty's subjects.[182] In turn, Denning LJ (as he then was) stated that a public nuisance was a nuisance that was so indiscriminate in its effects that it would not be reasonable to expect one person to take proceedings on their own responsibility to put a stop to it, but that it should be taken on the responsibility of community at large.[183] In the absence of authority, it is suggested that the 2003 Act's intention is to prevent licensed premises causing annoyance to the local community, in contradistinction to the public at large. In short, the licensing objective of the prevention of a 'public nuisance' under the Act should be more in line with the meaning of a private nuisance and therefore be limited to protecting a narrower class of individuals, such as local residents.[184]

The system of licensing is achieved through the provision of authorisations, through personal licenses, premises licenses, club premises certificates and temporary event notices. Personal licenses, premises licenses and club premises certificates are granted by the licensing authority where the premises are situated or, in the case of personal licenses, the licensing authority in which the applicant is normally resident. A licensing authority is required to carry out its licensing functions

[178] For a discussion of the provisions of the Licensing Act 2003, see R. McCracken et al, *Statutory Nuisance*, 4th edn (Bloomsbury, 2019) 10.33–10.39.

[179] 'Regulated entertainment' is any entertainment that takes place before a live audience and is provided for the purpose of entertaining an audience: Licensing Act 2003 Sch 1. It includes: (a) a performance of a play; (b) an exhibition of a film; (c) an indoor sporting event; (d) a boxing or wrestling entertainment; (e) a performance of live music; (f) any playing of recorded music; (g) a performance of dance; (h) entertainment of a similar description to that falling within (e), (f) or (g) where certain conditions are met, one of which is that the entertainment takes place in the presence of an audience (or spectators).

[180] Licensing Act 2003 s 4(2). In 2018 the Home Office issued a Revised Guidance under s 182 of the Licensing Act 2003. The Government stated that the legislation supported a number of other key aims and purposes, including protecting the public and local residents from crime, antisocial behaviour and noise nuisance caused by irresponsible licensed premises: para 1.8.

[181] [1957] 2 QB 169.

[182] [1957] 2 QB 169 at 184.

[183] [1957] 2 QB 169 at 191.

[184] In its Revised Guidance (fn 173 above) the Government stated that the expression, 'public nuisance' as used in the Act retained its common law meaning: para 2.16.

with a view to promoting the aforementioned, licensing objectives.[185] A licensing authority is required to determine its licensing policy in relation to the exercise of its licensing functions.[186] An authority could, for example, have a policy not to license establishments in a certain area, or to limit the type and size of establishment for which it will grant a licence. The licensing authority may also publish a cumulative impact assessment statement, to the effect that the licensing authority considers that the number of relevant authorisations in one or more parts of its area is such that it would be inconsistent with its licensing functions under the Act.[187] For example, the licensing authority could limit the number of licenses granted in a certain area in order to protect residents and, indeed, the public, from excessive noise.

An important tool at the disposal of the licensing authority as far as the suppression of noise is concerned is the power to attach conditions to the grant of a premises licence[188] and club certificates.[189]

It is made an offence to carry on a licensable activity on or from any premises otherwise than under, and in accordance with an authorisation, or to knowingly allow a licensable activity to be so carried on.[190] The 2003 Act makes provision for the exemption of certain activities in certain locations where a license is not required.[191]

Under s 160(1) of the 2003 Act a magistrates' court may make an order requiring all of the premises that are situated at or near a place of disorder or expected disorder and, in respect of which a premises license or temporary event notice has effect, to be closed for a period not exceeding twenty-four hours, specified in the order. However, a magistrates' court may only make such an order on the application of a police officer who is of the rank of superintendent or above.[192] The magistrates' court may not make such an order unless it is necessary to prevent disorder.[193] Where an order is made the following commit an offence if they knowingly keep any premises to which the order relates open during the period of the order.[194] The relevant individuals are:

(i) the manager of the premises;
(ii) in the case of licensed premises, the holder of the premises license in respect of the premises;
(iii) the designated premises supervisor (if any) under such a licence; and

[185] 2003 Act s 4(1).
[186] 2003 Act s 5(1).
[187] 2003 Act s 5A(1).
[188] 2003 Act s 18(2).
[189] 2003 Act s 72(2). In its Revised Guidance (fn 173, above) the Government stated that conditions relating to noise would usually concern steps appropriate to control the levels of noise emanating from premises: at para 217. The guidance went on to state that any conditions appropriate to promote the prevention of public nuisance should be tailored to the type, nature and characteristics of the specific premises and its licensable activities. Furthermore, licensing authorities should avoid inappropriate or disproportionate measures that could deter events that were valuable to the community, such as live music.
[190] 2003 Act s 136(1).
[191] 2003 Act s 173(1).
[192] 2003 Act s 160(2).
[193] 2003 Act s 160(3).
[194] 2003 Act s 160(4).

(iv) in relation to premises in respect of which a temporary event notice has effect, the premises user in relation to that notice.[195]

A person guilty of an offence is liable on summary conviction to a fine.[196]

Civic Government (Scotland) Act 1982

As far as Scotland is concerned, a licence is required for premises used as a place of public entertainment.[197] A licensing authority may attach conditions to a public entertainment licence, *inter alia*, fixing the date and the times when the premises may be open for the purposes of entertainment, or recreation.[198]

Licensing (Scotland) Act 2005

As far as Scotland is concerned, the Licensing (Scotland) Act 2005 regulates the sale of alcohol from premises. The Act allows a licensing board (which grants licenses to premises) to impose conditions that it considers necessary or expedient for the purposes of any of the licensing objectives that are contained in the Act.[199] The licensing objectives include, 'the prevention of public nuisances'. The expression 'public nuisance' is unfortunate since Scots law (unlike the law of England) does not recognise the concept of public nuisance. The expression 'public nuisance' as used in the 2005 Act has not, thus far, been determined by the courts. It is suggested, however, that the phrase would certainly cover noise from licensed premises. Many licensing boards have imposed conditions in the relevant license to the effect that no noise should be discernible at the perimeter of the premises.

RAVES

Raves, by their very nature, can be a source of noise nuisance in the neighbourhood. The Criminal Justice and Public Order Act 1994 (the 1994 Act) makes special provision for the control of what are commonly described as 'raves'.

As far as England and Wales are concerned s 63(1) of the 1994 Act gives the police power to remove persons attending or preparing for a rave. The section applies to a gathering on land, in the open air, of twenty or more persons (whether or not trespassers) at which amplified music is played during the night (with or without permission) and is such as, by reason of its loudness or duration, and the time at which it is played, is likely to cause serious distress to the inhabitants of the locality. The expression 'gathering' for the purposes of the section is one where the gathering extends over several days throughout the period during which amplified music is played at night (with or without intermissions). Music includes sound wholly or predominantly characterised by the emission of a succession of repetitive beats.

[195] 2003 Act s 160(5).

[196] 2003 Act s 160(6).

[197] Civic Government (Scotland) Act 1982 s 41(1). A place of public entertainment is defined as any place where members of the public are admitted or may use any facilities for the purposes of entertainment or recreation but does include certain premises such as athletic or sports grounds or educational establishments while these premises are being used as such: s 41(2).

[198] Civic Government (Scotland) Act 1982 s 41(3).

[199] Licensing (Scotland) Act 2005 s 27(6).

The section also applies to a gathering on land of twenty or more persons who are trespassing on the land, and it would be a gathering of a kind mentioned in s 63(1) if it took place on land in the open air.[200] If a police officer of at least the rank of superintendent reasonably believes that:

(a) two or more persons are making preparations for the holding there of a gathering to which s 63 applies,
(b) ten or more persons are waiting for such a gathering to begin there; or
(c) ten or more persons are attending such a gathering which is in progress,

the officer may give a direction that those persons, and other persons who come to prepare, or wait, for or to attend the gathering, are to leave the land and remove any vehicles, or other property, which they have with them on the land.[201] A direction, if not communicated to these persons by the police officer giving the direction, may be communicated to them by any constable at the scene.[202] Such persons are deemed as having had such a direction if reasonable steps have been taken to bring it to their attention.[203] Such a direction does not apply to an exempt person.[204]

If a person, knowing that a direction has been given that applies to them: (a) fails to leave the land as soon as is reasonably practicable; or (b) having left, again enters the land within a period of seven days, beginning on the day on which the direction was given, commits an offence and is liable to imprisonment or a fine, or both.[205]

It is a defence for the accused to show that they had a reasonable excuse for failing to leave the land as soon as reasonably practicable or, as the case may be, for again entering the land.[206]

A person commits an offence if they know that a direction has been given under s 63(2) that applies to them and they make preparations to attend a gathering to which this section applies within a period of twenty-four hours, starting when the direction was given.[207] Such a person is liable on summary conviction to imprisonment or a fine, or both.[208]

Section 63 does not apply in England and Wales to a gathering in relation to a licensable activity within s 1(1)(c) of the Licensing Act 2003 (provision of certain forms of entertainment) carried on, under and in accordance with, an authorisation within the meaning of s 136 of that Act.[209] Nor does s 63 of the 1994 Act apply in Scotland to a gathering in premises, which by virtue of s 41 of the Civic Government (Scotland) Act 1982, are licensed to be used as a place of public entertainment.

The 1994 Act makes special provision for raves, as far as Scotland is concerned. Section 63 confers powers to remove persons either attending or preparing for a rave.

---

[200] 1994 Act s 63(1A).
[201] 1994 Act s 63(2).
[202] 1994 Act s 63(3).
[203] 1994 Act s 63(4).
[204] In relation to land (or any gathering on land) 'exempt person' means the occupier, any member of their family and any employee or agent of theirs and any person whose home is situated on the land: 1994 Act s 63(10).
[205] 1994 Act s 63(6).
[206] 1994 Act s 63(7).
[207] 1994 Act s 63(7A).
[208] 1994 Act s 63(7B).
[209] 1994 Act s 63(9).

That section applies to a gathering on land in the open air of 100 or more persons (whether or not trespassers) at which amplified music is played during the night (with or without intermissions) and is, such as, by reason of its loudness and duration and the time at which it is played, likely to cause serious distress to the inhabitants of the locality.[210] For the purposes of the section the gathering is required to continue during intermissions in the music and, where the gathering extends over several days, throughout the period during which amplified music is played at night (with or without intermissions). Power is conferred on a police officer of at least the rank of superintendent if certain requirements are met.[211] These are that: (a) two or more persons are making preparations for the holding there of a gathering to which the section applies; (b) ten or more persons are waiting for such a gathering to begin there; (c) ten or more persons are attending such a gathering which is in progress. In such circumstances, the police officer may give a direction that those persons, and any other persons, who come to wait for or to attend the gathering, are to leave the land and remove other vehicles and property that they have with them on the land.

The remainder of the section is similar to that which applies to England and Wales.

Section 64 of the 1994 Act confers additional powers on the police in relation to raves. If a police officer of at least the rank of superintendent reasonably believes that circumstances exist in relation to any land that would justify the giving of a direction under s 63, in relation to a gathering to which that section applies, they may authorise[212] any constable to enter the land for the following purposes.[213] These purposes are to ascertain whether such circumstances exist and to exercise any power that is conferred on a constable under s 63 or s 64(4).[214] Under the latter if a direction has been given under s 63 and a constable reasonably suspects that any person to whom the direction applies has, without reasonable excuse, either: (a) failed to remove any vehicle[215] or sound equipment on the land that appears to the constable to either belong to them or to be in their possession or under their control; or (b) entered the land as a trespasser[216] with a vehicle or sound equipment within the period of seven days, beginning with the day on which the direction was given, the constable may seize and remove that vehicle or sound equipment.[217] However, the power conferred under s 64(4) does not authorise the seizure of any vehicle or sound equipment of an exempt person.[218]

If a constable in uniform reasonably believes that a person is on their way to a gathering to which s 63 applies, in relation to which a direction under s 63(2) is in

210 1994 Act s 63(1).

211 1994 Act s 63(2).

212 A constable who is so authorised can enter the land with or without warrant: 1994 Act s 64(3).

213 1994 Act s 64(1).

214 1994 Act s 64(2).

215 'Vehicle' has the same meaning as in s 61: 1994 Act s 64(6).

216 In Scotland entering the land with sound equipment in circumstances mentioned in s 64(4)(b) is not an exercise of access rights within the meaning of the Land Reform (Scotland) Act 2003: 1994 Act s 64(5A).

217 'Sound equipment' means equipment designed or adapted for amplifying music and any equipment suitable for use in connection with such equipment. 'Music' has the same meaning as used in s 63: 1994 Act s 64(6).

218 1994 Act s 64(5). See fn 198 for meaning of exempt person.

force, they may stop that person and direct them not to proceed in the direction of the gathering.[219] However, that power may only be exercised at a place within five miles of the boundary of the site of the gathering.[220] Furthermore, no direction may be given to an exempt person.[221]

If a person, knowing that a direction under s 65(1) has been given to them fails to comply with that direction they commit an offence and are liable on summary conviction to a fine.[222]

In Scotland a constable in uniform who reasonably suspects that a person is committing an offence under s 65, may arrest them without a warrant.[223]

Where a person is convicted of an offence under s 63 in relation to a gathering to which that section applies, and the court is satisfied that any sound equipment that has been seized from them under s 64(4), or which was in their possession or under their control at the relevant time has been used at the gathering, the court may make an order for forfeiture in respect of that property.[224]

The 1994 Act makes provision for the retention and charges of seized property.[225]

FIREWORKS

Fireworks can pose a physical risk to those who use them, as well as others. Fireworks can also be used in various forms of antisocial behaviour, some of which is the creation of neighbourhood noise. The Fireworks Act 2003, which relates to the whole of the UK, enables the Secretary of State to make regulations for securing that there is no risk that the use of fireworks[226] will have certain consequences, or for securing that the risk that the use of fireworks will have those consequences, is the minimum that is compatible with their being used.[227] Any person who contravenes a provision imposed by fireworks regulations is guilty of an offence.[228]

The Fireworks Regulations 2004[229] (the main purpose of which is to tackle the antisocial use of fireworks through regulation of their use and supply) make it an offence for any person under the age of eighteen to possess an adult firework[230] in a public place.[231] The Regulations also prohibit the possession of category four fireworks (i.e. professional display fireworks).[232] These prohibitions do not include

---

219 1994 Act s 65(1).
220 1994 Act s 65(2).
221 1994 Act s 65(3). An exempt person has the same meaning as in s 63: 1994 Act s 65(6).
222 1994 Act s 65(4).
223 1994 Act s 65(5).
224 1994 Act s 66(1).
225 1994 Act s 67.
226 'Fireworks' means devices that: (a) are fireworks for the purposes of the British Standard Specification relating to fireworks, published on 30 November 1988 (BS 7114) or any British Standard replacing it; or (b) would be fireworks for those purposes if they were intended as a form of entertainment: Fireworks Act 2003 s 1(1).
227 Fireworks Act 2003 s 2(1).
228 Fireworks Act 2003 s 11(1).
229 SI 2004/1836.
230 'Adult firework' is defined in reg 3 as a Category F2, F3 or F4 firework.
231 Fireworks Regulations 2004 reg 4(1). A 'public place' includes any place to which, at the material time, the public have or are permitted access whether on payment or otherwise: reg 4(2).
232 Fireworks Regulations 2004 reg 5.

persons employed in the business of professional displays, fireworks manufacturers or importers, etc.[233] The Regulations, subject to certain exceptions, also ban the use of adult fireworks during night hours.[234] However, the ban does not extend to the use of a firework during a permitted fireworks night[235] or any person who is employed by a local authority and who uses the firework in question either for the purposes of putting on a fireworks display by that authority at a national public celebration, or at a national commemorative event.[236]

The Regulations also require any person who supplies or exposes for supply any adult firework to be licensed in respect of each premises that are under their control, at which the fireworks are supplied, or exposed for supply.[237] If the person who supplies, or exposes for sale, any firework in premises that are not under their control, such a person requires to be in possession of a licence that has been granted to them. However, these requirements do not apply during certain prescribed periods,[238] or in certain circumstances.[239] An application for a licence is required to be made to the local licensing authority where the relevant premises that are under the applicant's control are situated or, if the premises are not under their control, the application is required to be made to the licensing authority where the principal business premises of the applicant are located.[240] A local licensing authority may only grant a licence to person ('A') if satisfied that A, or another person on A's behalf, holds a valid licence for the storage of the fireworks under the Explosives Regulations 2014,[241] or a licence for storage is not required under the Explosives Regulations 2014.[242]

A local licensing authority may either refuse to grant a licence, or may revoke a licence that it has granted, if the applicant has committed certain offences.[243] A person may appeal to the court against the decision of a local licensing authority to refuse to grant them a licence or to revoke a licence, and any such appeal requires to be made within twenty-eight days of the decision in question being notified to that person.[244]

Any person who either supplies (whether by retail or wholesale) or exposes for supply, any adult firework or sparkler in any premises, is required to display, in a prominent position in the premises, a notice that contains certain information.[245] Where adult fireworks are exposed for supply in other circumstances (such as the internet, mail order, etc.) the person who supplies such fireworks is required to give

---

233 Fireworks Regulations 2004 reg 6.

234 Fireworks Regulations 2004 reg 7(1). 'Night hours' is defined as the period beginning 11pm and ending 7am the following day: reg 7(3).

235 'Permitted fireworks night' is defined in reg 7(3).

236 Fireworks Regulations 2004 reg 7(2).

237 Fireworks Regulations 2004 reg 9(1).

238 Fireworks Regulations 2004 reg 9(2).

239 Fireworks Regulations 2004 reg 9(2A).

240 Fireworks Regulations 2004 reg 9(3).

241 SI 2014/1638.

242 Fireworks Regulations 2004 reg 9(4).

243 Fireworks Regulations 2004 reg 9(5).

244 Fireworks Regulations 2004 reg 9(8).

245 Fireworks Regulations 2004 reg 10(1). The relevant required information is that it is illegal to sell category F2 fireworks or category F3 fireworks to anyone under the age of eighteen and that it is illegal for anyone under the age of eighteen to possess either category F2 fireworks or category F3 fireworks in a public place; Fireworks Regulations 2004 reg 10(2).

that information to the person to whom the fireworks are supplied, or exposed for supply. Subject to certain exceptions, suppliers of adult fireworks are required to maintain a record for a period of three years, *inter alia*, of the name and address of the person to whom the fireworks is being supplied (subject to certain exceptions) and the date when the firework was supplied to them.[246] Subject to certain exceptions, a person who supplies adult fireworks is required, if requested by a local licensing authority, to provide any of such information to that authority, as is specified in the request.[247]

The Regulations also require the importer of any firework to provide customs and excise with certain information, including the name and address of the person who is to store the fireworks following their importation.[248]

As far as Scotland is concerned, the Fireworks (Scotland) Regulations 2004[249] make provision for the safe use of fireworks.

The use of adult fireworks[250] outside permitted hours[251] is prohibited.[252] The ban on the use of fireworks outside these hours is subject to certain exceptions.[253] The supply of adult fireworks is also prohibited outside permitted hours.[254] However, the ban is subject to certain exceptions.[255] The supply of fireworks in specified circumstances and in excess of the permitted quantity[256] at any one time is also prohibited.[257] Again, the ban is subject to certain exceptions.[258]

A local authority can grant a dispensation from the prohibition of the use of adult fireworks to any person mentioned in reg 3(2) to enable that person to use fireworks: (a) for the purpose of putting on a fireworks display, for their employer or in the course of their business (as the case may be); or (b) at a national public celebration or a national commemorative event.[259] The relevant person is any person who is employed by, or in business as, a professional organiser or operator of firework displays.[260] However, a local authority may not grant such a dispensation unless it is satisfied either: (a) that there is no risk that the use of fireworks, in accordance with the dispensation, will have any of the consequences mentioned in s 2(2) of the Fireworks Act 2003; or (b) that the use of fireworks, in accordance with the dispensation, will have any such consequences. This is the minimum that is compatible with their being used.[261] An application for a dispensation requires to be made to the local authority

---

[246] Fireworks Regulations 2004 reg 10(3).
[247] Fireworks Regulations 2004 reg 10(3A).
[248] Fireworks Regulations 2004 reg 11.
[249] SSI 2004/393.
[250] 'Adult firework' is defined in Fireworks (Scotland) Regulations 2004 reg 2.
[251] 'Permitted hours' is defined in Fireworks (Scotland) Regulations 2004 reg 3(3).
[252] Fireworks (Scotland) Regulations 2004 reg 3(1).
[253] Fireworks (Scotland) Regulations 2004 reg 3(2).
[254] Fireworks (Scotland) Regulations 2004 reg 3A(1). 'Permitted hours' is defined in reg 3A(2) as the period beginning 7am and ending at 6pm.
[255] Fireworks (Scotland) Regulations 2004 reg 3A(3).
[256] 'Permitted quantity' means fireworks with a total net mass of explosive substance of five kilograms: Fireworks (Scotland) Regulations 2004 reg 3B(2).
[257] Fireworks (Scotland) Regulations 2004 reg 3B(1).
[258] Fireworks (Scotland) Regulations 2004 reg 3B(3).
[259] Fireworks (Scotland) Regulations 2004 reg 4(1).
[260] Fireworks (Scotland) Regulations 2004 reg 4(2).
[261] Fireworks (Scotland) Regulations 2004 reg 4(3).

in whose area the applicant proposes to put on a fireworks display, national public celebration or national commemorative event.[262]

Police Scotland is responsible for enforcing the provisions of the Scottish Regulations.[263]

The Fireworks and Pyrotechnic Articles (Scotland) Act 2022 provides *inter alia* for fireworks licensing, as well as the restriction of supply and use of certain fireworks and pyrotechnic articles. The Act also makes provision for firework control zones.

PYROTECHNIC ARTICLES

Directive 2013/29/EU, which is a harmonisation measure, is aimed at harmonising the free movement of pyrotechnic articles (including fireworks) within the EU and also addresses securing a high level of protection of human health and safety and the protection of consumers and professional end users.[264] Furthermore, in ensuring a high level of protection, pyrotechnic articles are categorised by the manufacturer according to their type of use or their purpose and level of hazard, including their noise level.[265]

Category F1 fireworks are fireworks that present a very low hazard and negligible noise level, for use in confined areas. Category F2 fireworks are fireworks that present a low hazard and low noise level and are intended for outdoor use in confined areas. Category F3 fireworks are fireworks that present a medium hazard, which are intended for outdoor use in large open areas and whose noise level is not harmful to human health. Category F4 fireworks are fireworks that present a high hazard and which are intended for use only by persons with specialist knowledge (commonly known as fireworks for professional use) and whose noise level is not harmful to human health.

The Pyrotechnic Articles (Safety) Regulations 2015[266] implement the 2013 Directive and also Directive 2014/58/EU on the traceability of pyrotechnic articles.

Before placing a pyrotechnic article[267] on the market, a manufacturer must categorise it using the categories set out in Schedule 1 (categories of pyrotechnic article) according to its type of use or purpose and level of hazard, including its noise level.[268] The manufacturer is also required to ensure that it has been designed and manufactured in accordance with the essential safety requirements.[269] The essential safety requirements are contained in Schedule 2 to the Regulations and provide *inter alia* that the manufacturer of a firework is required to assign fireworks to different categories, categorised by net explosive content, safety distances, noise level or similar. The relevant category is also required to be indicated on the label of the firework. Specific conditions are required to be met in relation to each category of firework, namely, categories, categories one to four.

262 Fireworks (Scotland) Regulations 2004 reg 4(6).
263 Fireworks (Scotland) Regulations 2004 reg 5.
264 Directive 2013/29/EU, Preamble.
265 Directive 2013/29/EU art 6.
266 SI 2015/1553.
267 'Pyrotechnic article' is defined in reg 3.
268 Pyrotechnic Articles (Safety) Regulations 2015 reg 6.
269 Pyrotechnic Articles (Safety) Regulations 2015 reg 7.

Before a pyrotechnic article can be placed on the market the manufacturer is required to ensure that it is labelled visibly, legibly and indelibly, is clearly understandable and is in English.[270] The labelling of a pyrotechnic article must contain certain information, including the name, registered trade name or registered trademark of the manufacturer and the name, type and category of the pyrotechnic article.[271]

The Regulations also require a manufacturer to maintain a record of certain information of the pyrotechnic article, including the site of manufacture.[272] The manufacturer is also required to provide the enforcing authority with that information.[273] The manufacturer is also required to keep a register that contains certain information.[274] Any entry made in the register requires to be kept for a period of at least ten years.[275]

The Regulations also make provision as to the minimum age of persons to whom categories one to three fireworks can be supplied.[276] Category 4 fireworks cannot be supplied, except to a person with specialist knowledge.[277] The supply of certain category 2 and 3 fireworks is also prohibited.[278]

The relevant local authority (weights and measures) is responsible for enforcing the Regulations in relation to categories one to three, inclusive, fireworks.[279] The Health and Safety Executive is responsible for enforcing the Regulations in relation to category 4 fireworks.

The Regulations make provision for a variety of offences, including making it an offence for a manufacturer to contravene, or to fail to comply, with any requirement of reg 7 (design and manufacture in accordance with essential safety requirements) and regs 11 and 12 (labelling of pyrotechnic articles).[280]

It is also made an offence for a distributor to contravene or fail to comply *inter alia* with reg 25 (requirements that must be satisfied before a distributor makes an article available on the market) and reg 26 (prohibition on making available on the market where a pyrotechnic article is not considered to be in conformity with the essential safety requirements).[281]

BYELAWS

Prior to the passing of the Noise Abatement Act 1960, the sole legislative control in relation to noise took the form of byelaws. It was during the Victorian era, when the Industrial Revolution was at its zenith, that byelaws began to be made to a significant extent. Byelaws were generally directed at specific types of noise, for example, street noise. The content of such byelaws often provides the historian with valuable primary

270 Pyrotechnic Articles (Safety) Regulations 2015 reg 11(1).
271 Pyrotechnic Articles (Safety) Regulations 2015 reg 11(2), Schedule 3.
272 Pyrotechnic Articles (Safety) Regulations 2015 reg 20(4).
273 Pyrotechnic Articles (Safety) Regulations 2015 reg 20(2).
274 Pyrotechnic Articles (Safety) Regulations 2015 reg 21(2).
275 Pyrotechnic Articles (Safety) Regulations 2015 reg 21(3).
276 Pyrotechnic Articles (Safety) Regulations 2015 reg 31.
277 Pyrotechnic Articles (Safety) Regulations 2015 reg 32.
278 Pyrotechnic Articles (Safety) Regulations 2015 reg 33.
279 Pyrotechnic Articles (Safety) Regulations 2015 reg 52(1).
280 Pyrotechnic Articles (Safety) Regulations 2015 reg 62(1).
281 Pyrotechnic Articles (Safety) Regulations 2015 reg 62(3).

evidence of the social, as well as the environmental conditions, that were present during the period. For example, the byelaw challenged collaterally (that is, in legal proceedings) in the celebrated case of *Kruse v Johnson*[282] purported to prohibit the playing of musical instruments or singing in any public place within fifty yards of any dwelling house, after being ordered by any constable, or any inmate of such house to desist.

The council of a district and the council of any London borough may make bylaws for the good rule and government of any part of the district or borough, for the suppression of nuisances therein.[283] However, byelaws may not be made under the Act for any purpose, as respects any area, if provision for that purpose, as respects that area, is made by or is, or may be made under, any other enactment.[284] In Scotland, local authorities have similar power under s 201(1) of the Local Government (Scotland) Act 1973. Such power is ostensibly wide and is indeed only circumscribed by the requirement of reasonableness[285] and consistency with both the common and statutory law.[286]

INDUSTRIAL NOISE

Noise from various industrial sources has the potential to have a negative impact on the community. Pollution from industry will normally fall within the scope of the EU Industrial Emissions Directive.[287] One of the main aims of the Directive is to ensure the prevention and control of pollution by providing that each installation should only operate if it holds a permit or if it is registered.[288] Under the Directive 'pollution' includes noise that is harmful to human health or the quality of the environment.[289] Member States are placed under an obligation to ensure that no installation or combustion plant, waste incineration plant or waste co-incineration plant is operated without a permit.[290] A competent authority is required to grant a permit only if the installation complies with the requirements of the Directive.[291] Installations are required to be operated in accordance with certain principles.[292] These principles are that all appropriate preventative measures are taken against pollution; the best available techniques[293] are applied; and that no significant pollution is caused. A permit condition (which could relate to noise) is required to include measures necessary to secure compliance with these principles.[294]

---

282 [1898] 2 QB 91.
283 Local Government Act 1972 s 235(1).
284 Local Government Act 1972s 235(3).
285 *Kruse v Johnston* [1898] 2 QB 91.
286 *Powell v May* [1946] KB 330.
287 Directive 2010/75/EU.
288 Directive 2010/75/EU, Preamble.
289 Directive 2010/75/EU art 3.
290 Directive 2010/75/EU art 4.
291 Directive 2010/75/EU art 5.
292 Directive 2010/75/EU art 11.
293 'Best available techniques' is defined in art 3.
294 Directive 2010/75/EU art 14. See the Environment Agency guidance, 'Noise and vibration management: environmental permits' (21 July 2021), available at *http://www.gov.uk/government/publications/noise-and-vibration-management-environmental-permits* (last accessed 22 October 2022).

The Directive has been implemented by the Pollution Prevention and Control (Scotland) Regulations 2012[295] and the Environmental Permitting (England and Wales) Regulations 2016.[296]

WASTE

Under the EU's Waste Framework Directive[297] Member States were required to establish a framework to prevent, reduce and, in so far as is reasonably possible, eliminate from the outset, the sources of pollution or nuisance by adopting relevant measures in its management of waste.[298]

In England and Wales waste management activities are regulated through the Environmental Permitting (England and Wales) Regulations 2016[299] regime that has just been described. The Environment Agency has the vast majority of regulatory control over such activities.

In Scotland all waste management operations require a licence. Essentially, the EPA allows the Scottish Environmental Protection Agency (SEPA) to regulate waste treatment facilities by means of a licensing system. SEPA has wide powers as to the nature of the conditions that it can attach to a waste management licence. Under the EPA a licence is required to be granted on such terms, and also subject to such conditions as appear to SEPA to be appropriate.[300] The Scottish Ministers are empowered to make regulations governing the conditions that are, or are not, to be included in a licence.[301] The conditions that SEPA could include in the relevant licence could relate to noise from the relevant premises.

Certain waste management activities in Scotland fall to be regulated by SEPA under the Pollution Prevention and Control (Scotland) Regulations 2012.[302]

Landfill sites in Scotland are regulated by SEPA under the Landfill (Scotland) Regulations 2003 by means of a permitting system.[303] SEPA can effectively regulate the day-to-day operation of a landfill site by including conditions in the relevant permit it grants. As far as the regulation of noise from landfill sites is concerned, a permit is required to include a condition that measures are required to be taken to

295 SSI 2012/360.

296 SI 2016/1154. For a general discussion of Integrated Pollution, Prevention and Control and Permitting see F. McManus, *Environmental Law in Scotland – An Introduction and Guide* (EUP, 2016) Ch 9; F. McManus, 'Pollution Prevention and Control' in F McManus (ed), *Environmental Law in Scotland* (SULI/Thomson Reuters, looseleaf) Ch 11; R. Burnett-Hall and B. Jones, *Environmental Law*, 3rd edn (Sweet and Maxwell, 2012) Ch 23; S. Bell et al, *Environmental Law*, 9th edn (OUP, 2017). The Environment Agency has issued guidance to operators and applicants for permits, including how the environment agencies will assess noise from certain industrial processes and also what operators should do to manage noise and vibration. See 'Noise and vibration management: environmental permits' (as above, fn 294).

297 Directive 2008/98/EC.

298 Directive 2008/98/EC Preamble.

299 SI 2016/1154.

300 EPA s 35(3).

301 EPA s 35(6). See the Waste Management (Scotland) Regulations 2011 (SSI 2011/228) (as amended) regs 11–13B as to specific conditions that have been prescribed.

302 SSI 2012/360 Sch 1.

303 SSI 2003/235.

minimise the nuisances and hazards arising from the landfill in relation to noise and traffic.[304]

HOUSEHOLD NOISE

The fact that many domestic properties are insufficiently insulated to prevent the transmission of noise has proved problematic over the years. We have already seen that noise from everyday domestic activities that affects neighbours does not constitute a nuisance in law.[305] Ensuring that buildings have adequate sound insulation is the most effective means of securing that the residents of premises are protected against noise that emanates from outside the premises.

As far as new buildings in England and Wales are concerned, the Building Regulations 2010[306] provide that building work requires to be carried out so that it complies with the relevant provisions in Schedule 1 of the Regulations.[307]

Under Schedule 1 Part E1, dwelling houses, flats and rooms for residential purposes are required to be designed and constructed in such a way that they provide reasonable resistance to sound from other parts of the same building and from adjoining buildings.

Under Schedule 1 Part E2, subject to certain exceptions, dwelling houses, flats and rooms for residential purposes are required to be designed and constructed in such a way that: (a) internal walls between a bedroom or a room containing a water closet and other rooms; and (b) internal floors, provide reasonable resistance to sound.

Under Schedule 1 Part E3, the common internal parts of a building that contain flats or rooms, for residential purposes, are required to be designed and constructed in such a way as to prevent more reverberation around the common part than is reasonable. However, this provision only applies to corridors, stairwells, hallways and entrance halls that give access to the flat or room for residential purposes.

Under Schedule 1 Part E4, as far as schools are concerned, each room or other space in a school building is required to be designed and constructed in such a way that it has acoustic conditions and the insulation against disturbance by noise that is appropriate to its intended use.

An individual carrying out building work in relation to which Schedule 1 Part E1 imposes a requirement, or in relation to work that is required to be carried out to an existing building to ensure that it complies with Schedule 1 Part E1 by virtue of reg 6(1)(f) (requirements in relation to material change of use of the whole building) or reg 6(2)(b) (requirements in relation to material change of use of only part of the building) is required to ensure that appropriate sound testing is carried out in accordance with a procedure approved by the Secretary of State.[308] A copy of the results of the testing also requires to be given to the relevant local authority. However, this requirement does not apply (provided certain conditions are met) where the building work consists of the erection of a dwelling house or a building containing

[304] SSI 2003/235 reg 10(3) and Schedule 3.
[305] See p. 32 above.
[306] SI 2010/2214.
[307] SI 2010/2214 reg 4(1).
[308] SI 2010/2214 reg 41(1), (2).

flats, if the person carrying out the works notifies the local authority, before the work commences, that in order to meet the requirements of Schedule 1 Part E1, the person is using one or more of the design details approved by Robust Details Ltd.[309] The Robust Details Scheme is the alternative to pre-completion sound testing for satisfying the requirements of Part E of the Building Regulations. Using the scheme avoids the uncertainties of pre-completion sound testing.

A local authority may make such tests of any building works as may be necessary to establish that the work complies with the requirements of Schedule 1.[310]

As far as Scotland is concerned, the Building (Scotland) Regulations 2004[311] requires buildings to be built in such a way as to limit the transmission of source noise from normal domestic type activities between such areas to a level that will not threaten the health of, or cause inconvenience to, the building occupants.[312] However, this standard only applies to a building in different occupation, incorporating: (a) a detached dwelling; (b) attached residential buildings; or (c) a roof, walkway or access deck located directly above an area that is either a dwelling or a residential building.

Furthermore, every building must be designed and constructed in such a way as to limit the transmission of source noise from domestic type activities through a wall or floor between a room and internal space where noise is likely to occur to a level that will cause inconvenience to the building occupants.[313] However, this standard only applies to a wall or floor forming an apartment in a dwelling and a room in a residential building that is capable of being used for sleeping other than: (a) a wall between an ensuite bathroom and an apartment or room it serves; (b) a hospital; or (c) a place of lawful detention.

BS 8233 (2014) provides guidance on the control of noise in and around buildings. It applies to the design of new buildings or refurbished buildings undergoing a change of use. However, it does not provide guidance on assessing the effects of changes in the external noise levels to occupants in an existing building.

The *Code for Sustainable Homes* was launched by the UK Government in 2006 for use in the design and construction of new homes with a view to encouraging continuous improvement in sustainable home building. The code is now voluntary.

NOISE FROM MACHINERY AND EQUIPMENT

The Noise Emission in the Environment by Equipment for use Outdoors Regulations 2001[314] (which extends to the whole of the UK) makes provision for the control of noise from machinery and equipment. The Regulations apply to a wide range of equipment, from concrete breakers and picks, dumpers, excavators, landfill compactors and lawnmowers to power generators.[315] However, the Regulations do not apply to

[309] SI 2010/2214 reg 41(4).

[310] SI 2010/2214 reg 45.

[311] SI 2004/406.

[312] SI 2004/406 Schedule 5, para 1.

[313] SI 2004/406 Schedule 5, para 2.

[314] SI 2001/1701. The Regulations implement Directive 2000/14/EC the purpose of which was *inter alia* to harmonise the laws of Member States relating to noise emission standards in relation to equipment for outdoor use: art 1.

[315] SI 2001/1701 reg 3, Schs 1 and 2.

equipment placed on the market or put into service on or before 2 January 2002 that comply with any provisions that they would have been required to comply for them to be placed on the market in the UK on 2 July 2001.[316] A manufacturer of thirty-five categories of outdoor equipment is required to affix a label to the relevant product that shows its guaranteed sound power level, which is measured in accordance with the Regulations.[317] Furthermore, a manufacturer of a further twenty-two categories (within the thirty-five categories) of outdoor equipment is required to ensure that the guaranteed sound power level of the equipment does not exceed the permissible sound level for that product, as defined in the Regulations.[318] The guaranteed sound power level also requires to be marked on that equipment.

NOISE FROM HOUSEHOLD APPLIANCES

Noise from household appliances in dwellings can be a source of annoyance to neighbours, especially in flatted property.[319] The Household Appliances (Noise Emission) Regulations 1990[320] (which apply to the whole of the UK) apply to a range of appliances for use in dwellings, including appliances used for cleaning, the preparation and storage of food stuffs, heaters and air conditioners.[321] The Regulations prohibit the manufacturer or importer of any appliance (which has been manufactured or imported by them on or after 28 February 1990) from marketing any appliance that has either been manufactured or imported by them, unless the requirements of the Regulations have been complied with.[322] The Regulations require a manufacturer or importer of an appliance who takes any steps to inform any person to whom the appliance is to be, or may be, marketed of the level of airborne noise that is emitted by the appliance, that level requires to be determined in accordance with the Regulations.[323] The relevant level requires to be stated in a manner that is readily understandable by any person to whom the appliance is to be, or may be, marketed.[324] The relevant weights and measures department is responsible for enforcing the Regulations within its area.[325]

It is made an offence, subject to a penalty, to fail to comply with the Regulations without reasonable excuse.[326]

[316] SI 2001/1701 reg 6.
[317] SI 2001/1701 reg 7.
[318] SI 2001/1701 reg 8.
[319] See e.g. *Baxter v Camden LBC* [1999] 4 All ER 449.
[320] SI 1990/161. The Regulations implement Directive 86/594/EEC.
[321] SI 2001/1701 reg 2.
[322] SI 2001/1701 reg 3.
[323] SI 2001/1701 regs 4 and 5.
[324] SI 2001/1701 reg 4.
[325] SI 2001/1701 reg 6.
[326] SI 2001/1701 reg 9.

Chapter 7

Noise and Human Rights

INTRODUCTION

In this chapter we discuss the role human rights jurisprudence plays in relation to the control of noise. Human rights law has an important role in this respect, given the limitations of both common law and statutory nuisance, to secure redress by those affected by noise. For example, in the House of Lords case of *Baxter v Camden LBC (No 2)*[1] a tenant who resided in a block of flats that was owned by a local authority, raised an action against the authority, *inter alia*, on the grounds that, by reason of poor sound insulation in both the walls and ceilings which separated the various flats, she could hear almost everything her neighbours were doing. Whereas the claimant was being subjected to severe annoyance, the House of Lords held that the state of affairs did not rank as a nuisance on the grounds that the noise in question was everyday noise – that is to say, noise that was created by the ordinary (as opposed to the unreasonable) use by her neighbours of their respective properties. Another important limitation of the law of nuisance is that in order to be able to successfully raise an action in terms of the law of nuisance the claimant is required to have a proprietary interest in the land that is adversely affected by the adverse state of affairs, for example, noise.[2]

We now discuss the extent to which human rights jurisprudence can be enlisted by those who are affected by noise to secure redress.

The Human Rights Act 1998 (HRA) incorporates the European Convention of Human Rights (ECHR) into UK law.[3] Under art 8 and art 1 of the First Protocol of the ECHR have been invoked on a number of occasions by those affected by various forms of pollution, including noise.

Article 8 provides:

(1) Everyone has the right to respect for his private and family life, his home and his correspondence.
(2) There shall be no interference by a public authority with the exercise of this right except such as in accordance with the law and is necessary in a democratic society in the interests of national security, public safety or the economic well-being of the country, for the prevention of disorder or crime,

---

[1] [2001] 1 AC 1.
[2] *Hunter v Canary Wharf Ltd* [1997] AC 655.
[3] Human Rights Act 1998 ss 1, 2.

for the protection of health or morals, or for the protection of the rights and freedom of others.

Article 1 of the First Protocol provides:

> "Every natural or legal person is entitled to the peaceful enjoyment of his possessions. No one shall be deprived of his possessions except in the public interest and subject to the conditions provided for by law and by the general principles of international law."

UK CASES

Almost all of the UK cases on the subject of noise and human rights have related to noise from aviation. We look now at noise from military aviation and then noise from civil aviation.

Military aviation

In *Dennis v Ministry of Defence*,[4] which we have already discussed in the context of the law of nuisance, the claimants resided in a large estate. RAF Wittering was situated about two miles from the estate. RAF Wittering was used as a training base for Harrier Jump Jets. The Harrier was[5] a noisy aircraft. Indeed, at the time there was none noisier. The claimants alleged that the noise constituted an interference with their rights under the HRA. The claimants relied on art 8 and art 1 of the First Protocol of the HRA. Buckley J was prepared to hold that the noise from the aircraft infringed both art 8 and art 1 of the First Protocol to the ECHR, first, by virtue of the noise in question being sufficiently loud, and second, by dint of the effect of the noise on the market value of the property.

Noise from military aircraft formed the basis of *Jones v Ministry of Defence*.[6] In that case, the claimants, Mr and Mrs Jones ('J') resided in Anglesey. J owned property (known as 'Parc Cefni'), which was situated on the south shore of a reservoir that was situated in the centre of Anglesey. J intended to develop the land in order to create a holiday and leisure park. A mile to the west of Parc Cefni there was situated Mona Airfield (the airfield). The airfield had been used by the Royal Air Force as a relief landing ground for the nearby base at RAF Valley, and also as runway where trainee pilots undertook circuit drills using fast jets and turbo prop aircraft. J claimed that an increase in the noise, which had been created by the operations in and around the airfield since 2007, had blighted their land. J claimed that the noise constituted an actionable nuisance or, alternatively, that the noise had infringed their rights under art 8 and art 1 of the First Protocol to the ECHR. J sought a remedy by way of a declaration and/or damages.

J claimed that the overflying aircraft constituted a failure on the part of the Ministry of Defence to respect J's private and family life and their home. The judge held that the aircraft noise had disturbed J's lives and their home. However, in his view, such interference was in accordance with the law and was also in the interests of national security. He rejected J's submissions that the MoD's activities were

4 [2003] Env LR 17.

5 The Harrier was decommissioned in 2014.

6 [2021] EWHC 2276.

unreasonable and disproportionate. The judge held that the training of air force pilots and promoting cordial relations with our allies engaged the interests of national security.[7]

However, a more difficult question was whether a proper balance had been struck between the competing requirements of national security and J's human rights, such as to justify the conclusion that the interference was necessary. The judge held that a balance had been lawfully struck in the instant case for two reasons.[8] The first reason was that the MoD operated a noise amelioration scheme for householders affected by noise. The public purse afforded relief to those most affected by noise. The reason why J did not qualify for such assistance was that they had not established that the noise was sufficiently loud. The second reason was that the MoD had taken steps to minimise the noise of overflying jets. Pilots had been instructed to avoid the most sensitive parts of J's property. The judge rejected a possible suggestion that if a private individual's interests were being interfered with because of a public interest the individual was bound to be compensated.[9] The judge concluded that a breach of art 8 had not taken place.

The judge then went on to address J's claim in terms of art 1 of Protocol 1. The judge stated that 'peaceful' in the Protocol meant without interference.[10] It did not mean 'without noise'. J submitted that their possessions had been interfered with by aircraft noise. The judge held that J had invested in their land with the hope of running a profitable future business. However, that hope did not represent a hope that was capable of being protected by art 1.[11] In short, no breach of art 1 of Protocol 1 had taken place.[12]

Civil aviation

Noise from civil aviation formed the basis of *Hatton v United Kingdom*.[13] Essentially, an action was brought against the UK Government by a group of residents who lived under the flightpath of aircraft that used Heathrow Airport. The residents claimed that the government policy on night flights by aircraft at Heathrow flouted their rights under art 8 of the ECHR.

The Grand Chamber of the European Court of Human Rights recognised the principle that art 8 of the ECHR did not confer the right to a clean and quiet environment.[14] However, the court held that where an individual was both directly and seriously affected by noise, or some other form of pollution, it was possible that art 8 could be engaged. The court went on to state that art 8 could be contravened either by a positive act on the part of the government or by its failure to protect its citizens from pollution.[15] In both contexts regard was to be had to the fair balance

7 [2021] EWHC 2276 at [75].
8 [2021] EWHC 2276 at [76].
9 [2021] EWHC 2276 at [77].
10 [2021] EWHC 2276 at [80].
11 [2021] EWHC 2276 at [83].
12 For a discussion of *Jones* see (2021) 162 *Rep. B.* 4.
13 (2003) 37 EHRR 28.
14 (2003) 37 EHRR 28 at [96].
15 (2003) 37 EHRR 28 at [98]. See also *Powell and Rayner v United Kingdom* (1990) 12 EHRR 355. In that case, the claimants were owners of property situated near Heathrow Airport. They claimed

to be struck between the competing interests of the individual and of the community as a whole. Furthermore, in both contexts the state enjoyed a certain margin of appreciation in determining the steps that required to be taken to ensure compliance with the ECHR. The margin of appreciation varied in the context of a particular case.[16] The court was required to determine whether the UK had struck a fair balance between the economic well-being of the UK as a whole, and the interests of those who were affected by the noise.[17] The court held that whereas environmental protection should be taken into consideration by governments acting within their margin of appreciation, and by the courts in reviewing that margin, in the instant case it was not appropriate for the court to adopt a special approach by reference to a special status of environmental human rights.[18] The court also considered it relevant that those affected by noise could move elsewhere without financial loss.[19]

In the last analysis, the court found that there had been no violation of art 8 by the UK government.[20]

'Non-aviation' human rights case law

We now discuss cases other than those concerning the application of art 8 in terms of noise from aviation.

In *Lopez Ostra v Spain*[21] Lopez Ostra (LO) lived with her family in Lorca, Spain. The town of Lorca had a heavy concentration of leather industries. Several tanneries, all belonging to the same company, had a plant for the treatment of liquid and solid waste, which had been built with a state subsidy on municipal land twelve metres away from the applicant's home. The plant had begun operating in 1988 without a licence, as was required by national legislation. Shortly after the plant had commenced operation it released gas fumes, pestilential smells and contamination that caused health problems and nuisance to many people in Lorca, particularly those living in the applicant's district. The town council had evacuated the residents and had rehoused them, free of charge, during the summer and early autumn of

---

that the noise in question flouted their respective rights under art 8 of the ECHR. However, the court held that it had no jurisdiction to determine whether the noise from aircraft using the airport contravened the claimants' rights. The court stated, however, a national government acted within a wide margin of appreciation in deciding how aircraft noise should be controlled. It was not for the court to substitute for the assessment of the national authorities any other assessment of what might be the best policy in that difficult social and technical sphere: at [43].

16 (2003) 37 EHRR 28 at [103].

17 (2003) 37 EHRR 28 at [121], [122].

18 In *Fadayeva v Russia* (2007) 45 EHRR 10 where the court was required to decide whether the state had taken sufficient steps to prevent the claimant from being affected by pollution from a steel plant, the court held that in such cases the state enjoyed a wide margin of discretion in terms of art 8(2): at [134]. See also *Dmitriyev v Russia* Application No. 17840/06 at [53] where the court held that the state enjoyed a wide margin of appreciation in balancing the rights of the individual against those of the community.

19 (2003) 37 EHRR 28 at [127].

20 (2003) 37 EHRR 28 at [130]. For a discussion of *Hatton*, see A. Brown 'Article 8 noise pollution' (2003) *H.R. & UK Practice* 16; J. Hyam 'Hatton v United Kingdom in the Grand Chamber: One step forward, two steps back' (2003) 6 EHRLR 631; C. Reid, (2003) 98 *SPEL* 87; 'Night flying and human rights' F. McManus, 'Noise Pollution and Human Rights' (2005) 6 EHRLR 575; F. McManus 'Noise pollution and Human Rights' (2006) 166 *SPEL* 84; F. Stewart 'A Right to Silence' (2010) 55 JLSS 26.

21 (1995) 20 EHRR 277.

1988. In September the town council had ordered the cessation of one of the plant's activities but had allowed another to continue. LO had raised an action in the local court seeking protection of her fundamental rights. LO had complained *inter alia* of an unlawful interference with her home and her peaceful enjoyment of it. She requested that the court order the temporary or permanent cessation of its activities. However, the court had held that notwithstanding the fact that the plant had caused a nuisance by virtue of smells, fumes and repetitive noise, it had not infringed the fundamental rights claimed. LO appealed to the Supreme Court claiming that the polluting fumes, smells and repetitive noise had caused both her and her daughter health problems. In 1989 the Supreme Court dismissed her appeal. LO appealed against this decision to the European Court of Human Rights.

LO claimed that her rights in terms of art 8 of the ECHR had been violated. The Court held that severe environmental pollution could affect an individual's well-being and prevent them from enjoying their homes in such a way as to affect their private and family life adversely without, however, seriously endangering their health.[22] Whether the question was analysed in terms of a positive duty on the state to take reasonable and appropriate measures to secure the applicant's rights under art 8(1) as LO wished, or in terms of an interference by a public authority to be justified in accordance with art 8(2), the applicable principles were broadly similar.[23] That was to say, in both contexts, regard had to be had to the fair balance that required to be struck between the competing interests of the individual and that of the community as a whole. In any case, the state enjoyed a certain margin of appreciation. Furthermore, even in relation to positive obligations under art 8(1) in striking such a balance, art 8(2) might be of certain relevance.

The Court concluded by deciding that the state had not struck a fair balance between the interest of the town's economic well-being in having a waste-treatment plant and the applicant's effective enjoyment of her right to respect for her home and her private and family life.[24] There had been a violation of art 8.

Gomez v Spain[25] provides a good example of persons affected by noise invoking human rights law to recure redress. In that case, Ms Gomez (G) lived in a flat that was situated in a residential quarter of Valencia. Since 1974 Valencia City Council (VCC) had allowed licensed premises such as bars, pubs and discotheques to open in the vicinity of her home, making it impossible for people who lived in the area to sleep. G claimed that this state of affairs amounted to a breach of art 8 of the ECHR on the grounds that, whereas VCC was not the direct source of the noise, VCC has caused the adverse state of affairs in question to come into existence by issuing an unlimited number of licenses without taking the requisite measures to comply with the law. G further claimed that the level of night-time disturbance that had been caused by more than 127 nightclubs infringed the right to health as indicated by the World Health Organisation (WHO) guidelines. The court held that a breach of art 8 could take place by the intrusion of noise into the home.[26] Indeed, a serious breach of a person's right to respect for their home could take place if it prevented

22 (1995) 20 EHRR 277 at [51].
23 See also *Kapa v Poland* App. No. 75031/13, judgement 14 October 2021 at [150].
24 (1995) 20 EHRR 277 at [58].
25 (2005) 41 EHRR 40.
26 (2005) 41 EHRR 40 at [53].

them from enjoying the amenities of their home. The court went on to state that whereas the object of art 8 was essentially to protect the individual against arbitrary interference by public authorities, art 8 could place a duty on a public authority to adopt measures that were designed to secure respect for family life, even in the sphere of relations of individuals between themselves.[27] However, in both contexts, regard was to be had to the fair balance that had to be struck between the competing interests of the individual and that of the community as a whole. As to whether the noise in question flouted art 8, it sufficed that the relevant maximum permitted level of noise had exceeded the permitted noise levels (which VCC itself had established through its byelaws) and had continued for a number of years.[28] In conclusion, the court held that there had been a violation of art 8.[29]

In *Dees v Hungary*[30] noise pollution from traffic formed the basis of the applicant's ('D') claim to the European Court of Human Rights. D claimed that by virtue of the increase in volume of traffic on the road outside his house (which had been caused by trucks and other vehicles diverting past his house in order to stop paying a toll to use the local motorway) the house had become damaged by the vibrations from the traffic and had also become uninhabitable by the increased noise and vibrations. D claimed that as a consequence his rights under art 8 of the ECHR had been infringed. The court recognised that the ECHR protected the individual's right to respect for their home, meaning not simply the individual's right to the actual physical area, but also to the quiet enjoyment of that area within reasonable limits.[31] Furthermore, breaches of the right to respect of the home were not confined to concrete breaches, such as the unauthorised entry into a person's home, but could also include those that were diffuse such as noise, emissions, smells or other similar forms of interference. A serious breach could result in the breach of a person's right to respect for their home if such a breach prevented them from enjoying the amenities of their home. The court stated that although the object of art 8 was essentially that of protecting the individual against arbitrary interference by public authorities, it could also involve the authorities adopting measures designed to secure respect for private life and home, even in the sphere of the relations of individuals between themselves.

The court noted that the state had introduced certain measures to mitigate the noise from vehicles near D's home.[32] The court went on to recognise that the state enjoyed a certain margin of appreciation in determining the steps that were required to be taken in order to ensure compliance with the ECHR when it came to the

[27] (2005) 41 EHRR 40 at [55].

[28] (2005) 41 EHRR 40 at [60], [61]. In *Fadayeva* (above, fn 18) the court held that the adverse effects of the relevant pollutant required to attain a minimum level in order to engage art 8. The assessment of that minimum level was relative and depended on all circumstances of the case such as the intensity and duration of the nuisance and also the physical and mental effects of the pollutant. The general context of the environment also required to be taken into account. Article 8 would not be infringed if the detriment complained of was negligible in comparison with the environmental hazards inherent to life in every modern city: (2007) 45 EHRR 10 at 311. See also *Kapa v Poland* (above, fn 23) at [153].

[29] (2005) 41 EHRR 40 at [63].

[30] (2013) 57 EHRR 12.

[31] (2013) 57 EHRR 12 at [21].

[32] (2013) 57 EHRR 12 at [22].

regulatory and other measures intended to protect art 8 rights.[33] That consideration also applied in situations that did not concern a direct interference by public authorities with the right to respect for the home. The state also had a margin of appreciation involving the state's failure to put a stop to third party breaches of the right that was relied on by D. In the instant case, the state was required to balance the interests of road users with those of the inhabitants of the surrounding areas. The court recognised the complexity of the state's task in handling infrastructural issues, such as those in the instant case, where measures requiring considerable time and resources might be necessary. However, the court observed that the measures that had been taken by the authorities were insufficient, the upshot of which was that D had been exposed to excessive noise disturbance over a period of time. That had created a disproportionate individual burden for D. The court observed that since the noise pressure had significantly exceeded statutory levels, a state of affairs to which state measures had not responded appropriately could, of itself, amount to a violation of art 8.

In the last analysis, the court held that there had been a violation of art 8.[34]

Noise featured in *Oluic v Croatia*.[35] In that case, the applicant ('O') owned part of a house in Rijeka where she lived with her family. Since December 1999 a bar had been run by a third person in another part of the house. In 2001 O wrote to the Sanitary Inspectorate (SI) (a public authority responsible for noise nuisance abatement in the area where O lived) claiming that her flat had been constantly exposed to noise from the bar, which had been open from 7am until midnight. Measurements had been carried out in May 2001 by an independent expert firm of acousticians who found that the level of noise at night had exceeded the permitted level. Later in the year, the SI had ordered the company that owned the bar to reduce the level of noise from their equipment for the reproduction of music. The decision, however, was quashed by the Ministry of Health and was remitted to the SI. Further measurements were taken later. These measurements showed that noise from the bar exceeded the permitted levels. In 2002 the SI ordered the owner of the bar to add sound insulation to the walls and floor of the bar. However, a subsequent inspection revealed that the order had not been complied with. The SI then ordered an enforcement of the order. A subsequent inspection found that insulation had been installed but that it was insufficient. Further measurements that were taken of the noise from the bar in 2003 showed that the noise from the bar exceeded the permitted levels. Later in 2003 proceedings against the bar owner were terminated on the basis that the noise from the bar was not excessive. O then lodged an appeal that was dismissed by the administrative court, challenging the findings of the administrative bodies. Further measurements carried out in 2005 showed that the noise level in O's flat exceeded the permitted level. O then lodged a complaint with the Supreme Court about the length of the proceedings before the administrative court. The complaint was accepted and the former ordered the latter to come to a decision within three months. In April 2007 the administrative court quashed the decisions of the lower bodies and ordered them to establish whether the noise from

---

[33] (2013) 57 EHRR 12 at [23].

[34] (2013) 57 EHRR 12 at [24].

[35] App. No. 61260/08, judgement 20 May 2010.

the bar was still excessive. Later in the same year, a second-instance administrative body annulled the decisions that had been made in 2003 on the basis that the noise that came from the bar was excessive and also that the insulation between the flat and the bar was insufficient.

Between December 2007 and December 2008 the SI took more measurements, which showed that the level of noise was again excessive. In January 2009 the SI ordered the owner of the bar to reduce the noise level. However, a month later measurements showed that the noise levels had not exceeded the set standards. O then brought an action against the state, claiming that it had failed to protect her from the excessive noise that had emanated from the bar.

First, the government argued that O had failed to exhaust to exhaust domestic remedies in the administrative proceedings.[36] The court held, however, that before one could enlist the aid of the court one was required to make use of normal domestic remedies that were effective, sufficient and accessible.[37] If there were a number of domestic remedies an individual could make use of any such remedies that addressed their essential grievance. In other words, when a remedy had been pursued there was no need for the applicant to pursue another remedy that had the same objective. In the instant case, the remedies that O had invoked were aimed at securing the same objective as the appropriate civil proceedings, namely abating the noise from the bar.[38] Therefore, the applicant was not required at the same time to bring civil proceedings to bring a civil action or to use any other remedy. Therefore, the government's argument that the applicant had failed to exhaust effective domestic remedies, in so far as it related to her failure to pursue a civil action against the owner of the bar, fell to be rejected.[39]

Second, the government maintained that the applicant had failed to use all available remedies in the administrative proceedings that had instituted and also that some of the proceedings were still pending.[40]

Third, the government claimed that the level of noise to which O had been exposed had not reached the necessary level of severity for art 8 to be engaged.[41] Fourth, the government claimed that the present case concerned a dispute between two private individuals and not an interference by state authorities with any of the applicant's rights which were protected under art 8.[42] The court held, however, that both the exhaustion of domestic remedies in the administrative proceedings and the issue as to the applicability of art 8 to the circumstances of the case should be joined to the merits, since they were closely linked.[43]

The Court held that whereas there was no explicit right in the ECHR to a clean and quiet environment, where an individual was directly and seriously affected by noise or other pollution art 8 could be engaged.[44] The Court went on to state that

[36] App. No. 61260/08 at [33].
[37] App. No. 61260/08 at [35].
[38] App. No. 61260/08 at [36].
[39] App. No. 61260/08 at [37].
[40] App. No. 61260/08 at [38].
[41] App. No. 61260/08 at [39].
[42] App. No. 61260/08 at [43].
[43] App. No. 61260/08 at [41].
[44] App. No. 61260/08 at [45].

whereas art 8 was essentially aimed at protecting the individual against arbitrary interference by public authorities, it could involve the authorities adopting measures that were designed to secure respect for private life, even in the sphere of relations between private individuals themselves.[45] However, in determining whether art 8 had been breached, the applicable principles were broadly the same, namely, regard had to be paid to the competing interests of the individual and of the community, as a whole. The instant case concerned an allegation that the relevant public authority had failed to put a stop to third parties breaching O's rights under art 8.[46]

The Court then went on to determine whether the noise to which O had been subjected contravened art 8. In order to contravene art 8 the noise was required to attain the minimum level of severity.[47] The assessment of that minimum depended on all the circumstances of the case, such as the intensity and duration of the nuisance and its physical and mental effects. The Court considered the fact that the noise levels to which the applicant had been exposed had exceeded the permitted levels that had been set by the relevant byelaw, between 2001 and 2008.[48] Furthermore, the Court took into account the fact that the noise from the bar had exceeded the international standards that had been set by the WHO and also most European countries.[49] The Court then went on to hold that by virtue of both the volume of the noise, the fact that it had occurred during the night and had exceeded the permitted levels and had continued a number of years and also nightly, that the level of disturbance had reached the minimum level of severity that required the relevant authorities to implement measures in order to protect the applicant from such noise.[50] The Court stated that the administrative authorities had delayed for a long period in taking remedial action against the owner of the bar.[51] The administrative court had also delayed four years in reaching its decision. This delay in dealing with night-time disturbances had resulted in O suffering an infringement of her right to respect for her home. Furthermore, the level of noise that O had been exposed to for a number of years had reached the required level of severity for art 8 to be breached.[52] The Court also observed that the national authorities had allowed this situation to persist for almost eight years while the various proceedings before the administrative authorities and the administrative court were pending, thus rendering these proceedings ineffective.

The Court held that in these circumstances the state had failed to discharge its positive obligation to guarantee O's right to respect for her home and private life.[53] Therefore, there had been a violation of art 8 of the ECHR.

First, *Oluic* reaffirms the fact that the European Court of Human Rights recognises the fact that noise that impacts on the enjoyment of one's home is capable of flouting art 8 of the ECHR. Second, *Oluic* emphasises the point that in determining whether art 8 has been infringed not only is the Court entitled to

[45] App. No. 61260/08 at [46].
[46] App. No. 61260/08 at [48].
[47] App. No. 61260/08 at [49].
[48] App. No. 61260/08 at [54]–[59].
[49] App. No. 61260/08 at [60].
[50] App. No. 61260/08 at [62].
[51] App. No. 61260/08 at [63], [64].
[52] App. No. 61260/08 at [65].
[53] App. No. 61260/08 at [66].

consider the relevant domestic law of the country in which the complainant lives, the Court is also entitled to take into account WHO environmental noise standards and also any acceptable noise levels other European countries have set. Third, *Oluic* establishes the principle that one is not required to bring civil proceedings against the author of a noise nuisance before enlisting the aid of the European Court of Human Rights. Fourth, in determining whether art 8 had been contravened, the court is entitled to take into account the length of time the relevant domestic courts take to reach a decision concerning the relevant noise complaint.

Noise featured again in the interesting case of *Zammit Meampel v Malta*.[54] Every year, on the occasion of certain village feasts firework displays were set up in the fields, which were situated close to the applicants' residence. The applicants ('Z') alleged that each time fireworks were let off from the area they were exposed to risk and peril to their life, physical health and personal security. Moreover, the heavy debris produced caused considerable damage to the residence. Z claimed *inter alia* that their rights under art 8 had been infringed by virtue of the Chief of Police having issued permits to allow fireworks to be let off near Z's residence without Z having had the opportunity to comment on the matter, and also by the fact that the area had not been declared a restricted area following the advice of a group of experts. In consequence, they complained that they were suffering a disproportionate interference with their right to respect for their private life and home.

The Court stated that the noise in question was not caused by the state, or by organs of the state, in that the noise was created by private individuals.[55] The Court stated that whereas the case could be seen as one that gave rise principally to the positive obligations of the state rather than an interference by the state, the Court was not required to finally decide the question since the test was essentially the same. That was to say, the question was whether the law, as applied in the present case, struck a fair balance between the competing rights of the individuals who were affected by the disturbance and the community as a whole. In order to justify the letting off of fireworks in the vicinity of Z's property, the Maltese government referred not only to the cultural and religious interests of the Maltese community but also to the economic interests of the country as a whole.[56] The Court observed that the state enjoyed a certain margin of appreciation in determining the steps that required to be taken to ensure compliance with the Convention when it came to the determination of regulatory, or other measures, that were intended to protect art 8 rights. That position also held good in situations that did not concern the direct interference by public authorities with the right to respect for the home but involved the authorities' failure to take action to put a stop to third party breaches of the right that was relied on by the applicant.[57] The Court stated that in cases that involved environmental issues, as in the present case, the state required a wide margin of appreciation.[58]

[54] Application No. 24202/10, judgement 22 November 2011.
[55] Application No. 24202/10 at [63].
[56] Application No. 24202/10 at [64].
[57] Application No. 24202/10 at [65].
[58] Application No. 24202/10 at [66].

The Court noted that the damage to Z's property had been both minimal and reversible.[59] Furthermore, whereas the mortality rate relating to the fireworks industry in Malta was alarming, such incidents occurred less frequently during fireworks displays than during the manufacture of fireworks. Z could have taken action against those responsible for the damage through ordinary civil proceedings. However, the Court accepted that the repeated letting off of fireworks, at sound levels reaching at least 120 decibels for two weeks each year, even though intermittently, created considerable inconvenience for Z. That inconvenience required to be balanced against the interests of the community. The Court accepted that in this context the authorities were entitled, having regard to the general nature of the measures taken, to identify distances from where third parties could perform the relevant displays, considering the geographical situation in Malta and its population density.[60] The state had also addressed its mind to the dangers that were inherent in the use of fireworks and had provided for a certain degree of protection.[61] Quite apart from the regulation of firework displays by way of permitting, regulations were in place in respect of transporting and uploading of fireworks. The letting off of fireworks was monitored by police inspectors and firefighters. Insurance covering the activity was also mandatory. The Court added that in determining whether the correct balance had been struck between the rights of Z and of the community as a whole, the mitigation measures carried considerable weight. Furthermore, the Court set store by the fact that Z had been fully aware of the very state of affairs of which they complained before they had acquired their property.[62] The Court held that that was a weighty factor in the relevant balancing exercise, irrespective of the fact that they were entitled to live there.

In the last analysis, the authorities had not overstepped their margin of appreciation by failing to strike a fair balance between the rights of individuals affected by those regulations to respect for their family life and home and the conflicting interests of others and of the community as a whole.[63] Therefore, there had been no violation of art 8 by the State.

CONCLUSIONS

The courts have established the following general principles in relation to the application of art 8 of the ECHR in terms of noise.

First, noise that exceeds a certain level (which has been described by the courts as the 'minimum level') is capable of engaging art 8. Whether the minimum level has been exceeded depends on all circumstances of the case. The court can consider whether the creation of the noise has contravened national legislation, the intensity, duration, physical and mental effects of the noise, and also whether relevant noise exceeds WHO environmental noise guidelines and those of other European countries. These factors are not exhaustive.

[59] Application No. 24202/10 at [67].
[60] Application No. 24202/10 at [68].
[61] Application No. 24202/10 at [69].
[62] Application No. 24202/10 at [72].
[63] Application No. 24202/10 at [73].

Second, art 8 can be contravened by a positive act on the part of the state and also by the state's failure to prevent its citizens from being affected by noise that has been caused by third parties.

Third, the state enjoys a fairly wide margin of appreciation in balancing the rights of the individual who has been affected by noise and those of the general community.

Chapter 8

Transport Noise

AIRCRAFT NOISE

We turn our attention, first, to the regulation of noise from civil aircraft and second, to noise from military aircraft.

Civil aircraft

Aircraft can cause noise problems for the community when the aircraft is taking off or landing at an airport, when the aircraft is in flight or when it is manoeuvring or even stationary with engines or auxiliary power units running (generically described as 'ground noise'). Therefore, the relevant statutory controls can roughly be divided into controls that relate to noise from the flight (or navigation) of aircraft, and controls that specifically relate to noise to aircraft from aerodromes.

Flight noise

Given that the flight paths of aircraft during take-off and landing are often directly over houses and other occupied premises, the noise that is generated by aircraft may cause considerable annoyance to individuals who are living beneath such flightpaths. However, the Civil Aviation Act 1982 (the 1982 Act) provides that no action may lie in respect of either trespass or nuisance by reason only of the flight of an aircraft over any property at a height above the ground that, having regard to wind, weather and all the circumstances of the case, is reasonable, or the ordinary incidents of such flight, provided that the provisions of any Air Navigation Order and of any orders under s 62[1] have been complied with.[2]

Furthermore, aircraft noise (from both civil and military aircraft) does not constitute a statutory nuisance, in terms of the Environmental Protection Act 1990 (EPA).[3]

The application of s 76(1) of the 1982 Act to noise from helicopters fell to be discussed in the Court of Appeal case of *Peires v Bickerton's Aerodromes Ltd*.[4] In that case the claimant lived in close proximity to the defendant's aerodrome. She brought an action for damages and an injunction to restrain the defendant from the

---

1 Repealed.

2 Civil Aviation Act 1982 s 76(1).

3 Environmental Protection Act 1990 s 79(6), (6A).

4 [2017] 1 WLR 2865. For a discussion of *Peires* see (2017) 184 *SPEL* 143.

continuation of a nuisance, which she alleged was caused by noise from exercises that were carried out by helicopters, on that part of the aerodrome which was situated closest to her property. Those exercises were part of the mandatory training requirements for a helicopter pilot. The exercises in question consisted of helicopters landing, taking off, hovering, turning through 180 degrees and landing again. The defendant asserted that the claimant's action was barred, *inter alia*, by s 76(1) of the Act. However, the trial judge rejected the statutory defence on the basis that s 76(1) of the Act was designed to cover journeys that consisted of aircraft passing over property. Therefore, the exercises, the noise from which was the subject matter of the action, did not amount to 'flight' in terms of the Act and the relevant orders. The trial judge, therefore, concluded that the noise in question amounted to a nuisance and granted an injunction that limited the helicopter exercises for a fixed duration during certain days of the week.[5]

The defendant successfully appealed to the Court of Appeal. The appeal essentially centred on the meaning of 'flight' in terms of the Act and the relevant orders. The court held that the expression 'flight' in that context was not confined to lateral travel by an aircraft from one fixed point to another.[6] Rather, the expression included an operation under which a helicopter rose a certain distance, then turned and landed.[7] Furthermore, there was nothing in s 76(1) of the Act that made it a precondition of immunity, which was conferred by the section, that the flight or the ordinary incidents of the flight, must be reasonable.[8] Rather, the only specified requirement as to reasonableness was in relation to the height of the aircraft 'having regard to wind, weather, and all the circumstances of the case'. The trial judge had made no finding that the height of the aircraft was unreasonable having regard to these factors. In the instant case, the claimant's action comprised a complaint that concerned both the frequency and the duration of the noise, rather than the height of the aircraft.

The appeal was, therefore, allowed.[9]

Section 60(3) allows Air Navigation Orders to be made, *inter alia*, as to the conditions under which and, in particular the aerodromes to or from which, aircraft entering or leaving the UK may fly, and as to the conditions under which aircraft may fly from one part of the UK to the other. Under the Air Navigation Order 2016 the Secretary of State may make regulations known as Rules of the Air *inter alia* prescribing the manner in which aircraft move or fly.[10] It is an offence to fail to comply with the Rules.[11] The current rules of the air are the Rules of the Air Regulations 2015 (the Rules).[12] The Rules prohibit *inter alia* the take off or landing of aircraft within a congested area of any city, town or settlement, except at an aerodrome, in accordance with procedures notified by the Civil Aviation Authority

[5] See (2016) 178 *SPEL* 143.
[6] [2017] 1 WLR 2865 at 2874.
[7] [2017] 1 WLR 2865 at 2875.
[8] [2017] 1 WLR 2865 at 2876.
[9] [2017] 1 WLR 2865 at 2877.
[10] Air Navigation Order 2016 (SI 2016/765) art 249(1).
[11] Air Navigation Order 2016 art 265.
[12] SI 2015/840. These rules were made under the Air Navigation Order 2007 (repealed).

(the CAA).[13] This provision could be used to prevent those living in the city, etc. from being affected by aircraft noise.

Aircraft noise certification

Whereas the potential noise problems from aircraft can be reduced by controlling the flight of aircraft flying over Britain, much more important is the requirement to reduce the noise that emanates from aircraft at source. Aircraft noise has been controlled, since the 1970s, by the setting of noise limits in the form of Standards and Recommended Practices (SARPS) contained in Annex 16 to the Convention on International Civil Aviation (the Chicago Convention).[14] Noise provisions are contained in Volume 1 of Annex 16, which requires certain aircraft to be certified before being allowed to operate. The primary purpose of noise certification is to ensure that the latest available noise reduction technology is incorporated into aircraft design and that this is demonstrated by procedures that are relevant to day-to-day operations. This will result in a reduction of noise around airports. In the UK noise certificates are issued by the CAA.

Before Brexit, the EU had made a number of Directives (which had been transposed into UK law) and Regulations, which were based on agreements that were made under the aegis of the ICAO. As far as the UK is concerned the relevant provisions of both the Chicago Convention and the relevant EU Directives are implemented by orders made under s 60(3)[15] of the Civil Aviation Act 1982. EU Regulation 748/2012[16] also makes provision, *inter alia*, for the issue of noise certificates in relation to aircraft.

Propeller-driven aircraft

The Aeroplane Noise Regulations 1999[17] make provision for the noise certification for UK registered propeller-driven aeroplanes, falling within one of the categories set out in Volume 1 of Annex 16 to the Chicago Convention. Subject to certain exceptions, such aircraft cannot be used in the UK unless there is in force in respect of that aeroplane a noise certificate that has been granted by the CAA.

Jet propelled aircraft

EU Regulation 2018/1139 provides that noise and emissions from aircraft require to comply with the environmental protection requirements, which are contained in

---

[13] Rules of the Air Regulations 2015 Schedule 1 s 3. See also EU Regulation No. 923/2012 of 26 September 2012, SERA3105 (retained), which specifies minimum heights for aircraft flying over congested areas of inter alia cities, towns and settlements.

[14] See *https://www.icao.int/environmental-protection/Pages/Reduction-of-Noise-at-Source.aspx* (last accessed 27 October 2022).

[15] The Civil Aviation Act 1982 s 60(3)(r) provides that an Air Navigation Order may make provision for prohibiting aircraft from taking off or landing in the UK unless there are in force in respect of those aircraft such certificates of compliance with standards as to noise as may be specified in the Order and except upon compliance with the conditions of those certificates.

[16] EU retained legislation.

[17] SI 1999/1452 reg 4.

Volume 1 of Annex 16 of the Chicago Convention.[18] As far as the UK is concerned, the CAA is required to ensure, *inter alia*, that in exercising its functions (which would include the noise certification of aircraft) that the CAA conforms with the provisions of the Chicago Convention.[19] Furthermore, the CAA is required to ensure that it is required to receive and assess applications that are made to it, in accordance with the provisions of Volume 1 of Annex 16 to the Chicago Convention.[20]

Non-Part 21 Aircraft

The Air Navigation (Environmental Standards for Non-Part 21[21] Aircraft) Order 2008 makes provision for the noise certification of Non-Part 21 aircraft.[22] Under the Order, subject to certain exceptions, a microlight aircraft may not land or take off in the UK unless there is in force for the aeroplane a noise certificate, and any conditions subject to which the certificate was issued have been complied with.[23] In the case of a microlight aircraft that is registered in the UK the noise certificate requires to be issued by the CAA.[24] The Order also makes provision for UK registered state aircraft, or research aircraft, for which there is no Part 21 equivalent type.[25] No such aircraft may take off or land in the UK unless there is in force for that aircraft a noise certificate issued by the CAA in accordance with the Order, and any conditions subject to which the certificate was issued, have been complied with.[26]

AERODROME NOISE

The CAA is placed under a duty under s 5(1) of the 1982 Act when it exercises any aerodrome licensing or certification function,[27] in relation to an aerodrome that has been specified in an order that has been made by the Secretary of State for the purposes of s 5, to have regard to the need to minimise, so far as is reasonably practicable, any adverse effects on the environment and any disturbance to the public from *inter alia*, noise and vibration.

---

18 EU Regulation 2018/1139 art 9.

19 EU Regulation 2018/1139 art 75.

20 EU Regulation 2018/1139 arts 9 and 62.

21 'A Non-Part 21 aircraft' means an aircraft that is not required, by virtue of the basic Regulation and any implementing rules adopted in accordance with that Regulation, to hold a Part 21 certificate: reg 3. The basic Regulation means Regulation (EU) No 2018/1139 of the European Parliament and of the Council of 4 July 2018 on common rules and, *inter alia*, establishing a European Union Aviation Safety Agency.

22 SI 2008/3133.

23 SI 2008/3133 art 4(1).

24 SI 2008/3133 art 4(2).

25 'Part 21' means the annex to so-entitled Commission Regulation (EC) No 1702/2003 of 24 September 2003 laying down implementing rules *inter alia* for the airworthiness and environmental certification of aircraft; SI 2008/3133 art 3.

26 SI 2008/3133 art 7(2).

27 One of the CAA's functions is to license aerodromes: 1982 Act s 3. A licensing function is a function that is carried out by the CAA under an Air Navigation Order with respect to the licensing of aerodromes: *ibid* s 5(2). An aerodrome certification function is a function carried out by the CAA under the Aerodromes Regulation with respect to the certification of aerodromes. 'Aerodromes Regulation' means Commission Regulation (EU) No 139/2014 laying down requirements and administrative procedures relating to aerodromes pursuant to Regulation (EC) No 216/2008.

Under s 77(1) of the 1982 Act provision may be made by an Air Navigation Order for regulating the conditions under which noise and vibration may be caused by aircraft on an aerodrome, and the Order may provide that s 77(2) (below) applies to such noise and vibration. Article 218(1) of the Air Navigation Order 2016 provides that the Secretary of State may prescribe the conditions under which noise and vibration may be caused by aircraft (including military aircraft) on government aerodromes, national licensed aerodromes, certified aerodromes or on aerodromes at which the manufacture, repair or maintenance of aircraft is carried out by persons carrying on business as manufacturers or repairers of aircraft. Article 218(2) provides that s 77(2) applies to any aerodrome in relation to which the Secretary of State has prescribed conditions, in accordance with art 218(1).

Section 77(2) provides that no action may lie, in respect of the law of nuisance, by reason only of the noise and vibration of aircraft on the aerodrome, provided that the provisions of the Order are complied with.

Designated aerodromes

The 1982 Act gives the Secretary of State wide ranging control over aircraft noise from aerodromes that are designated as 'designated aerodromes'. Aerodromes are so designated by way of an order made under s 80 of the Act.

Section 78(1) of the 1982 Act allows the Secretary of State (by way of a notice that is published in the prescribed manner) to place a duty on the operator of an aircraft, which is to take off or land at a designated aerodrome, to secure that after the aircraft either takes off or before it lands at the aerodrome certain requirements for limiting or mitigating the effect of noise and vibration from the aircraft (which are specified in the notice) are met. This power is used by the Secretary of State to determine the flight paths that aircraft are required to follow after taking off or landing at the airport to reduce the impact of aircraft noise on houses situated below the flightpaths.

The Civil Aviation (Notices) Regulations 1978[28] makes provision for the relevant notification procedure. Publication is effected by way of a notice published in the CAA publication entitled *United Kingdom Air Pilot* or *Notam*.[29]

Under s 78(2) if it appears to the Secretary of State that any requirement specified in relation to a designated aerodrome (and published in accordance with s 78(1)) has not been complied with as respects any aircraft, the Secretary of State may, after giving the operator of the relevant aircraft a hearing and also considering any representations made by the operator, direct the person managing the aerodrome that until the Secretary of State revokes their direction, facilities at the aerodrome are withheld to the extent specified in the direction from the aircraft of the operator. The person who is managing the aerodrome is placed under a duty to comply with the direction.

Furthermore, under s 78(3), if the Secretary of State considers it appropriate for the purpose of avoiding, limiting or mitigating the effect of noise and vibration connected with the taking off or landing of an aircraft at a designated aerodrome

[28] SI 1978/1303.
[29] SI 1978/1303 reg 2.

to prohibit aircraft from taking off or landing, or limit the number of occasions on which aircraft take off or land at the aerodrome, during certain periods (for example, during the night) the Secretary of State is given wide power to take appropriate measures. The Secretary of State may, by a notice published in the prescribed manner, prohibit aircraft of descriptions specified in the notice from taking off or landing at the aerodrome (otherwise in an emergency of a description so specified) during the periods so specified. The Secretary of State may also specify the number of occasions on which specified aircraft may be permitted to take off or land at the aerodrome (otherwise in an emergency of a description so specified). The Secretary of State may also determine the persons who will be entitled to arrange for aircraft, of which they are operators, to take off or land at the aerodrome during the relevant periods and, in respect of each of these persons, the number of occasions on which aircraft of a particular description of which they are the operator may take off or land at the aerodrome during these periods. The person managing the aerodrome is placed under a duty to secure that the prohibitions or restrictions relating to the aerodrome, which are imposed by the notice, are complied with.

Under s 78(4) a particular occasion or series of occasions on which aircraft take off or land at an aerodrome fall to be disregarded for the purpose of s 78(3) in respect of that aerodrome, if:

(i) on that occasion, or series of occasions, the aircraft take off or land in circumstances specified, in relation to that aerodrome, by the Secretary in a notice which has been published in the prescribed manner; and
(ii) the person for the time being managing the aerodrome or a person authorised by him for the purpose, determines that the occasion, or series of occasions, should be so disregarded. In such circumstances, the person managing the aerodrome requires to notify the Secretary of State in writing, within a week of it occurring, of any occasion (whether a single occasion or series of occasions) to which s 78(4) applies.

The 1982 Act makes further provision in relation to s 78(3). Under s 78(5) a duty is placed on the Secretary of State, before they make a determination in relation to an aerodrome as to the persons who will be entitled to arrange for aircraft to take off or land at the aerodrome during specified periods, and the number of occasions on which aircraft of a particular description of which they are the operator, may take off or land at the aerodrome during these periods, the Secretary of State is required to consult any body appearing to them to be representative of operators of aircraft using the aerodrome.

Section 78(5) also gives the Secretary of State power, if it appears to them that an aircraft is about to take off in contravention of any prohibition or restriction imposed under s 78(3) to authorise any person to detain the aircraft for such period as that person considers appropriate for the purpose of preventing the contravention. Such a person may enter upon any land for that purpose. Similar powers are conferred on a person, authorised for the purpose (or in turn, a person authorised by that person) by the person who, for the time being, is managing the aerodrome.

Section 78(5) of the 1982 Act further provides that the Secretary of State may, by notice given in the prescribed manner to the person managing an aerodrome to which a notice under s 78(3) relates, determine that a particular occasion, or series of occasions on which aircraft take off or land at an aerodrome, is to be disregarded for the purposes of a notice under that subsection.

The powers that the Secretary of State can exercise under s 78(3) formed the basis of *R v Secretary of State*.[30] In July 1993 the Secretary of State announced his intention to introduce a new system of night-time flying restrictions at Heathrow, Gatwick and Stansted airports, based on the amount of noise (using a quota system) that was produced by the aircraft used at the respective aerodromes. The upshot of such a policy would have been that it would have been possible for aircraft operators to increase the total number of take offs and landing movements by using quieter aircraft. The local authorities in the surrounding area challenged that policy by way of judicial review, claiming that individuals residing in the area would be adversely affected by the new regime if it came into force. It was held that it was not lawful for the Secretary of State to limit the number of night flights from a designated aerodrome by means of a quota system, based on the noise generated by the aircraft using the aerodrome, in contradistinction to the number of aircraft using the aerodrome.

In 2017 the UK government set out its policy in relation to night-time flights at the designated aerodromes for the period extending from 2017–2022.[31] An environmental objective for that period was to limit, or reduce, the number of people significantly affected by noise at night, including through encouraging the use of quieter aircraft, while maintaining the existing benefits of night flights.[32] The achievement of this objective is to be measured *inter alia* by employing a quota count[33] per aircraft movement over the course of a season (i.e. summer and winter) and also the number of movements taking place during the night quota period.[34]

Under s 78(6) the Secretary of State may give to the person managing a designated aerodrome such directions as they consider appropriate for the purpose of avoiding, limiting or mitigating the effect of such noise and vibration connected with the taking off or landing of aircraft at the aerodrome. The person who at the time is managing the aerodrome is placed under a duty to comply with the directions.[35]

In order that noise at the designated aerodrome can be measured, s 78(8) of the 1982 Act allows the Secretary of State (after giving the person managing the aerodrome a hearing) by order, to require them at their own expense, *inter alia*, to provide, maintain and operate noise measuring equipment in the vicinity of the aerodrome in accordance with any specified instructions given by the Secretary of State. The person managing the aerodrome may also be required to make reports concerning the noise that has been measured by the equipment to the Secretary of

---

30 [1994] 1 WLR 74.

31 Decision Document, *Night Flight Restrictions at Heathrow, Gatwick and Stansted* (Department of Transport, 2017).

32 Decision Document at 4.

33 A quota count (QC) is a classification based on certified noise levels that allocates a certain number of points (0–16) to an aircraft, that is to say the louder the aircraft the higher is the count.

34 The night period starts at 11pm and ends at 7am the following morning. Currently, Gatwick airport has an allowance of 11,200 movements and a 5,150 QC in the summer period, and 3,250 movements and a 1,785 QC in the winter.

35 Directions given under s 78(6) of the 1982 Act may be given for the purpose of avoiding, limiting or mitigating the effect of the noise and vibration either generally or in any particular area or areas: *ibid* s 78(6A).

State. The person who for the time being is managing the aerodrome is required to comply with the provisions of the order.

Section 78(9) makes provision for the case of the person who is managing the aerodrome failing to comply with the order. In such circumstances, the Secretary of State, after giving them a hearing, may *inter alia* take such steps as the Secretary of State considers appropriate for remedying the failure. The Secretary of State can also recover relevant expenses from the person managing the aerodrome. It is also an offence, subject to a penalty, to fail to comply with such an order.

To date, only Heathrow, Gatwick and Stansted in London have been designated for the purposes of s 78 of the 1982 Act.[36] At the time of writing[37] there are no designated aerodromes for the purposes of either ss 78 or 79 in Scotland.

Noise preferential routes at airports

An important device to reduce the impact of noise on the ground on those living in the immediate vicinity of airports from aircraft taking off at the airports, is the use of noise preferential routes (NPRs).[38] NPRs have been used by the UK Government, under s 78 of the 1982 Act, for the purpose of regulating noise at London's designated airports.[39] Some local authorities have also imposed special orders (containing NPR provisions) on non-designated airports, under s 106 of the Town and Country Planning Act 1990, to mitigate the noise impact from aircraft on local communities within their local authority areas. Furthermore, some airports, as good practice, have established NPRs on a voluntary basis.[40]

Noise control schemes – non designated aerodromes

An aerodrome operator[41] may establish a noise control scheme under s 38A of the 1982 Act for the purpose of avoiding, limiting or mitigating the effect of noise connected with the taking off or landing of aircraft at a non-designated aerodrome. A noise control scheme may:

(i) require operators of aircraft that are to take of or land at the airport to ensure that specific requirements (i.e. as specified in the scheme) are complied with in relation to the aircraft, either after they take off or land at the aerodrome;
(ii) prohibit aircraft of specified descriptions from taking off or landing at the aerodrome during specified periods;
(iii) specify the maximum number of occasions on which aircraft of specified descriptions can take off or land at the aerodrome during specified periods; and

36 These aerodromes were designated under the Civil Aviation (Designation of Aerodromes) Order 1981 (SI 1981/651), which was made under s 29 of the Civil Aviation Act 1971. The 1981 Order remains in force by virtue of the savings provisions contained in Schedule 14 to the 1982 Act.

37 June 2022.

38 See the *Guidance to the Civil Aviation Authority on Environmental Objectives Relating to the Exercise of its Air Navigation Functions* (Department of Transport, 2014) paras 5.1–5.14.

39 *Guidance to the Civil Aviation Authority* at para 5.15.

40 Routes conforming to the NPRs at designated and non-designated airports are published by the Department for Transport in the UK Aeronautical Information Publication (AIP).

41 An aerodrome operator is defined as the person owning or managing an aerodrome: 1982 Act s 38A(11).

(iv) impose other restrictions for limiting the cumulative amount of noise caused by aircraft of specified descriptions taking off or landing at the aerodrome during specified periods.[42]

If a noise control scheme imposes requirements in relation to the taking off or landing of an aircraft at an aerodrome, the requirements so imposed have effect in relation to the aircraft only while the aircraft is within such an area as is specified in an order made by the Secretary of State.[43] If no such area has been so specified the requirements apply only while the aircraft is within an area represented by a circle with a radius of forty kilometres from the centre of the longest runway at the aerodrome.

Before making an order, the Secretary of State is required to consult certain bodies.[44] The Secretary of State is required to consult: the CAA, the aerodrome operator; representatives of the operators of aircraft using the aerodrome; local authorities in whose areas the aerodrome (or any part of it) is situated; other local authorities whose areas are in the neighbourhood of the aerodrome, and any other body appearing to the Secretary of State to be representative of persons concerned with the locality in which the aerodrome is situated.

Where a noise control scheme imposes requirements in relation to the taking off or landing at an aerodrome, the scheme may provide for the aerodrome operator to require the payment of a penalty if any such requirement is not complied with.[45] The scheme requires to afford the operator of the aircraft the opportunity to make representations relating to the penalty to the aerodrome operator, either before or after the penalty is imposed.[46] If the scheme affords an opportunity to make representations after a penalty is imposed, the scheme requires to provide for the aerodrome operator to cancel the penalty if it considers it appropriate to do so having considered those representations.[47]

Noise insulation grants– designated aerodromes

While the reduction of noise at source from aircraft is the most desirable form of noise control, a substantial benefit can be achieved by insulating premises exposed to noise from aircraft. Under s 79 of the 1982 Act, the Secretary of State may, by statutory instrument in respect of designated aerodromes, make a scheme requiring the person for the time being managing an aerodrome to make a grant towards the cost of insulating buildings, or part of relevant buildings, against noise that is attributable to the use of the aerodrome. At the time of writing there are no extant grant schemes in operation.[48]

[42] 1982 Act s 38A(2).
[43] 1982 Act s 38B(2).
[44] 1982 Act s 38B(5).
[45] 1982 Act s 38C(2).
[46] 1982 Act s 38C(4).
[47] 1982 Act s 38C(5).
[48] The Insulation Grant Schemes for Heathrow and Gatwick Airports have been revoked: SI 2014/3233.

Environmental information and guidance, etc.

Section 84(1) of the Civil Aviation Act 2012 places a duty on the CAA to publish information and advice relating to the environmental effects of civil aviation[49] in the UK and how human health is, or may be, affected by such effects and the measures taken, or proposed to be taken, with a view to reducing, controlling or mitigating the adverse environmental effects of civil aviation in the UK. Furthermore, under s 84(2)(3) the CAA may publish guidance and advice (which is required to be kept under review) with a view to reducing, controlling or mitigating the adverse environmental effects of civil aviation in the UK.

Under s 70(2) of the Transport Act 2000 the CAA is required to take account of any guidance on environmental objectives given to the CAA by the Secretary of State. The Secretary of State issued guidance to the CAA under s 70(2) in 2014.[50]

Military aircraft

Noise from military aircraft, especially low-flying aircraft, can cause much higher levels of noise on the ground than civilian aircraft. The problem of low flying is aggravated by the fact that the design of military aircraft is such that they have a greater capacity to create noise than civil aircraft. Furthermore, the legal controls discussed so far in the book are largely inapplicable to military aircraft. However, the Crown can be sued for noise that contravenes art 8 of the ECHR and also in terms of common law nuisance.[51]

The Ministry of Defence also operates a noise amelioration scheme for householders affected by noise in the immediate vicinity of military airfields.[52]

Planning controls

Town and country planning has an important role to play in controlling noise from airports. This topic is dealt with later in the book.[53]

Hovercraft noise

The Hovercraft Act 1968 provides that Orders in Council may be made *inter alia*, to regulate both the noise and vibration from hovercraft.[54] Such orders may also provide that no civil action may lie, or proceedings under Part III of the EPA may be brought in relation to nuisance, if the Order is complied with. At the time of writing,[55] no such order has been made.

---

[49] 'Civil aviation' means civil airports, associated facilities and aircraft using such airports; Civil Aviation Act 2012 s 84(7).

[50] See *Air Navigation Guidance 2017: Guidance to the CAA on its environmental objectives when carrying out its air navigation functions, and to the CAA and wider industry on airspace and noise management* (Department for Transport, 2017).

[51] See e.g. *Dennis v MoD* [2003] Env LR 741; and *Jones v MoD* [2021] EWHC 2276; *King v Advocate General for Scotland* 2009 CSOH 169.

[52] The Ministry of Defence sets out its policy concerning noise from military aircraft in JSP 418: Leaflet 04-1, 'Environmental Noise'.

[53] See Ch. 10.

[54] Hovercraft Act 1968 s 1(1).

[55] March 2022.

TRAFFIC NOISE

In 1990 the Noise Review Working Party considered road traffic noise as the most serious of all transportation noise problems.[56] More recently, in 2018 the World Health Organisation drew attention to the fact that at least 100 million people in the EU were affected by road traffic noise, and in Western Europe alone at least 1.6 million healthy years of life were lost as a result of road traffic noise.[57]

Whereas Parliament has made noise from civil aircraft largely immune from civil action,[58] it has not been similarly indulgent as far as road traffic noise is concerned. However, whilst road traffic noise is not immune from civil action, road traffic noise is excluded from constituting a statutory nuisance in terms of s 79(1) of the EPA.[59]

Liability in nuisance

Private nuisance[60]

As far as civil liability is concerned, vehicle noise that interferes with the enjoyment of land could constitute a private nuisance.

Public nuisance

Furthermore, noise from a vehicle using a public road could constitute a public nuisance[61] in England and Wales. In the Court of Appeal case of *Attorney General v PYA Quarries Ltd*,[62] which concerned an action that was brought by local residents who were adversely affected by the projection of stones, grit and dust from the defendants quarry, Lord Denning MR stated that a public nuisance was nuisance that was so widespread in its range, and so indiscriminate in its effect, that it would not be reasonable to expect one individual to take proceedings on their own to put a stop to it, but that it should be taken on the responsibility of the community at large.[63] Whether the group of individuals is sufficiently numerous to raise an action in public nuisance is a question of fact in every case.[64] In such circumstances, an individual could seek redress by way of a relator action for an injunction brought by the Attorney General. However, if an individual who is affected by a state of affairs that constitutes a public nuisance can show that they have suffered personal injury, damage or inconvenience (as would be the case with interference by noise) that was substantially more serious than that suffered by others who are exposed to the same nuisance, the claimant would be able to bring a civil action for public nuisance.[65]

---

56 Report of the Noise Review Working Party (HMSO 1990) at 13.
57 *Environmental Noise Guidelines* (WHO, 2018) Foreword.
58 See p. 111.
59 EPA s 79(6A).
60 See Chapter 2 above.
61 For a discussion of public nuisance see C. Witting, *Street on Torts*, 16th edn (OUP) at 456–462 incl. See also *Clerk and Lindsell on Torts*, 23rd edn at 19–69.
62 [1957] 2 QB 169 at 191.
63 See also *AG British Columbia ex rel Eaton* (1963) 39 DLR (2d) 48. It was held that seven neighbouring families who protested against noise from a speedway constituted a sufficient class of the public to raise an action in terms of public nuisance.
64 *PYA Quarries* above, at 184 (per Romer LJ).
65 *Rose v Miles* (1815) 4 M and S 101; 105 ER 773.

Furthermore, under s 222 of the Local Government Act 1972 a local authority is empowered to bring proceedings in its own name (i.e. without the concurrence of the Attorney General) for injunctive relief where it considers it expedient to do so for the protection of the interests of the inhabitants.

Regulation of road traffic noise

There is no legal limit as regards road traffic noise beyond the requirements of the Noise Insulation Regulations, which are discussed below.[66] However, the approach to the problem of road noise in the UK has been to regulate vehicle construction and use in order to reduce the capacity of vehicles to generate noise on roads.

As far as the statutory control of noise from vehicles is concerned, s 41(1) of the Road Traffic Act 1988 (the 1988 Act) allows the national authority[67] to make regulations that govern the use of motor vehicles on roads, their construction and equipment and the conditions under which they can be used. Section 41(2) allows specific provision to be made in the regulations *inter alia* with respect to noise. It is made an offence to fail to comply with regulations that have been made under s 41 relating to the construction and use requirement in the regulations, or uses on a road a motor vehicle that does not comply with such a requirement, or causes a motor vehicle to be so used.[68]

The main regulations that govern the construction and use of vehicles are the Road Vehicles (Construction and Use) Regulations 1986.[69] Under reg 54 every vehicle that is propelled by an internal combustion engine requires to be fitted with an exhaust system that includes a silencer, both of which require to be kept good and efficient working order. Regulations 55–57 make provision in respect of noise limits that vehicles must not exceed. Furthermore, under reg 97 no motor vehicle may be used on a road in such a manner as to cause any excessive noise that could have been avoided by the exercise of reasonable care on the part of the driver.

Section 54(1) of the 1988 Act gives the Secretary of State power to make regulations that prescribe requirements (i.e. 'type approval requirements') relating to the design, construction and equipment of vehicles. Under s 55(1) if the Secretary of State is satisfied that a vehicle of a class in relation to which regulations that have been made under s 54 apply, and that the vehicle complies with the relevant type approval requirements, the Secretary of State may approve that vehicle as a type vehicle. Under s 55(2) where the Secretary of State approves a vehicle as a type vehicle they are required to issue a type approval certificate, stating that the vehicle complies with the relevant type approval requirements. A plethora of type approval regulations have been made, the vast majority of which have no bearing at all on noise. However, the Road Vehicles (Approval) Regulations 2020[70] specify certain requirements relating to the reduction of vehicle noise, for example, that a vehicle is

[66] See pp. 124–5 incl.

[67] 'National authority' means in relation to a function so far as is exercisable within devolved competence, within the meaning of the Scotland Act 1998, the Scottish Ministers, otherwise, the Secretary of State: Road Traffic Act 1988 s 41(2A).

[68] Road Traffic Act 1988 s 42.

[69] 1988 SI/1078.

[70] SI 2020/818.

fitted with an exhaust system, including a silencer, and also requirements relating to noise testing.[71]

The above legislation includes the regulation of noise from motorcycles. In addition to these controls, the Motor Cycle Noise Act 1987[72] prohibits a person who is carrying on a business to supply, offer or agree to supply, or expose, or have in their possession for the purpose of suppling, an exhaust system for a motor cycle or a silencer, or any component other than a silencer, or fixing for such a system, unless the system, silencer or component complies with the provisions of regulations made by the Secretary of State. The Motor Cycle Silencer and Exhaust Systems Regulations 1995[73] makes provision *inter alia* for the marking of silencers, as well as for packaging, labelling and accompanying instructions.

Location and design of roads

The location and design of new roads has an obvious bearing on the capacity of vehicles to discomfort the public by noise. The Department of Transport and the Welsh Office issued guidance to highways and roads authorities in 1988 in a memorandum entitled, *Calculation of Road Traffic Noise*[74] to allow them to calculate road traffic noise. The memorandum describes procedures for calculating such noise and also provides guidance appropriate to the calculation of road traffic noise, for the purposes of highway design, road schemes, land use planning and for the purpose of calculating entitlement under the Noise Insulation Regulations.[75]

Road traffic regulation

The Road Traffic Regulation Act 1984[76] allows a traffic authority, for a road outside Greater London, to make a traffic regulation order in respect of the road where it appears to the authority making the order that it is expedient to make it *inter alia* for preserving or improving the amenities of the area through which the road runs.

Powers of police to seize vehicles

In England and Wales if a police constable in uniform has reasonable grounds for believing that a motor vehicle[77] is being used in any manner that is causing or is likely to cause alarm, distress or annoyance to any member of the public, the constable has power *inter alia* to seize the vehicle, under the Police Reform Act 2002 (the 2002 Act).[78] A police constable has similar powers where he has reasonable grounds for believing that a motor vehicle has been used in similar circumstances.[79] However, a vehicle may not be seized unless he has warned the person who appears to the police

[71] SI 2020/818 Schs 1 and 2.
[72] Motor Cycle Noise Act 1987 s 1(1).
[73] SI 1995/2370 reg 3.
[74] *Calculation of Road Traffic Noise* (HMSO, 1988).
[75] See p. 125 below.
[76] Road Traffic Regulation Act 1984 s 1(1).
[77] 'Motor vehicle' means any mechanically propelled vehicle, whether or not it is intended or adapted for use on roads: Police Reform Act 2002 s 59(9).
[78] Police Reform Act 2002 s 59(1), (3).
[79] 2002 Act s 59(2).

constable to be using the vehicle that is causing alarm, distress or annoyance, that he will seize it if that use continues, or is repeated, and it appears to him that the use has continued or has been repeated after the warning.[80] In certain circumstances, the 2002 Act provides that it is not necessary that a warning is given to the person using the vehicle.[81]

MISCELLANEOUS CONTROLS, ETC. OVER TRANSPORT NOISE

Planning law and noise mapping

Planning law and noise mapping have a role to play as far the control of noise from roads and aerodromes is concerned. These topics will be dealt with later in the book.[82]

Noise – effect on value of property

The value of property may depreciate as a result of the construction or use of public works, for example, works associated with the construction of a highway or an aerodrome. The Land Compensation Act 1973 (the 1973 Act) makes provision for the payment of compensation in such circumstances. Under s 1(1) of the Act if the value of an interest in land[83] is depreciated by physical factors[84] that are caused by the use of public works,[85] then, if the interest qualifies for compensation under the 1973 Act, and the person who is entitled to the interest makes a claim under the Act, compensation is payable by the responsible authority[86] to the person making the claim. However, compensation is not payable under the Act, in respect of the physical factors caused by the use of any public works, other than a highway, unless immunity from actions in nuisance in respect of that noise is conferred (whether expressly or by implication) by an enactment relating to these works or, in the case of an aerodrome and physical factors caused by aircraft – the aerodrome is one to which s 77(2) of the 1982 Act (immunity from actions in nuisance)[87] for the time being, applies.[88]

Sound insulation

As has been seen, the vast bulk of the legislation relating to transport noise is aimed at suppressing noise at source. However, the impact of noise on those living in

---

[80] 2002 Act s 59(4).

[81] 2002 Act s 59(5).

[82] See Ch. 10.

[83] Section 2 of the Land Compensation Act 1973 defines the interests that qualify for compensation under s 1.

[84] 'Physical factors' include noise and vibration: 1973 Act s 1(2). Physical factors caused by an aircraft arriving or departing from an aerodrome are treated, for the purposes of the Act, as caused by the use of the use of the aerodrome, whether or not the aircraft is within the boundaries of the aerodrome. However, the source of the physical factors must be situated on, or in the public works, the use of which is alleged to be their cause: s 1(5).

[85] 'Public works' include a highway and any aerodrome: 1973 Act s 1(3).

[86] The responsible authority under s 1(1) is in relation to a highway, the appropriate highway authority and, in relation to other public works, the person managing those works: 1973 Act s 1(4).

[87] See p. 155 above.

[88] 1973 Act s 1(6).

the vicinity of public works can be mitigated by insulating buildings against the transmission of noise. Under s 20 of the 1973 Act the Secretary of State may make regulations either imposing a duty, or conferring a power, on responsible authorities to insulate buildings against noise, which is either caused or expected to be caused, by the construction or use of public works, or to make grants in respect of the cost of such insulation.[89] The Noise Insulation Regulations 1975[90] make provision for the noise insulation of premises affected by road traffic noise.

Under reg 3(1) where the use of a highway to which the Regulation relates,[91] causes, or is expected to cause noise at a level that is not less than the specified level,[92] the appropriate highway authority is required either to carry out or make a grant in respect of the cost of carrying out, insulating work in or to an eligible building as defined in reg 7 (below). The duty that is imposed on the responsible authority under reg 3(1) applies to a highway and also to a highway in relation to which an additional carriageway either has been, or is about to be constructed, if the highway or additional carriageway was, or will be, first open to public traffic after 16 October 1972.[93]

Under reg 4 a highway authority has power to carry out, or make such grants, in relation to the use of a highway first open to public traffic after 16 October 1969 and before 17 October 1972.

Under reg 7(1) a noise insulation grant is only available, subject to certain exceptions, in respect of dwellings and other buildings used for residential purposes that will not be more than 300 metres from the nearest point on the carriageway of the highway, after the construction of that highway, or of an additional carriageway therefor, or the alteration thereof, as the case may be.

Insulation work carried out pursuant to the Regulations requires to be carried out in accordance with certain specifications.[94]

The Department of Transport memorandum *Calculation of Road Traffic Noise*, which has been mentioned above,[95] describes the procedures for calculating noise from road traffic, which are necessary to enable entitlement under the Noise Insulation Regulations to be determined.

Similar legislation to the above, namely, the Land Compensation (Scotland) Act 1973 and the Noise Insulation (Scotland) Regulations 1975[96] apply in Scotland.

---

[89] 1973 Act s 20(1).

[90] SI 1973/1763.

[91] Regulation 3 relates to: (a) a highway; and (b) a highway for which an additional carriageway has been or is to be constructed, if the highway or additional carriageway was or will be first open to the public traffic after 16 October 1972.

[92] 'Specified level' means a noise level of L 10 (18-hour) of 68 dB(A); SI 1973/1763 reg 2. For the purposes of regs 3 and 4 the use of a highway causes, or is expected to cause, noise at a level not less than the specified level if: (a) the relevant noise level is greater by at least 1dB(A) than the prevailing noise level and is not less than the specified level; and (b) noise caused or expected to be caused by traffic using, or expected to use, that highway makes an effective contribution to the relevant noise level of at least 1dB(A): SI 1973/1763 reg 3(2).

[93] SI 1973/1763 reg 3(3).

[94] SI 1973/1763 reg 9, Sch 1.

[95] See p. 123.

[96] SI 1975/460.

RAIL TRAFFIC NOISE

Noise from trains can constitute a significant environmental problem. Such noise may emanate from the action of trains travelling on rails, as well as noise from shunting operations. The vast majority of railway lines in the UK were constructed during the nineteenth century by way of private Acts of Parliament, when railway construction had assumed fever pitch. Since the power to construct a railway derived from Acts of Parliament, the defence of statutory authority (which is a complete defence) would be applicable in relation to an action in nuisance.[97] The upshot of this is that it would not be possible to take action, by way of private nuisance, or in terms of statutory nuisance, in relation to noise from the relevant railway provided that the creation of the relevant noise was the inevitable consequence of that which was authorised by the relevant Act.[98]

In England and Wales, s 158(1), (2) of the Planning Act 2008 confers statutory authority, in terms of civil or criminal proceedings, for carrying out development in relation to which consent is granted by an order granting development consent and doing anything else authorised by an order granting such consent. This defence is only available in relation to relevant nuisance actions. The defence of statutory authority under the Act would apply to noise from railways, which are nationally significant infrastructure projects,[99] in terms of s 14(1)(k) of the Planning Act 2008.[100]

At present the Transport and Works (Scotland) Act 2007[101] allows the Scottish Ministers to make an order relating to, or to other matters connected with, the construction or operation of a transport system, including a railway that starts, ends and remains in Scotland. However, there is no authority on whether the defence of statutory authority would be applicable in respect of noise from trains that used a new railway line that was authorised under an order made under the Act.

Sound insulation

The Noise Insulation (Railways and Other Guided Transport Systems) Regulations 1996[102] make provision for the sound insulation of premises affected by rail traffic noise. The Regulations apply in relation to initial works, additional works or altered works that form part of a transport system in relation to a railway, a tramway and a system using modes of guided transport falling within the scope of the Regulations,

[97] See p. 4 for a discussion of the defence of statutory.

[98] *Allen v Gulf Oil Refining Ltd* [1981] AC 1001. See p. 41. The High-Speed Rail (London-West Midlands) Act 2017 makes provision for defences in relation to proceedings for statutory noise nuisance, under the EPA ss 79 and 80 (see above) and ss 60 and 61 of the Control of Pollution Act 1974 relating to the control of noise and prior consent for work on construction sites.

[99] Development consent is required for nationally significant infrastructure projects: Planning Act 2008 s 31.

[100] A railway falls within the scope of Planning Act 2008 s 14(1)(k) provided that the railway will be, when constructed, wholly in England and the railway will (when constructed) be part of a network operated by an approved operator. The railway also requires to be of more than two kilometres in length: Planning Act 2008 s 25(1).

[101] Transport and Works (Scotland) Act 2007 s 1.

[102] SI 1996/428.

such works being provided or used in the exercise of statutory powers.[103] However, ground-born vibration falls outwith the scope of the Regulations.[104]

The responsible authority is required to either to carry out, or make a grant, in respect of the cost of carrying out insulation work, either in or to an eligible building (as defined in reg 7 below) when on, or after, the relevant date[105] the movement of vehicles using, or expected to use, initial works or additional works, as the case may be, causes or is expected to cause noise at a level not less than the prescribed level.[106]

The responsible authority has the power either to carry out or make a grant in respect of the cost of carrying out, insulation work in or to any eligible building, either when on, or after, the relevant date, the movement of vehicles using, or expected to use, altered works causes or is expected to cause noise at a level that is not less than the prescribed level.[107]

Under reg 7(1) the duty on the part of the responsible authority to carry out insulating work, or make a grant in terms of the Regulations, is confined (subject to certain exceptions) to 'eligible buildings', that is to say, to dwellings and other buildings that are used for residential purposes that will be not more than 300 metres from the nearest point of the nearest running rail, or if the relevant system has no running rail, the nearest point of the nearest apparatus corresponding thereto, of the initial, additional, or altered works, as the case may be.

Regulation 8 gives the responsible authority power to either carry out, or make a grant in respect of the cost of carrying out insulating work, in or to, an eligible building, in circumstances where the construction of initial works or additional works or the carrying out of altered works, either causes or is expected to cause noise at a level that in the opinion of the responsible authority either seriously affects or will seriously affect for a substantial period of time, the enjoyment of an eligible building adjacent to the site on which the works are being or are to be carried out. The power on the part of the responsible authority to make such grants does not

---

[103] SI 1996/428 reg 3(1).

[104] SI 1996/428 reg 3(2).

[105] 'Relevant date' means the date on which the initial works, additional or altered works, as the case may be, completed on or after the commencement date, were first used after their completion: SI 1996/428 reg 2(1).

[106] SI 1996/428 reg 4(1). When movement of the vehicles takes place during the daytime period (i.e. 18 hours between 6am and midnight) the relevant noise level requires to be greater by at least 1dB(A) than the prevailing daytime noise level (as defined in reg 2(1), and is not less than the specified daytime noise level (i.e. 68dB L_eq, day time), and the noise caused, or expected to be caused, by that movement makes an effective contribution to the relevant noise level of at least 1dB(A): SI 1996/428 reg 4(2). When movement takes place during the night-time period (i.e. six hours between midnight and 6am) the relevant noise level requires to be greater by at least 1dB(A) than the prevailing night-time noise level and is not less than the specified night-time level (i.e. 63 dB L_eq, night-time), and the noise caused or expected to be caused, by that movement makes an effective contribution to the relevant noise level of at least 1dB(A).

[107] SI 1996/428 reg 5(1). When movement takes place during the daytime period the relevant noise level requires to be greater by at least 1dB(A) than the prevailing daytime noise level and not less than the specified daytime level, and the noise caused or expected to be caused by that movement makes an effective contribution to the relevant noise level of at least 1dB(A). When noise takes place during the night-time period, the relevant noise level requires to be greater by at least 1dB(A) than the prevailing night-time noise level, and not less than the specified night-time level, and the noise is caused, or expected to be caused, by that movement makes an effective contribution to the relevant noise level of at least 1dB(A): SI 1996/428 reg 5(2).

extend, however, to eligible buildings in relation to which a duty or power has arisen under regs 4 or 5 (above).

Regulation 9 makes provision for the calculation of the level of noise for the purposes of regs 4 and 5. A responsible authority is required to use the method of calculation contained in the publication *Calculation of Railway Noise 1995*[108] and Supplement 1 thereto.

[108] *Calculation of Railway Noise 1995* (Department of Transport, 1995).

Chapter 9

Noise Mapping

INTRODUCTION

Noise mapping in the UK owes its existence, as does much of UK environmental law, to the EU. Directive 2002/49/EC (the END Directive) was the most important measure the EU had taken in relation to ambient noise. Environmental noise mainly consists of noise from transport sources such as road, rail and aviation. The END addresses this problem. The END represents the flagship of the EU in its attempt to address environmental noise. The END's main objective is to establish a common approach intended to avoid, prevent or reduce, on a prioritised basis, the harmful effects, including annoyance, caused by exposure to environmental noise.[1] That policy is to be implemented *inter alia* by the determination of exposure to environmental noise, through noise mapping by methods of assessment that are common to the Member States, and by ensuring that information on environmental noise, and its effects, is made available to the public. The scope of the END is wide-ranging and applies to environmental noise that humans are exposed to, particularly in built-up areas, in public parks or other quiet areas in an agglomeration,[2] in quiet areas in the open country,[3] near schools, hospitals and other noise-sensitive buildings and areas.[4] However, the END does not apply to noise caused by the exposed person themselves, noise from domestic activities, noise created by neighbours, noise at work places or noise inside means of transport or due to military activities in military areas.

COMPETENT AUTHORITIES

Under the END Directive Member States are required to designate the appropriate levels of competent authorities and bodies responsible for implementing the END.[5]

---

1 Council Directive 2002/49/EC art 1. 'Environmental noise' is defined as unwanted or harmful outdoor sound created by human activities, including noise emitted by means of transport, road traffic, air traffic and from sites of industrial activity such as those defined in Annex I to Council Directive 96/61/EC concerning integrated pollution and control: art 3.

2 'Agglomeration' means part of a territory, delineated by a Member State, having a population in excess of 100,000 persons and a population density such that Member States consider it to be in an urbanised area. A quiet area in an agglomeration means an area delimited by the competent authority, for instance, which is not by the Council Directive 2002/49/EC art 3.

3 'A quiet area in the open country' means an area delimited by the competent authority, that is undisturbed by noise from traffic, industry or recreational activities: Council Directive 2002/49/EC art 3.

4 Council Directive 2002/49/EC art 2.

5 Council Directive 2002/49/EC art 4.

This includes authorities responsible for making and, where relevant, approving noise maps[6] and action plans for agglomerations, major roads,[7] major railways,[8] major airports[9] and also, collecting noise maps and action plans.[10]

NOISE INDICATORS

Member States are required to use noise indicators L den(lower case) and L night (lower case) as referred to in Annex I for the preparation and revision of strategic noise mapping in accordance with art 7 (below).[11]

ASSESSMENT METHODS

The values of L den (lower case) and L night (lower case) require to be determined by means of assessment methods that are defined in Annex II.[12]

STRATEGIC NOISE MAPPING

Member States were required to ensure that, no later than 30 June 2007, strategic noise maps showing the situation in the preceding calendar year had been made out and, where relevant, approved by the relevant competent authorities for all agglomerations with more than 250,000 inhabitants and for all major roads that have more than six million vehicle passages a year and major airports within their territories.[13] Member States are required to adopt measures to ensure that no later than 30 June 2012, and thereafter every five years, strategic noise maps showing the situation in the previous calendar year have been made and, where relevant, approved by the competent authorities for all agglomerations and for all major roads and major railways within their territories. Strategic noise maps are required to satisfy the minimum requirements laid down in Annex IV. Strategic noise maps are required to be reviewed, and revised, if necessary, at least every five years after the date of their preparation.

[6] 'Noise mapping' means the presentation of data on an existing or predicted noise situation in terms of a noise indicator, indicating breaches of any relevant limit value in force, the number of people affected in certain area or the number of dwellings exposed to certain values of a noise indicator in a certain area: Council Directive 2002/49/EC art 3.

[7] 'Major road' means a regional, national, or international road, designated by the Member State, which has more than three million vehicle passages per year: Council Directive 2002/49/EC art 3.

[8] 'Major railway' means a railway, designated by the Member State, which has more than 30,000 train passages per year: Council Directive 2002/49/EC art 3.

[9] 'Major airport' means a civil airport designated by the Member State that has more than 30,000 train passages per year: Council Directive 2002/49/EC art 3.

[10] 'Action plans' means plans designed to manage noise issues and effects, including noise reduction if necessary: Council Directive 2002/49/EC art 3.

[11] Council Directive 2002/49/EC art 5.

[12] Council Directive 2002/49/EC art 6.

[13] Council Directive 2002/49/EC art 7.

ACTION PLANS

Member States were required to ensure that, no later than 18 July 2008, the competent authorities had drawn up action plans designed to manage, within their territories, noise issues and effects, including noise reduction, if necessary for:

(a) places near the major roads that had more than six million vehicle passages a year, major railways that had more than 60,000 train passages a year, and major airports;
(b) agglomerations with more than 250,000 inhabitants. Such plans were also required to aim to protect quiet areas against an increase in noise.[14]

Measures within the plans were at the discretion of the competent authorities. However, the plans were required to address priorities that could be identified by the exceeding of any limit value, or by other criteria that was chosen by the Member States, and apply, in particular, to the most important areas, as established by strategic noise mapping. Member States were required to ensure that, no later than 18 July 2013, the competent authorities had drawn up action plans, notably to address priorities that could be identified by the exceeding of any relevant limit value, or by other criteria chosen by the Member States for the agglomerations, and for the major roads, as well as the major railways within their territories.

The action plans are required to be reviewed, and revised if necessary, when a major development occurs affecting the existing noise situation and at least every five years after the date of approval of those plans. Member States are required to ensure that the public is consulted about proposals for action plans and that the results of the participation are considered. The public is required to be informed of any decisions taken.

INFORMATION TO THE PUBLIC

Member States are required to ensure that the strategic noise maps that they have made and have adopted, and the action plans that they have drawn up, are available and disseminated to the public in accordance with relevant EU legislative Acts.[15] Such information can be made available by means of available information technologies. The information requires to be clear, comprehensible and easily accessible. A summary setting out the most important points requires to be provided.

The END has been implemented in the UK and Northern Ireland by subordinate legislation. As far as England is concerned, the END is implemented by the Environmental Noise (England) Regulations 2006.[16] The Secretary of State has general responsibility in relation to measures relating to the assessment, management and control of environmental noise.[17]

---

[14] Council Directive 2002/49/EC art 8.

[15] Council Directive 2002/49/EC art 9. In particular, Directive 2003/4/EC (public access to environmental information) and Directive 2007/2/EC (establishing an infrastructure for Spatial Information in the European Community (INSPIRE)).

[16] SI 2006/2238.

[17] SI 2006/2238 Preamble. In England DEFRA is responsible for creating noise maps and drawing up action plans for most of the major sources of noise. The exception is that airport operators (with

IDENTIFICATION OF NOISE SOURCES

The Secretary of State was required to identify, by no later than 31 December 2006, all:

(a) first round agglomerations[18];
(b) first round major roads[19];
(c) first round major railways[20]; and
(d) major airports.[21]

The Secretary of State was required, by 31 December 2011 to publish maps identifying all:

(a) agglomerations[22];
(b) major roads[23];
(c) major railways[24];
(d) and major airports.[25]

From 2016 the Secretary of State is required to publish maps identifying:

(a) agglomerations;
(b) major roads;
(c) major railways; and
(d) major airports,

as necessary, if they consider that the most recently published maps made pursuant to reg 3(2), are no longer appropriate.[26]

---

the exception of designated airports) are responsible for noise mapping and drawing up action plans.

[18] 'First round agglomeration' means an area having a population in excess of 250,000 persons and a population density equal to or greater than 500 people per km 2 and which the Secretary of State considers to be urbanised: SI 2006/2238 reg 3(5).

[19] 'First round major road' means: trunk roads; motorways that are not trunk roads, or principal or classified roads; roads that have more than six million vehicle passages a year; and roads that the Secretary of State considers to be regional, national or international: SI 2006/2238 reg 3(7).

[20] 'First round major railway' means railways that have more than 60,000 train passages per year: SI 2006/2238 reg 3(9).

[21] 'Major airports' means civil airports that have more than 50,000 movements per year (a movement being a take off or a landing) excluding those purely for training purposes on light aircraft: SI 2006/2238 reg 3(11) and see also SI 2006/2238 reg 3(1).

[22] 'Agglomeration' means an area having a population in excess of 100,000 persons and a population density equal to or greater than 500 people per km 2 and which the Secretary of State considers to be urbanised: SI 2006/2238 reg 3(6).

[23] 'Major roads' are trunk roads, motorways that are not trunk roads or principal or classified roads, have more than three million vehicle passages per year and which the Secretary of State considers to be regional, national or international; SI 2006/2238 reg 3(8).

[24] 'Major railway' means railways that have more than 30,000 train passage per year.

[25] 'Major airport' has same meaning as described in fn 21 (above) and see also SI 2006/2238 reg 3(2).

[26] SI 2006/2238 reg 3(3).

STRATEGIC MAPS

General requirements for strategic noise maps

Strategic noise maps are required to satisfy the requirements contained in Schedule 1 to the Regulations.[27] A competent authority is required to apply the noise indicators L den (lower case) and L night (lower case)[28] as referred to in Annex 1 of the END Directive and the supplementary noise indicators[29] when making or revising strategic noise maps.[30]

Strategic noise maps –noise sources other than non-designated airports

The Secretary of State is made the competent authority for the making, review and revision of strategic noise maps, for noise sources other than non-designated airports.[31] The Secretary of State was required to make and adopt strategic noise maps showing the situation in the preceding calendar year for all:

(a) first round agglomerations;
(b) first round major roads;
(c) first round major railways; and
(d) major airports.[32]

No later than 30 June 2012, and thereafter, every five years, the Secretary of State is required to make, and adopt, strategic noise maps showing the situation in the previous calendar year, for all:

(a) agglomerations;
(b) major roads;
(c) major railways; and
(d) major airports.[33]

The Secretary of State is required to review and, if necessary, revise any strategic noise map that they have made or have adopted whenever a major development occurs that affects the existing noise situation.[34]

Strategic noise maps – non-designated airports

As far as non-designated airports are concerned, the relevant airport operator is made the competent authority for the purposes of strategic noise mapping.[35]

---

[27] SI 2006/2238 reg 4(1).

[28] The values of L den (lower case) and L night (lower case) require to be determined by computation at the assessment position and by means of the assessment methods set out in Annex 2 to the END Directive: SI 2006/2238 reg 4(3). The assessment position means the assessment height in para 7 of Annex 4 to the END: SI 2006/2238 reg 4(3A).

[29] 'Supplementary noise indicators' means a noise indicator as defined in Sch 3: SI 2006/2238 reg 4(6).

[30] SI 2006/2238 reg 4(2).

[31] SI 2006/2238 reg 6.

[32] SI 2006/2238 reg 7(1).

[33] SI 2006/2238 reg 7(2).

[34] SI 2006/2238 reg 7(3).

[35] SI 2006/2238 reg 10.

Strategic noise maps – non-designated major airports

As far as non-designated major airports are concerned the airport operator was required, no later than 31 March 2007, and every 5 years thereafter, to make a strategic noise map showing the situation in the preceding calendar year for the airport and submit that map with input data and metadata[36] to the Secretary of State.[37]

From time to time, and whenever a major development occurs affecting the existing noise situation, the airport operator is required to review and, if necessary, revise any strategic noise map that has been made and adopted under reg 23 (below).[38] The airport authority must submit any strategic noise map that has been so revised, with input data and metadata, to the Secretary of State within three working days of its revision.[39]

Strategic noise maps – non-designated other airports

As far as non-designated airports, other than major airports, are concerned, the airport operator was required, no later than 31 March 2007, to make a strategic noise map showing the situation in the preceding calendar year for any relevant first round agglomeration[40] and submit that map, along with input data and metadata, to the Secretary of State.[41] No later than 31 March 2012, and thereafter every five years, the airport operator is required to make a strategic noise map showing the situation in the preceding calendar year for any relevant agglomeration[42] and submit that map, along with input data and metadata, to the Secretary of State.[43]

From time to time, and whenever a major development occurs that affects the existing noise situation, the airport operator is required to review and, if necessary, revise any strategic noise map that has been made and has been adopted under reg 23 (below).[44] The airport authority is required to submit any strategic noise map so revised, along with input data and metadata, to the Secretary of State within three working days of its revision.[45]

The most recent noise maps that have been produced by DEFRA, on behalf of the Secretary of State, were published in 2017.[46]

---

36 Both 'input data' and 'metadata' are defined in reg 9(1).

37 SI 2006/2238 reg 11(2).

38 SI 2006/2238 reg 11(3).

39 SI 2006/2238 reg 11(4).

40 'Relevant first round agglomeration' means a first round agglomeration in which air traffic from the airport results in air traffic noise of: (a) an L den (lower case) value of 55dB(A) or greater; or (b) an L night (lower case) value of 50dB(A) or greater, anywhere within the first round agglomeration: SI 2006/2238 reg 12(6).

41 SI 2006/2238 reg 12(2).

42 'Relevant agglomeration' means an agglomeration in which noise from air traffic from the airport results in air traffic noise of: (a) an L den (lower case) value of 55dB(A) or greater; or (b) an L night (lower case) value of 50dB(A) or greater, anywhere within the agglomeration: SI 2006/2238 reg 12(6).

43 SI 2006/2238 reg 12(3).

44 SI 2006/2238 reg 12(4).

45 SI 2006/2238 reg 12(5).

46 See *Strategic Noise Mapping: Explaining which noise sources were included in 2017 strategic noise mapping data sets* (DEFRA, 2019). Maps were made using computer modelling techniques, based on information such as traffic flow or vehicle; type data: *Ibid* at 1.

Quiet areas

The Secretary of State is required to identify quiet areas in first round agglomerations and also quiet areas in agglomerations in such published form as the Secretary of State considers appropriate.[47] The Secretary of State is required to keep the identification of quiet areas in first round agglomerations, and agglomerations, under review and make revisions where the Secretary of State considers it appropriate.[48]

ACTION PLANS

By way of introduction, action plans are based on the results of noise mapping, which occurs on a five-year cycle. Round 1 noise mapping took place in 2007. Subsequent action plans were adopted in 2010. Round 2 noise mapping took place in 2012, and the subsequent action plans were adopted in January 2014. The most recent mapping (i.e. Round 3) took place in 2017. In July 2019 DEFRA published three noise action plans in response to that noise mapping.[49]

We now discuss the relevant law.

The Secretary of State may compile a consolidated noise map in respect of any area covered by more than one strategic noise map.[50]

The Secretary of State is required to set out limit values, or other criteria, for the identification of priorities for action plans in such published form as the Secretary of State considers appropriate.[51] The Secretary of State is required to keep the relevant criteria under review and, where the Secretary of State considers it appropriate, make revisions.

Action plans – general requirements

Any action plan that has either been drawn up, or revised, is required *inter alia* to:

(i) aim to prevent and reduce environmental noise where necessary, and particularly where exposure levels can induce harmful effects on human health;
(ii) aim to preserve environmental noise quality where it is good;
(iii) be designed to manage noise issues and effects, including noise reduction, if necessary;
(iv) aim to protect quiet areas in first round agglomerations and agglomerations against an increase in noise; and
(v) address priorities that must be identified having regard to the relevant criteria.[52]

---

47 SI 2006/2238 reg 13(1).

48 SI 2006/2238 reg 13(2).

49 See *Noise Action Plan: Agglomerations (Urban Areas)*; *Noise Action Plan: Railways* and *Noise Action Plan: Roads* (DEFRA, 2 July 2019). The action plans were prepared after public consultation; see *Noise action plans: summary of responses and government response* (DEFRA, updated 2 July 2019).

50 SI 2006/2238 reg 14(1). A 'strategic noise map' means a strategic map made or revised pursuant to regs 7, 11 or 12 and adopted pursuant to reg 23: SI 2006/2238 reg 14(2).

51 SI 2006/2238 reg 14A.

52 SI 2006/2238 reg 15(1).

An action plan, and any revision of an action plan, must be based upon and apply, in particular, to the most important areas established by all strategic noise maps that are made or revised pursuant to regs 7, 11 or 12 (and adopted pursuant to reg 23[53]) and concern any part of the area addressed by the action plan.[54] The action plan must also be based upon and apply, in particular, to the most important areas as established by a consolidated noise map to the extent that it concerns any part of an area addressed by the action plan.

Action plans – noise sources other than airports

The Secretary of State is the competent authority for drawing up, reviewing and the revision of action plans in England.[55]

The Secretary of State was required, no later than 18 July 2008, to draw up action plans for:

(a) places near first round major roads;
(b) places near first round major railways; and
(c) first round agglomerations.[56]

The Secretary of State was required, no later than 18 July 2013, to draw up action plans for:

(a) places near major roads;
(b) Places near major railways; and
(c) agglomerations.[57]

The Secretary of State is required to review and, if necessary, revise the action plan whenever a major development occurs that affects the existing noise situation.[58] The action plan also requires to be reviewed and, if necessary, revised at least every five years after the date on which an action plan is adopted under reg 24 (below).

Action plans – airports

The airport operator is made the competent authority in relation to:

(a) major airports; and
(b) non-designated other airports, if aircraft noise results in an L den (lower case) value of 55dB(A) or greater, or an L night (lower case) value of 55 dB(A) or greater anywhere in first round agglomerations, or agglomerations.[59]

The airport operator was required to draw up an action plan for places near the airport and submit that action plan to the Secretary of State, no later than 30 June 2008.[60] The airport operator was required, no later than 30 June 2013, to draw up an

[53] See below.
[54] SI 2006/2238 reg 15(3).
[55] SI 2006/2238 reg 16.
[56] SI 2006/2238 reg 17(1).
[57] SI 2006/2238 reg 17(2).
[58] SI 2006/2238 reg 17(3), (4).
[59] SI 2006/2238 reg 18.
[60] SI 2006/2238 reg 19(1).

action plan for places near the airport and submit that action plan to the Secretary of State.[61]

The airport operator is required to review and, if necessary, revise the action plan whenever a major development occurs that affects the existing noise situation.[62] The action plan must also be reviewed, and if necessary revised, at least every five years after the date on which it was adopted under reg 24. An action plan must be submitted to the Secretary of State within three working days of its revision.[63]

Public participation

In preparing and also revising action plans for noise sources other than airports, and also airports, the competent authority is required to ensure that:

(a) the public is consulted about proposals for action plans;
(b) the public is given early and effective opportunities to participate in the preparation and review of the action plans;
(c) the results of that public participation are taken into account;
(d) the public is informed of any decisions taken; and
(e) reasonable time frames are provided, allowing sufficient time for each stage of public participation.[64]

ADOPTION OF STRATEGIC NOISE MAPS AND ACTION PLANS

The Secretary of State is required to adopt a strategic noise map that has been submitted to them under reg 11 (non-designated major airports) or reg 12 (non-designated other airports) if the map meets the requirements of reg 4 (general requirements).[65] The Secretary of State is under a similar duty in relation to a revised strategic noise map, or in relation to a map that either has been made or has been revised by them. However, if the Secretary of State considers that a noise map that has been submitted to them under regs 11 or 12 does not meet the requirements of reg 4, the Secretary of State may either amend and adopt the map, or they may reject the map.[66] If the Secretary of State rejects a strategic noise map, he is required to notify the competent authority that submitted it of the reasons why the map was not adopted, and also of the date by which the map must be revised and resubmitted.[67] The competent authority is then required to submit the revised strategic noise map to the Secretary of State by the date specified in the notification.[68] The aforementioned requirements also apply in respect of a revised strategic noise map.[69] If the Secretary

[61] SI 2006/2238 reg 19(3). This requirement applies only if airport operator was not required to draw up an action plan in the previous round because it was not the competent authority on or before 30 June 2008: *Ibid* reg 19(2).

[62] SI 2006/2238 reg 19(4)(5).

[63] SI 2006/2238 reg 19(6). The Secretary of State issued guidance to airport operators on noise action plans in 2017; see *Airport Noise Action Plans: Guidance* (DEFRA, July 2017).

[64] SI 2006/2238 reg 20(1).

[65] SI 2006/2238 reg 23(1).

[66] SI 2006/2238 reg 23(2).

[67] SI 2006/2238 reg 23(3).

[68] SI 2006/2238 reg 23(4).

[69] SI 2006/2238 reg 23(5).

of State amends a strategic noise map, or a revised strategic noise map, he is required to take such steps as they consider appropriate for ensuring that the map complies with the requirements of reg 4.[70]

Adoption of action plans

If the Secretary of State considers that an action plan that has been submitted to him under reg 19 (airports), or an action plan that has been drawn up or revised by them, meets the requirements of reg 15 (general requirements) the Secretary of State may adopt the action plan.[71] The Secretary of State has a similar power in relation to a revised action plan that has been submitted to him. However, if the Secretary of State considers that an action plan submitted to him in terms of reg 19 does not meet the requirements of reg 15, or that an action plan has not been adopted by him, the Secretary of State is required to either amend and adopt the plan, or reject that plan.[72] If the Secretary of State rejects an action plan they are required to notify the competent authority that submitted the plan of the reasons why the plan was not adopted, and also of the date by which the plan must be revised and resubmitted.[73] The competent authority is required to submit the revised action plan by the date specified in the notification.[74] The aforementioned requirements apply to a revised action plan as they do in relation to an action plan.[75] If the Secretary of State either amends an action plan, or a revised action plan, they are required to take such steps as they consider appropriate for ensuring that the action plan, or the revised action plan, complies with the requirements of the Regulations.[76]

POWERS OF THE SECRETARY OF STATE

The Secretary of State may at any time require the competent authority to provide information in relation to its functions under the Regulations.[77]

Information to the public and guidance

Any strategic noise map or any action plan that is made available to the public before it is adopted is required to include prominently displayed wording to the effect that it is a draft that is subject to adoption by the Secretary of State.[78] Any strategic map that has been adopted, or any consolidated noise map that has been compiled by the Secretary of State, or any action plan that has been adopted by the Secretary of State, is required to be published by the Secretary of State and also accompanied by a summary that sets out the most important points.[79]

---

[70] SI 2006/2238 reg 23(6).
[71] SI 2006/2238 reg 24(1).
[72] SI 2006/2238 reg 24(2), (3).
[73] SI 2006/2238 reg 24(4).
[74] SI 2006/2238 reg 24(5).
[75] SI 2006/2238 reg 24(6).
[76] SI 2006/2238 reg 24(7).
[77] SI 2006/2238 reg 26(1).
[78] SI 2006/2238 reg 29(1).
[79] SI 2006/2238 reg 29(2).

Guidance

The Secretary of State may issue guidance to a competent authority, in relation to the exercise of its functions under the Regulations.[80] In turn, the competent authority is required to have regard to such guidance.[81]

SCOTLAND

The Environmental Noise (Scotland) Regulations 2006[82] implemented the END Directive in Scotland. The Scottish Ministers (other than for airports) are responsible for making, reviewing and revising strategic noise maps.[83] The relevant airport operator is the competent authority for exercising such functions in relation to an airport.[84] The Scottish Ministers are responsible for drawing up, reviewing and revising action plans for noise sources other than airports.[85] The airport operator is the competent authority for exercising such functions in relation to airports.[86] The Scottish Ministers are responsible for the adoption of strategic noise maps and action plans.[87]

80 SI 2006/2238 reg 30(1).
81 SI 2006/2238 reg 30(2).
82 SSI 2006/465.
83 SSI 2006/465 reg 7.
84 SSI 2006/465 reg 8.
85 SSI 2006/465 reg 14. Technical guidance on noise action planning, namely *CNMA to NMA Guidance Document* was updated 6 September 2017. See also *Guidance for possible measures to manage noise from road and rail* (undated).
86 SSI 2006/465 reg 16.
87 SSI 2006/465 reg 21.

Chapter 10

Planning and Noise

The law relating to town and country planning has an important role to play in the control of noise in the environment. In this chapter we first consider environmental impact assessment, then strategic environmental assessment and thereafter, turn our attention to the control of development, under the Town and Country Planning Acts.

ENVIRONMENTAL IMPACT ASSESSMENT

Environmental impact assessment (EIA) is a key legal mechanism that has emerged in the last thirty-five years. It has its origins in the USA in the 1960s.[1] There it was a response to both the growing environmental movement of that era[2] and also, in no small measure, to the concerns about the US interstate highway system during the 1960s.[3] EIA enables decision-makers, mainly in the form of planning authorities as far as the UK is concerned, to take account of the environmental impact of their decisions. In essence, the importance of EIA is that information, about the likely environmental impacts of certain development projects, is properly considered before a decision is taken as to whether they should proceed. EIA is a process, or procedure, that comprises a drawing-together in both a formal and systematic way of assessments of projects that are likely to have significant environmental effects. This process helps to ensure that the importance of the predicted effects, and the scope for reducing them, are properly understood not only by the public, but by the relevant competent authority before it makes its decision.[4] The use of EIA conduces to transparency on the part of actions that are taken by decision-makers, and also increases the opportunities for the public to participate in the planning process. Since its adoption in the US National Environmental Policy Act of 1969, EIA has become an important tool of domestic environmental management world-wide.[5]

EIA DIRECTIVE AND ITS IMPLEMENTATION IN THE UK

The European Commission's Second Action Programme on the environment, in 1977, reiterated the approach that had been expressed in the First Action Programme,

[1] See the US National Environmental Policy Act 1969.
[2] See R. Carson, *Silent Spring* (1962).
[3] S. Tromans, *Environmental Impact Assessment*, 2nd edn (Bloomsbury, 2012) at 2.
[4] Department of Environment (now DEFRA) Circ. 02/1999, *Environmental Impact Assessment* para 9.
[5] Birnie, Boyle and Redgwell, *International Law and the Environment*, 4th edn (OUP, 2021) at 184.

namely that effects on the environment should be taken into account at the earliest possible stage in all the technical planning and decision-making processes.[6] The UK was initially opposed to the European Commission's proposals for a Directive on EIA.[7] Such opposition was largely based on the definition of the projects that would fall within the scope of an EIA Directive and also the delays and litigation that the implementation of the Directive would have on the planning process. The 1985 Directive, namely Directive 85/337/EEC, represented a political compromise.[8] The 1985 Directive has been subsequently amended several times. It was codified in 2011 by Directive 2011/92/EU (the 'Directive') which, in turn, has been amended by Directive 2014/92/EU. The Preamble to the 2011 Directive provides that development consent for public and private projects that are likely to have significant effects on the environment should be granted only after an assessment of the likely significant effects of those projects have been carried out.

Article 2 requires Member States to adopt all measures that are necessary to ensure that before consent is given, projects that are likely to have significant effects on the environment by virtue, *inter alia*, of their nature, size or location, are made subject to a requirement for development consent and an assessment with regard to their effects. Importantly, the article provides that EIA may be integrated into the existing procedures for consent to projects in Member States.

What is a project?

The Directive defines a project as the execution of construction works or other interventions in the natural surroundings and landscape, including those involving the extraction of mineral resources.[9] Normally, to be classed as a project there requires to be some form of construction or physical intervention. In Brussels in the case of *Hoofdsedilyk Gewest v Vlaams Gewest*[10] the European Court of Justice held that a consent, which simply allowed an airport to continue to operate, was not a project that fell within the scope of the Directive on the basis that no works or physical interventions to the airport were involved nor did the relevant consent constitute a stage in a procedure that could lead either to such works or physical interventions. However, where a proposal is simply part of a larger scheme that, when looked at *in toto*, would constitute a project that falls within the scope of the Directive, an EIA would be required. What is at issue here is what has been referred to as 'salami slicing', namely splitting a large development project into smaller units that, looked at in isolation, would fall below the thresholds that would require an EIA.[11] The Directive is not simply confined to new projects but also includes the modification of existing projects.[12]

[6] European Community Policy and Action Programme on the Environment, OJ C139, 13.6.1977 p1, para [203].
[7] For a discussion of the opposition of the UK Government, see S. Tromans (fn 3) at 2.19.
[8] S. Tromans (fn 3) at 2.22.
[9] Directive 2011/92/ EU art 1.
[10] [2012] Env LR 9.
[11] See e.g. *Commission v Spain* [2004] ECR 1-08253.
[12] See e.g. *R (Baker) v Bath and North East Somerset Council* [2009] EWHC 595.

While the UK courts have never fully addressed the point, in the Court of Appeal case of *Bowen-West v Secretary of State for Communities and Local Government*[13] Laws LJ suggested that whether or not a proposal was part of a larger scheme could be either a question of law or one of judgement for the decision-maker.[14] Again, in *R (Save Britain's Heritage) v Secretary of State for Communities and Local Government*[15] Stadlen J stated that the question whether a development was an intrinsic part of any inevitably wider whole was a matter of fact and judgement for the decision-maker.

'Development consent' is defined in the Directive as 'the decision of the competent authority or authorities, which entitles the developer to proceed with the project'.[16] However, the Directive does not cover decisions that involve merely the detailed regulation of activities, consent for which has already been given.[17] Generally, a project that falls within the scope of the Directive would fall within the definition of 'development' in terms of both s 55 of the Town and Country Planning Act 1990 (TCPA 1990) and also s 26 of the Town and Country Planning (Scotland) Act 1997 (TCPSA 1997) and, therefore, be subject to planning control. In such cases, the EIA process would be governed by the regulations which we now discuss.

TOWN AND COUNTRY PLANNING (ENVIRONMENTAL IMPACT ASSESSMENT) REGULATIONS 2017[18]

The Town and Country Planning (Environmental Impact Assessment) Regulations 2017 (the 'Regulations')[19] essentially implement art 2 of the Directive, as amended. It should be observed, at the outset that, in contrast to the Directive, the Regulations do not employ the expression 'project' in terms of environmental impact assessment. In contrast, the Regulations use the term, 'development' in terms of what falls to be regulated by the planning regime.

It should be stressed, however, that the Regulations only relate to development that requires consent in terms of town and country planning legislation. The Regulations do not apply to development that requires consent under other legislation. Such development is subject to separate environmental impact assessment legislation.

Prohibition on grant of planning permission or subsequent consent without an EIA

The Regulations prohibit either a planning authority, the Secretary of State or an inspector from granting planning permission, or subsequent consent, for an EIA

13 [2012] Env LR 22 at para [26].

14 See also *R v Swale BC ex p Royal Society for the Protection of Birds* [1991] JPL 39 and *R (Save Britain's Heritage) v SoS for the Communities and Local Government* [2014] Env LR 9.

15 2014 Env LR 9 at para [145].

16 Directive 2011/92/EU art 1.

17 [1999] Env LR 623 at 630 (per Lord Hoffmann).

18 SI 2017/571.

19 For UK Government guidance on the Town and Country Planning (Environmental Impact Assessment) Regulations 2017, see *Guidance: Environmental Impact Assessment* (Dept. for Levelling Up, Housing and Communities and Ministry of Housing, Communities and Local Government, 2014, updated most recently on 13 May 2020).

development unless an EIA has been carried out in respect of that development.[20] An EIA development is defined as either a Schedule 1 development or a Schedule 2 development that is likely to have significant effects on the environment, by virtue of such factors as its nature, size and location.[21]

Schedule 1 development

Schedule 1 of the Regulations implements Annex I of the Directive. Schedule 1 includes twenty-three different categories of development, including crude oil refineries, nuclear power stations, iron and steel works, construction of lines for long distance railway traffic, airports, with a basic runway length of 2,100 metres or more, motorways and express roads. Almost exclusively, each category in Schedule 1 has its own threshold by means of which one determines whether the development ranks as a Schedule 1 development. Whereas some thresholds are based on the size of the relevant development, other thresholds are 'triggered' by the output of the relevant development. Furthermore, any change to or extension to a Schedule 1 development ranks as such a development, provided that such a change or extension, in itself, meets the relevant threshold, if any, of the development set out in the Schedule.[22]

Schedule 2

Generally speaking, a Schedule 2 development is one that is likely to have a lesser environmental impact than a Schedule 1 development. Examples of a Schedule 2 development include intensive fish farming, quarries and open cast mining, deep drilling, windfarms, brewing and malting, industrial estate development projects, construction of airfields (unless included in Schedule 1) and the construction of roads (unless included in Schedule 1).

Environmental assessment process

EIA is defined as a process consisting of:

(a) the preparation of an environmental statement;
(b) any consultation, publication and notification required by, or by virtue of (the Regulations) or any other enactment in respect on an EIA development; and
(c) the steps required under reg 26.[23]

EIA is required to identify, describe and assess, in an appropriate manner, in the light of each individual case, the direct and indirect significant effects of the proposed development on *inter alia* population and human health.[24] The relevant planning authority, or the Secretary of State, must ensure that they either have, or have access as necessary to, sufficient expertise to examine the environmental statement.[25]

---

[20] SI 2017/571 reg 3.
[21] SI 2017/571 reg 2(1).
[22] SI 2017/571 Schedule 1 para 24.
[23] SI 2017/571 reg 4(1).
[24] SI 2017/571 reg 4(2).
[25] SI 2017/571 reg 4(5).

Screening

Where a planning authority, or the Secretary of State, is required to determine whether a Schedule 2 development is an EIA development, the relevant planning authority is required to consider, *inter alia*, any information that has been provided by the applicant, and also any of the selection criteria that is set out in Schedule 3 as are relevant to the development.[26] Schedule 3 lists a number of criteria including:

(i) the characteristics of the development;
(ii) the location of the development; and
(iii) the types and characteristics of the potential impact of development.

Of particular relevance to noise, under '(i)' are included pollution and nuisances, and also the risks to human health.

Where a planning authority adopts a screening opinion under reg 6(6), or the Secretary of State makes a screening direction under reg 7(5), the planning authority, or the Secretary of State, are required to state the main reasons for their conclusion with reference to the relevant criteria listed in Schedule 3.[27] If it is determined that the proposed development is not an EIA development, the planning authority or the Secretary of State is required to state any features of the proposed development and measures envisaged to avoid or prevent what would otherwise have been significant adverse effects on the environment. The Secretary of State may make a screening direction either on their own volition, or if requested to do so in writing by any person.[28]

A person who is minded to carry out a development may request the relevant planning authority to adopt a screening opinion.[29] The request must be accompanied, *inter alia*, by a plan sufficient to identify the land, a description of the development and a description of the aspects of the environment likely to be significantly affected by the development.[30] The person providing the information is required to take into account, *inter alia*, the criteria set out in Schedule 3.[31] The relevant planning authority is required to adopt a screening opinion within three weeks, beginning with the date of receipt for a request for such an opinion, or such longer period, not exceeding ninety days from the date on which the person making the request submits the relevant information, as may be agreed in writing with the person making the request.[32] If a planning authority adopts a screening opinion, the planning authority is required to send a copy to the person who made the request.[33]

Where a relevant planning authority either fails to adopt a screening opinion within the relevant period or adopts an opinion to the effect that the development

[26] SI 2017/571 reg 5(4).
[27] SI 2017/571 reg 5(5).
[28] SI 2017/571 reg 5(6).
[29] SI 2017/571 reg 6(1).
[30] SI 2017/571 reg 6(2).
[31] SI 2017/571 reg 6(4).
[32] SI 2017/571 reg 6(6).
[33] SI 2017/571 reg 6(9).

is an EIA development, the person who requested the opinion may request the Secretary of State to make a screening direction.[34]

The screening process takes place at a relatively early stage of the planning process, the upshot of which is that there may be some uncertainty about the full possible potential environmental impact of the proposed development. However, the screening opinion is required to be based on sufficient information to allow the planning authority to make an informed decision as to whether the development is likely to have a significant effect on the environment.[35] Whether there is sufficient information depends on the particular circumstances. A planning authority can adopt a screening opinion, notwithstanding the fact that its decision is based on less than complete information. In the Court of Appeal case on *R (Bateman) v Cambridgeshire DC*[36] Bick-Moore LJ stated that a screening opinion did not involve a detailed assessment of the factors relevant to the grant of planning permission. That came later. The judge added that a screening opinion involved a decision that was almost inevitably based on incomplete information. Again, in *R (Thakeham Village Action Ltd.) v Horsham DC*[37] Lindblom J (as he then was) stated that a planning authority was not bound to require an EIA, notwithstanding that there was some uncertainty about the likely effects of the development. The fact that a screening decision involves a matter of judgement or opinion was re-emphasised by the Court of Appeal in *R v Jones v Mansfield DC*[38] where Dyson LJ stated that whether a proposed development was likely to have significant effects on the environment involved an exercise of judgement or opinion. It was not a question of hard fact to which there could be only one possible correct answer in any given case. The role of the court should be limited to one of review, on *Wednesbury* grounds.

The point that a screening judgement takes part at an initial stage of the environmental assessment process and need not involve a rigorous assessment by the planning authority was succinctly expressed by Beatson J in *Zeb v Birmingham City Council*[39] who stated that detailed reports were not required. What was required was an initial assessment of an intended proposal.

In *R (Birchall Gardens LLP) v Hertfordshire CC*[40] Holgate J reiterated the point that had been made in *Bateman*, to the effect that a screening assessment did not involve a detailed assessment of factors relevant to the grant of planning permission. Nor did it include a full assessment of any identifiable environmental effects. It included only a decision, almost inevitably on the basis of less than complete information, as to whether an EIA needed to be taken at all. The court should not impose too high a burden on planning authorities in relation to the screening process.

---

34 SI 2017/571 reg 6(10). The person who requests the Secretary of State make a screening direction is required to submit the information specified in reg 7 with the request.

35 *R (Cooperative Group Ltd) v Northumberland CC* [2010] Env LR 40 at [8] (per Judge Pelling).

36 [2011] EWCA Civ 157 at [20].

37 [2014] Env LR 21 at [29].

38 [2004] Env LR 21 at [17].

39 [2010] Env LR 30 at [25].

40 [2017] Env LR 17 at [66]. See also *Swire v Ashford BC* [2021] EWHC 702. For a discussion of *Swire* see (2021) *208 SPEL* 141.

The judge went on to add[41] that whether there was sufficient information before the planning authority for it to issue a screening opinion, and whether a development was likely to have significant environmental effects, were both matters of judgement for the planning authority. Such decisions could be challenged only on the grounds of irrationality or for other public law error.

As far as the content of the screening opinion is concerned, in the Court of Appeal case of *R (Bateman) v South Cambridgeshire CC*[42] stated that when it was adopting a screening opinion, the planning authority was required to provide sufficient information to enable anyone interested in the decision to see that proper consideration had been given to the possible environmental effects of the development and to understand the reasons for that decision. Such information could be contained in the screening opinion itself or in separate reasons, if necessary combined with additional material provided on request.

Whereas a planning authority is not required to set out at length in its screening opinion, the considerations that it has taken into account in adopting a screening opinion, the essence of its reasoning, must be plain.[43] In the Court of Appeal case of *R (Friends of Basildon Golf Course) v Basildon DC*[44] Pill LJ stated that the decision taken on a screening opinion was required to be carefully and conscientiously considered, and was also required to be based on information that was both sufficient and accurate. The opinion was not required to be elaborate but at the same time, was required to demonstrate that the issues had been understood and considered. Finally, in *Birchall Gardens*[45] Holgate J held that the level of detail that was required in a screening opinion depended on the complexity, or otherwise, of the issues that fell to be considered. The judge went on to emphasise that in issuing a screening opinion the planning authority was not issuing a decision letter in a planning appeal. Rather, in issuing a screening opinion, the planning authority was issuing a screening opinion for a narrower purpose.

ENVIRONMENTAL STATEMENTS

An environmental statement (ES) is simply a statement by means of which one can assess the environmental effects of a project. The ES has been described as the cornerstone of the EIA regime.[46] Tromans argues that the importance of the ES lies not simply in the information it contains, but in its presentation of that information in comprehensive and accessible form to members of the public, including a non-technical summary.[47] The ES is the most visible part of the EIA process and is the main source of environmental information that is available to a planning authority.

[41] [2017] Env LR 17 at [67].
[42] [2011] EWCA Civ 157 at [21].
[43] *R (Thakeham Village Action) v Horsham DC* [2014] Env LR 21 at [28] (per Lindblom J).
[44] [2011] Env LR 16 at [62].
[45] [2017] Env LR 17 at [84].
[46] *Berkeley v SoS for the Environment, Transport and the Regions* [2001] 2 AC 603 at 608 (per Lord Bingham).
[47] S. Tromans (fn 3) at para 4.11.

Scoping opinion

A person who is making an EIA application can request the relevant planning authority to state, in writing, its opinion (i.e. 'scoping opinion') as to the scope and level of detail of the information that requires to be provided in the ES.[48] A request for a scoping opinion is required to include, *inter alia*, a plan that is sufficient to identify the land, a brief description of the nature and purpose of the development, its location and an explanation of the likely significant effects of the development on the environment.[49] A planning authority must not adopt a scoping opinion in response to a request until it has consulted the consultation bodies.[50] However, the planning authority is required to adopt a scoping opinion within five weeks (or such longer period as may be agreed in writing with the person making the request), beginning on the date of the receipt of the request. A copy must be sent to the person who made the request. Before adopting an environmental statement, a planning authority is required to take into account, *inter alia*, any information provided by the applicant about the proposed development, the specific characteristics of the particular development and the environmental features that are likely to be significantly affected by the development.[51]

Where a planning authority fails to adopt a scoping opinion within the relevant period the person who requested the opinion may request the Secretary of State to make a scoping direction as to the information to be provided in the environmental statement.[52]

Environmental statement – content, publicity, etc.

An EIA application (i.e. an application for planning permission for an EIA development) is required to be accompanied by an environmental statement.[53] Whilst the Regulations do not prescribe the precise form that the ES should take, the ES is required to contain certain information, as follows:

(a) a description of the proposed development, comprising information on the site, design, design, size and other relevant features of the development;
(b) a description of any likely significant effects of the proposed development on the environment;
(c) a description of any features of the proposed development, or measures envisaged, in order to avoid, prevent or reduce and, if possible, offset significant adverse effects on the environment;
(d) a description of the reasonable alternatives studied by the developer, which are relevant to the proposed development and its specific characteristics, and an indication of the main reasons for the option chosen, taking into account the effects of the development on the environment;

[48] Town and Country Planning (Environmental Impact Assessment) Regulations 2017 reg 15(1).
[49] 2017 Regulations reg 15(2).
[50] 2017 Regulations reg 15(4). The consultation bodies are listed in reg 2(1).
[51] 2017 Regulations reg 15(6).
[52] 2017 Regulations reg 15(7).
[53] 2017 Regulations reg 18(1).

(e) a non-technical summary of the information referred to in subparagraphs (a) to (d); and
(f) any additional information specified in Schedule 4, relevant to the specific characteristics of the particular development, or type of development, and to the environmental features likely to be significantly affected.[54]

An ES must also be based on the most recent scoping opinion or direction that has been issued under regs 15 or 16 so far as the proposed development remains the same as that which was subject to that opinion or direction.[55] The ES is also required to include the information that is reasonably required for reaching a reasoned conclusion on the significant effects of the development on the environment, taking into account current knowledge and methods of assessment. The ES is also required to contain the results of any relevant UK environmental assessment that are reasonably available to the person preparing the environmental statement, with a view to avoiding duplication of assessment. Finally, the ES is required to be prepared by competent experts.

In the House of Lords case of *Berkeley v Secretary of State for the Environment*[56] Lord Hoffman stated that an environmental statement must comprise a single and accessible compilation (as opposed to a number of separate documents) that is produced by the applicant at the very start of the application process. However, the ES need not contain detailed and exhaustive information of the potential environmental impact of a development. Moreover, the courts are prepared to allow any inadequacies and omissions (including apposite remedial, or mitigation measures, which may be required to be adopted in the future) in the ES to be addressed by the planning authority in the publicity and consultation process, which is incorporated in the EIA Regulations as a whole. In *R (Blewett) v Derbyshire CC*[57] Dove J emphasised that EIA applications were made on the basis of 'full information'. However, the Regulations were not based on the premise that the ES would contain the full information. The process was designed to identify any deficiencies in the ES in order that the local planning authority had the full picture, so far as it could be ascertained, when it came to consider the environmental information, of which the environmental statement would be but a part.

The courts accord planning authorities wide discretion as to the content of an ES. In *Kent v First Secretary of State*[58] the claimant was an objector to a proposed waste development. The First Secretary had called in the relevant planning application and had granted planning permission for the development. The application had been accompanied by an ES, which indicated which types of waste, would and would not be accepted at the site and also contained a qualitative risk assessment. The claimant claimed, *inter alia*, that the waste, which was to be disposed of at the site, was not described with sufficient particularity in the relevant ES. It was further claimed that the ES was defective in that it had not included a quantitative risk assessment. However, it was held that, whilst an environmental statement was required to

[54] 2017 Regulations reg 18(3).
[55] 2017 Regulations reg 18(4).
[56] [2001] 2 AC 603 at 617.
[57] [2004] Env LR 29 at [68].
[58] [2005] Env LR 30.

contain sufficient information to allow a planning authority to make an informed judgement as to whether the development was likely to have a significant effect on the environment, it was for the decision-maker to decide whether the information contained in the document was sufficient to meet the definition of an ES, in terms of the Regulations, subject to review on *Wednesbury* grounds.[59]

Publicity, etc. re the environmental statement

It is of fundamental importance that the public is notified of any ES in respect of an EIA application to a planning authority. Where the ES accompanies a planning application, the normal procedures relating to publicity for planning applications would apply. However, the Regulations make provision for publicity of the ES where an application for planning permission has been made without an environmental statement and the applicant proposes to submit such a statement.[60] In such circumstances, the applicant is required to publish in a local newspaper circulating in the locality in which the land is situated, a notice stating *inter alia*: the applicant's name; that an application is being made for planning permission (or subsequent consent) to the planning authority; the name and address of the planning authority, or that of the Secretary of State (in the case of an application that has been made to the Secretary of State); the address, or location, and nature of the proposed development; an address in the locality in which the land is situated at which the ES may be inspected; that any person who wishes to make representations should submit them in writing to the planning authority, or to the Secretary of State (in the case of an application made, or referred to the Secretary of State, or of an appeal); and the address to which representations should be sent.[61]

The relevant planning authority is required to make the ES available for inspection on a website maintained by, or on behalf, of the planning authority.[62] An applicant for planning permission, or subsequent consent, or an appellant who submits an ES in connection with an appeal, is required to ensure that a reasonable number of copies are available at the address that has been named in notices published, or posted, in terms of the Town and Country Planning (Section 62A Applications) Order 2013 or reg 20.[63]

Where an EIA application is determined by a local planning authority, the authority is required to promptly, *inter alia*, inform the public of the decision by local advertisement or by such other means as are reasonable in the circumstances, and the main reasons and considerations on which the decision is based.[64] Similar requirements apply in relation to an EIA application or appeal that has been determined by the Secretary of State or by an inspector.[65]

[59] [2005] Env LR 30 at [76]. See also *Gathercole v Suffolk CC* [2020] EWCA Civ 1179. See (2021) 203 *SPEL* 19. See also *Kenyon v Secretary of State for Housing, Communities and Local Government* [2020] EWCA Civ 302. See (2020) 199 *SPEL* 62.
[60] 2017 Regulations reg 20(1).
[61] 2017 Regulations reg 20(2).
[62] 2017 Regulations reg 20(7).
[63] 2017 Regulations reg 23.
[64] 2017 Regulations reg 30(1).
[65] 2017 Regulations reg 30(2), (3).

Scotland

The Town and Country Planning (Environmental Impact Assessment) (Scotland) Regulations 2017[66] make similar provisions as the above in relation to Scotland.[67] The Scottish Ministers exercise similar powers in Scotland as those possessed by the Secretary of State in England. In Scotland an environmental statement is referred to as an 'environmental impact report'.

Conclusions

EIA has generated a plethora of case law in the UK. However, EIA is simply a procedure with which the relevant planning authority must comply before deciding whether a proposed development should be given planning permission. The process ensures that the potential environmental impacts of a proposed development are taken into account by the planning authority. In the planning decision-making process, the potential environmental impact as elicited by the EIA procedure ranks as a material consideration. As such, the importance, or weighting, that a planning authority accords to the EIA is at the discretion of the planning authority and is only challengeable on *Wednesbury* grounds.[68] It automatically follows, of course, that the EIA process may indicate that the proposed development would have a significant adverse effect on the environment (that is, a so-called 'negative EIA') but notwithstanding this fact, the planning authority can quite legitimately decide to give the proposed development planning permission. However, frequently, the EIA process has been regarded by pressure groups who oppose a development as a formidable hurdle that developers must overcome in order to obtain planning permission. EIA is not intended to be a preventative process. Rather, it is a facilitative process that is conducive, at least in theory, to better decision-making by planning authorities.

STRATEGIC ENVIRONMENTAL ASSESSMENT

Essentially, a strategic environmental assessment (SEA) is an assessment of the potential environmental impacts of plans and programmes by competent authorities. SEA therefore has an important role to play as far as the control of noise is concerned.

Speaking generally, whereas EIA operates at a micro level, a SEA operates at a macro level. In common with EIA, the SEA is purely procedural in nature. However, both regimes are largely complimentary. The purpose of an SEA is to prevent major effects on the environment being predetermined by earlier planning measures, before the EIA stage is reached.

---

[66] SSI 2017/102. See Circ. 1/2017, Scottish Government, 16 May 2017.

[67] For a discussion of EIA, in Scotland see F. McManus and R. Hefron, 'Environmental Impact Assessment' in F. McManus (ed), *Environmental Law in Scotland* (SULI/Thomson Reuters) Looseleaf, Ch 20; F. McManus, *Environmental Law in Scotland* (Edinburgh University Press, 2016) pp 278–295, and F. McManus *Scottish Environmental Law Essentials* (Edinburgh University Press, 2020) pp 160–167.

[68] See e.g. *Tesco v SoS* [1995] 1 WLR 759.

THE SEA DIRECTIVE 2001/42/EC

Introduction

In common with the EIA, the SEA is EU-driven. A principal objective of the Directive is to provide for a high level of protection of the environment and to contribute to the integration of environmental considerations into the preparation and adoption of plans and programmes, with a view to promoting sustainable development by ensuring that an environmental assessment is carried out of certain plans and programmes that are likely to have significant effects on the environment.[69] In essence, the purpose of an SEA is to prevent major effects on the environment being predetermined by earlier planning measures before the EIA stage is reached.[70] While the EIA Directive is aimed at individual projects, the SEA requires assessment of plans and programmes that, in turn, set the framework for those individual projects which fall within the scope of the EIA Directive. The SEA Directive has the objective of introducing more transparency into the preliminary process that surrounds project development and also allows contributions to be made to the development of a strategic plan by the public.[71] The SEA Directive is more procedural in nature than the EIA Directive, in that it will identify potential impacts from plans and programmes but does not lead directly to reducing impacts, which is the function of the EIA process. The SEA Directive also does not impose any substantive duties on the relevant authority. Rather, it seeks to improve the quality of decision-making for development by requiring the authority to assess the potential environmental effects of a particular plan or programme before its adoption.[72]

Scope of strategic environmental assessment

It is mandatory for an environmental assessment (SEA) to be carried out for all plans and programmes that fall within the scope of the SEA Directive that are likely to have significant environmental effects.[73] An environmental assessment is required to be carried out for all plans and programmes that are prepared for forestry, fisheries, energy, industry, transport, waste management, water management, telecommunications, tourism, town and country planning, or land use, and which set the framework for future development consent of projects that require an EIA or which, in view of the likely effect on sites, have been determined to require an assessment in terms of arts 6 or 7 of Directive 92/43/EEC (the Habitats Directive). However, plans and programmes that simply determine the use of small areas at local level, require an environmental assessment only where the Member States determine that they are likely to have significant environmental effects. The SEA Directive, therefore, makes an important link between SEA and EIA.

---

[69] Directive 2001/42/EC art 1.

[70] *R (Buckinghamshire CC) v Secretary of State for Transport* [2014] 1 WLR 324 at 339 (per Lord Carnwath).

[71] *Ashdown Forest Economic Development LLP v Secretary of State for Local Government* [2014] EWHC 406 at [102] per Sales J. Overruled by the Court of Appeal; [2015] EWCA Civ 681.

[72] *R (Friends of the Earth, England, Wales and Northern Ireland Ltd) v The Welsh Ministers* [2016] Env LR 1 at [12].

[73] Directive 2001/42/EC art 3. The Directive does not use the word 'strategic'.

The criteria which are required to be taken into account in determining whether the plan or programme will have a significant environmental effect are set out in Annex II of the Directive. The criteria include having regard, in particular, to environmental problems that are relevant to the plan or programme, the probability, duration, frequency, and reversibility of the effects, the risks to human health or the environment and the cumulative nature of the effects.

The SEA is required to be carried out during the preparation of the plan, or programme, and before its adoption or submission to the relevant legislative procedure.[74]

Meaning of 'plans and programmes'

The SEA Directive defines 'plans and programmes' as plans or programmes, as well as any modifications to them, that are subject to preparation and/or adoption by an authority at national, regional or local level, or that are prepared by an authority for adoption through a legislative procedure and which are required by legislative, regulatory or administrative provisions.[75]

In *Inter-Environment Bruxelles ASBL v Region de Bruxelles-Capitale*[76] it was held that for a plan or programme to fall within the scope of the SEA Directive, the adoption of the relevant plan was not required to be compulsory. Plans and programmes whose adoption was regulated by national legislative or regulatory provisions that determined the competent authorities for adopting them and the procedure for preparing them fell within the scope of the SEA Directive. Furthermore, a procedure for the total or partial repeal of a land use plan fell within the scope of the SEA Directive. In *Cala Homes (South) Ltd v Secretary of State for Communities and Local Government*[77] the Court of Appeal held that a proposed revocation of regional strategies (which formed part of the development plan) by the government, in order to return decision-making to local planning authorities, fell within the scope of the requirements of the SEA Directive.

The issue as to what constitutes a plan or programme that falls within the scope of the SEA Directive was considered by the Supreme Court in *Walton v The Scottish Ministers*.[78] The case concerned a challenge to the Aberdeen Western Peripheral Route (AWPR). Proposals for a western peripheral route around Aberdeen had been in existence since the 1950s. The factual background to the case was that in 2001 a non-statutory regional transport partnership, known as the North East Scotland Transport Partnership (NESTRANS), was established with support from the Scottish Ministers. Its remit was to develop a regional transport strategy for the northeast of Scotland. NESTRANS membership included relevant local authorities and also Scottish Enterprise. The regional transport strategy, which was developed to cover the period to 2011, was described in a NESTRANS report published in 2003. That strategy was described as the Modern Transport System (or MTS). It comprised the local transport strategies that had been adopted by the relevant roads

[74] Directive 2001/42/EC art 4.
[75] Directive 2001/42/EC art 2.
[76] Case 567/210; [2010] Env LR 30.
[77] [2012] EWCA Civ 639.
[78] 2013 SC (UKSC) 67.

authority. Numerous schemes were described and costed in the report. One scheme included the AWPR. In 2003, the Minister for Transport announced that the AWPR would be promoted by the Scottish Ministers as a trunk road. However, in 2004, in the face of a campaign against the routing of the AWPR along a certain 'corridor', the minister instructed that work on that corridor should be reviewed and also that four other options should be re-examined. In 2005, the Minister of Transport announced that the route would comprise a 'hybrid route' (the 'Fastlink'), that is to say, a route that differed from the options that had previously been considered in the earlier consultation exercise, in that Fastlink broadly comprised the whole of one option and part of another. In 2006 draft trunk road schemes, *inter alia*, under s 7 of the Roads (Scotland) Act 1984, together with an EIA, were published. Objections were made to the proposed Fastlink. One objection included a letter from Walton ('W'), the pursuer. A public inquiry was held. However, its remit was confined to technical and environmental issues. In 2009 the Scottish Ministers announced their decision to proceed with the scheme, which was approved by the Scottish Parliament in 2010.

W argued that the MTS was a plan or programme that fell within the scope of the SEA Directive and that the decision to construct Fastlink was a modification of that plan or programme. Therefore, the decision was itself a plan or programme within the meaning of the SEA Directive. Furthermore, there had been a failure to comply with the requirements of the SEA Directive since there had been no public consultation.

The Supreme Court reserved its opinion as to whether either the MTS, or its associated strategies, constituted a plan or programme that fell within the scope of the SEA Directive.[79] However, the court held that the decision to construct Fastlink was not a modification of the MTS within the meaning of the SEA Directive. The decision had been taken by the Scottish Ministers in the course of executing a specific project and had related solely to that project. Furthermore, the decision had not been taken in the exercise of any power to modify the MTS, or otherwise set a legal or administrative framework for future development consent of projects. Furthermore, the relevant development had been implemented in accordance with the procedures that were laid down for specific road projects under the Roads (Scotland) Act 1984.

The Supreme Court had another opportunity to determine the meaning of the expression 'plan or programme' in terms of the SEA in *R (Buckinghamshire CC) v Secretary of State for Transport*.[80] In 2012 the Secretary of State for Transport published a Command Paper entitled, *High Speed Rail: Investing in Britain's Future-Decisions and Next Steps*[81] (DNS), which set out the Government's strategy for the promotion construction and operation of a new national high speed rail network, known as High Speed Two (HS2) from London to Birmingham, Manchester and Leeds. One of the issues that fell to be decided by the court was whether the DNS constituted a plan or programme within the meaning of the SEA Directive.

[79] Lord Carnwath expressed serious doubts (at [99]) that the MTS was a plan or programme that fell within the scope of the SEA Directive, given the informal character of the NESTRANS exercise.

[80] [2014] 1 WLR 324.

[81] Cmnd. 8274.

Lord Carnwath was prepared to accept *obiter* that the DNS could rank as a plan or programme that fell within the scope of the SEA.[82] However, his Lordship concluded that since the DNS did not constrain the decision-making process of the authority that was responsible (that is, Parliament), the DNS fell outwith the scope of the SEA Directive.[83]

For Lord Sumption (who tacitly accepted that the DNS could be a 'plan or programme') the DNS fell outwith the scope of the SEA Directive, since it was nothing more than a proposal.[84]

In *R (Friends of the Earth UK Ltd) v Secretary of State for Housing, Communities and Local Government*[85] the court was required to decide whether the revised National Planning Policy Framework (NPPF) required a strategic environmental assessment, on the ground that it constituted a plan or programme that fell within the scope of the SEA Directive. Dove J held that, given the fact that the NPPF was not a measure that was required by legislative, regulatory or administrative provisions that either regulated or determined the procedure for adopting it, and was a voluntary measure, the NPPF fell outwith the scope of the SEA Directive.[86]

By way of conclusion, it should be mentioned that, in Scotland, the Scottish Ministers are under a duty to prepare a National Planning Framework (NPF) and keep the same under review.[87] In other words, the NPF in Scotland would fall within the scope of art 2 of the SEA Directive, by virtue of being required by a legislative provision.

Environmental report

If an environmental assessment is required, an environmental report (ER) must be prepared.[88] The ER is required to identify, describe and evaluate the likely significant effects on the environment of implementing the plan or programme (together with reasonable alternatives) taking into account the objectives and the geographical scope of the plan or programme.

In *R (Friends of the Earth, England, Wales and Northern Ireland) v Welsh Ministers*[89] it was held that 'reasonable alternatives' did not include all possible alternatives. It required an evaluative judgement as to which alternatives should be included. That evaluation was a matter for the decision-maker, which was subject to challenge only on public law grounds.

The ER is also required to include the information that may be reasonably required, taking into account current knowledge and methods of assessment, the contents and level of detail of the plan or programme, its stage in the decision-making process and the extent to which certain matters are more easily assessed at different levels in that process, in order to avoid duplication of the assessment. The

82 [2014] 1 WLR 324 at 334.
83 [2014] 1 WLR 324 at 339.
84 [2014] 1 WLR 324 at 361.
85 [2019] Env LR 26.
86 [2019] Env LR 26 at [52]. For a discussion of the case see (2019) 193 *SPEL* 62.
87 Town and Country Planning (Scotland) Act 1997 s 3A(6).
88 Directive 2001/42/EC art 5.
89 [2016] Env LR 1 at [88].

information that is required to be provided in the ER is contained in Annex I to the SEA Directive. The ER must also include a non-technical summary.

In *Spurrier v Secretary of State for Transport*[90] it was held that the information that was required to be included in an ER was a matter for the judgement of the authority preparing the plan or programme. Such a judgement was a matter for the evaluative assessment of the authority, subject only to review on normal public law principles, including *Wednesbury* unreasonableness.

IMPLEMENTATION OF THE SEA

The SEA Directive is implemented in England by the Environmental Assessment of Plans and Programmes Regulations 2004[91] (the 2004 Regulations). However, in a book of this nature, only a brief overview of the Regulations can be given.

Extent

The 2004 Regulations apply to a plan or programme relating solely to the whole, or part, of England, or to England (whether as to the whole or part) and to any other part of the UK.[92]

Consultation bodies

The 2004 Regulations make provision for consultation bodies in relation to plans and programmes falling within the scope of the Regulations. The Countryside Agency; the Historic Buildings and Monuments Commission for England (English Heritage); English Nature; and the Environment Agency, are made the relevant consultation bodies, only in relation to so much of the plan or programme as relates to England.[93] However, in relation to a plan or programme to which the Regulations apply that relates to Scotland, the relevant consultation bodies are the Scottish Ministers; the Scottish Environment Protection Agency; and Scottish Natural Heritage.[94]

Environmental assessment for plans and programmes

The 2004 Regulations make provision for the environmental assessment of plans and programmes. Where the first formal preparatory act of the plan or programme takes place after 21 July 2004 and the plan or programme is prepared for:

(a) agriculture, forestry, fisheries, energy, industry, transport, waste management, water management, telecommunications, tourism, town and country planning or land use; and
(b) sets the framework for future development consent of projects listed in Annex I or II of the Directive on the assessment of the effects of certain public and private projects on the environment,

[90] [2019] EWHC 1070 at [433].
[91] SI 2004/1633.
[92] SI 2004/1633 reg 3(2).
[93] SI 2004/1633 reg 4(1).
[94] SI 2004/1633 reg 4(3).

the responsible authority[95] is required to either carry out, or secure the carrying out, of an environmental assessment during the preparation of the plan or programme and before its adoption, or submission, to the relevant legislative procedures.[96] An environmental assessment is also required in relation to a plan or programme that, in view of the likely effect on sites, has been determined to require an assessment, in terms of arts 6 or 7 of the Habitats Directive.[97] However, an environmental assessment is not required to be carried out for any plan or programme that determines the use of a small area at local level, or for a modification to a plan or programme of a description that falls within the scope of reg 5(2) and (3) (above), unless it has been determined under reg 9(1) (below), that the plan, programme or modification, as the case may be, is likely to have significant environmental effects.[98] Similarly, an environmental assessment is not required to be carried out if the plan, programme or modification is the subject of a direction under reg 10(3)(below).

If an environmental assessment is required for a plan or programme, the responsible authority is required to take account of the environmental report for the plan or programme as well as, *inter alia*, opinions received from the relevant consultation bodies.[99] As far as plans or programmes that determine the use of small areas (or plans that consist of minor modifications to such plans) the responsible authority is required to determine whether such a plan, etc. is likely to have significant environmental effects.[100] Before making such a determination, the responsible authority is required to apply the criteria specified in Schedule 1 of the Regulations, and also consult the consultation bodies.[101] Where the responsible authority determines that the plan or programme is unlikely to have significant environmental effects and therefore does not require an environmental assessment, the authority is required to prepare a statement of its reasons for such a determination.[102] The responsible body is also required *inter alia* to publicise such a determination.[103]

Preparation of environmental report

Where an environmental assessment is required, the responsible authority is required to prepare an environmental report.[104] The environmental report is required to identify, describe and evaluate the likely significant effects on the environment of implementing the plan or programme, and also reasonable alternatives, taking into account the objectives and the geographical scope of the plan or programme.[105] Schedule 2 specifies the information that requires to be included in the environmental report.[106]

95 The 'responsible authority' in relation to a plan or programme is the authority by which or on whose behalf, it is prepared: SI 2004/1633 reg 2(1).
96 SI 2004/1633 reg 5(1), (2).
97 SI 2004/1633 reg 5(3).
98 SI 2004/1633 reg 5(6).
99 SI 2004/1633 reg 8(2), (3).
100 SI 2004/1633 reg 9(1).
101 SI 2004/1633 reg 9(2).
102 SI 2004/1633 reg 9(3).
103 SI 2004/1633 reg 11(2).
104 SI 2004/1633 reg 12(1).
105 SI 2004/1633 reg 12(2).
106 SI 2004/1633 reg 12(3).

Consultation procedures

Every draft plan or programme for which an environmental report has been prepared under reg 12 (above), as well as its accompanying environmental report, requires to be made available for the purposes of consultation.[107] After preparation of the relevant documents the responsible body is required to send a copy of the documents to each consultation body.[108] The responsible body is also required to take such steps as it considers appropriate to bring the preparation of the relevant documents to the attention to the persons who, in the responsible body's opinion, are either affected, or likely to be affected, or have an interest in the decisions involved in the assessment and adoption of the plan or programme concerned, as required under the SEA Directive ('public consultees'). The public consultees are required to be informed *inter alia* of the address of the website at which the relevant documents may be viewed and downloaded free of charge, the fact that the documents can be obtained by email from the responsible authority, and also that the relevant documents can be obtained by post from the responsible authority (provided that it is reasonably practicable for the authority to provide a copy by post). The responsible bodies are required to invite the consultation bodies and the public consultees to express their opinion on the relevant documents and the period within which opinions must be sent. The period must be of such length as will ensure that the consultation bodies and the public consultees are given an effective opportunity to express their opinion on the relevant documents.[109] The responsible authority is required *inter alia* to publish the relevant documents on a public website at which the relevant documents may be viewed and downloaded, free of charge, and also provide a copy of the relevant documents by email, to any person who requests such a copy.[110]

As soon as reasonably practicable after the adoption of the plan or programme for which an environmental assessment has been carried out in terms of the Regulations, the responsible authority is required *inter alia* to publish the plan or programme as adopted, its accompanying environmental report and a statement containing the particulars specified in reg 16(4) ('the relevant documents') on a public website at which the documents may be viewed and downloaded free of charge and provide a copy of the relevant adoption details by email, to any person who requests a copy, as soon as reasonably practical after receipt of that person's request.[111] The responsible authority is also required to take such steps as it considers appropriate to bring the attention of the public to the title of the plan or programme, the date on which it was adopted and also the address of the website at which the relevant adoption documents may be viewed and downloaded free of charge. The responsible authority is also required to take steps to inform the public that the adoption documents may be obtained by email and post from the responsible authority, provided that it is reasonably practicable for the authority to provide a copy by post.

As soon as reasonably practicable after the adoption of a plan or programme the responsible authority is required to inform the consultation bodies and also the

[107] SI 2004/1633 reg 13(1).
[108] SI 2004/1633 reg 13(2).
[109] SI 2004/1633 reg 13(3).
[110] SI 2004/1633 reg 13(4).
[111] SI 2004/1633 reg 16(1).

persons who, in relation to the plan or programme, were public consultees for the plan or programme of certain matters.[112] Such matters include the fact that the plan or programme has been adopted; the address of the website at which a copy of the plan or programme, as adopted, as well as its accompanying environmental report, may be viewed, or from which a copy may be obtained.[113]

Both the public and the consultation bodies require to be informed, *inter alia*, how environmental considerations have been integrated into the relevant plan or programme, how the environmental report has been taken into account, and also how the results of any consultations have been taken into account.[114]

Monitoring the plan or programme

The responsible authority is required to monitor the significant environmental effects of the plan or programme, with the purpose of identifying unforeseen adverse effects at an early stage and being able to undertake appropriate remedial action.[115]

Scotland

The SEA Directive is implemented in Scotland by the Environmental Assessment (Scotland) Act 2005. The provisions of the Act are broadly similar to those of the Environmental Assessment of Plans and Programmes Regulations 2004 discussed above. However, considerations of space preclude any discussion of the Act.[116]

TOWN AND COUNTRY PLANNING

A proposed development may pose a potential source of noise impact to the general environment. The advantage of the development management system as a mechanism for pollution prevention, is that polluting activities can be prevented at source.[117] The planning system ranks as an anticipatory control that exemplifies the preventative principle, now well-ingrained in UK environmental law and policy. Indeed, it has been argued that the UK can claim to have adopted the principle long before such a principle became fashionable, and also before it featured in EU policy.[118]

Town and country planning has an important role to play in relation to the control of noise.[119] The modern system of town planning in the UK was founded in 1947.

[112] SI 2004/1633 reg 16(2).

[113] SI 2004/1633 reg 16(3).

[114] SI 2004/1633 reg 16(4).

[115] SI 2004/1633 reg 17(1).

[116] For a discussion of SEA in Scotland see F. McManus and R. Hefron, 'Environmental Impact Assessment' in F. McManus (ed), *Environmental Law in Scotland* (SULI/Thomson Reuters) paras 20.45–20.69; F. McManus, *Environmental Law in Scotland* (Edinburgh University Press, 2016) pp 289–295, and F. McManus, *Scottish Environmental Law Essentials* (Edinburgh University Press, 2020) pp 167–175.

[117] M. Purdue, 'The relationship between development control and specialist pollution controls: which is the tail and which the dog' [1999] JPL 585.

[118] See M. Purdue, 'The impact of EC Environmental Law on Planning Law in the United Kingdom' in J. Holder, *The Impact of EC Environmental Law in the United Kingdom* (Wiley, 1997) 231 at 231/232.

[119] For a discussion of town and country planning see S. Bell, D. McGillivray et al, *Environmental Law*, 9th edn (OUP, 2017) Ch 12. See also A. Bowes, *A Practical Approach to Planning Law*, 14th edn (OUP, 2019) and R. Duxbury, *Telling and Duxbury Planning Law and Procedure*, 16th edn (OUP, 2018).

The Town and Country Planning Act 1947[120] and the Town and Country Planning (Scotland) Act 1947,[121] in effect, introduced a new system for the regulation of the development of land in the UK. Indeed, the town and county planning legislation has been described as a 'daring experiment in social control of the environment'.[122] In essence, the legislation vested the regulation of the development of land in the UK in the state. Put simply, if one wanted to develop land, one required planning permission. Owners of property no longer enjoyed the absolute right to build, or change the use of land, without planning permission.

Noise is required to be considered either when a development may create additional noise, or the proposed development would be sensitive to noise.

First, the law relating to England is covered, and then attention turns to Scotland, with special reference to planning and the control of noise. However, in a book of this nature only a brief overview can be given.

England

Role of central government in planning

Central government has overall responsibility for town and country planning in England. The Department for Levelling Up, Housing and Communities is currently responsible for planning policy in England (DLHC). The NPPF sets out the government's planning policy for England and how the government expects such policies to be applied.[123] The NPPF states that the planning system is to contribute to the achievement of sustainable development.[124] One of the objectives to achieve sustainable development is an environmental objective, which includes minimising pollution.[125] The NPPF requires that the planning system should be genuinely plan-led and should, *inter alia*, provide a framework for addressing environmental priorities.[126] The NPPF also requires that transport issues require to be considered from the earliest stages of plan-making and development proposals in order that, *inter alia* the environmental impacts of traffic and transport infrastructure can be identified, assessed and taken into account, including appropriate opportunities for avoiding, or mitigating, any adverse effects.[127]

Central government is also responsible for providing planning guidance to planning authorities. As far as noise is concerned, DLHC has published *Guidance on Noise*, which advises how planning can manage potential noise impacts in new development.[128]

---

120 Repealed.

121 Repealed.

122 J. Rowan-Robinson, *Scottish Planning Law and Procedure* (W Green/SULI) at 13, citing C. Haar, *Land Use Planning in Free Society* (Harvard University Press, 1951).

123 The NPPF was first published on 27 March 2012 and subsequently updated. A new version of the NPPF was published on 20 July 2021.

124 NPPF para 7.

125 NPPF para 8.

126 NPPF para 15.

127 NPPF para 104.

128 Department for Levelling Up, Housing and Communities and Ministry of Housing Communities and Local Government, 6 March 2014 (updated 22 July 2019). See also Planning Policy Statement 23: *Planning and Pollution Control* (Office of the Deputy Prime Minister, 2004).

Role of local government in planning

Local authorities, that is, local planning authorities are, in effect, at the heart of the planning system. Since the inception of the modern planning system it has been recognised that elected members are familiar with their localities and, therefore, best placed to determine how land in the area should be developed. In this respect, local planning authorities are responsible for the preparation of development plans (now 'development plan documents') and also granting planning permission.

Development plans

Development plans act as a guide as to how land in a particular area should be developed. For example, a development plan could specify that premises that have the potential to generate noise are kept separate from buildings (such as houses, schools and hospitals) that may be adversely affected by noise. However, development plans have no immediate effect other than as a statement of what the local planning authority considers is desirable.[129] Development plans, however, are of great importance in planning control, in that they influence planning authorities when they decide whether or not to grant planning permission for a proposed development. Indeed, in the UK we have a 'plan-led' planning system. Under s 70(2) of the TCPA 1990 in deciding whether or not to grant planning permission a local planning authority is required to have regard *inter alia*, to the provisions of the development plan so far as is material to the application and to any other material considerations. Under s 38(6) of the Planning and Compulsory Purchase Act 2004 a local planning authority is required to determine a planning application in accordance with the development plan, unless material considerations indicate otherwise.

'Other material considerations'

The TCPA 1990 does not define the term 'material considerations'. In effect, the courts have been required to determine the meaning of the phrase. As far as the control of potential noise from a development, first, one is required to ascertain whether noise as well as other forms of pollution ranks as a material consideration and, second, if noise, etc. does rank as a material consideration, to what extent, if any, can one take into account the effect of any regulatory controls (which would be exercised, for example, by the Environment Agency) that would apply to the premises after the premises become operational? These very issues fell to be addressed by the Court of Appeal in *Gateshead Metropolitan BC v Secretary of State for the Environment*.[130]

In that case, the Northumbrian Water Group (NWG) had submitted an outline planning application to Gateshead Metropolitan Borough Council (GMBC) for the construction and operation of a clinical waste incineration plant. Since the plant was a prescribed process, in terms of the Environmental Protection Act 1990 (EPA), it was necessary for the prospective operators of the plant to obtain authorisation to carry on the process of incineration from HM Inspectorate of Pollution (HMIP, now the Environment Agency) in addition to obtaining planning permission. Planning

[129] S. Bell and D. McGillivray et al (fn 118) at 406.
[130] [1995] Env LR 37.

permission was refused by the planning authority on the ground that potential pollution from the incinerator would have a negative impact on the environment. NWG appealed to the Secretary of State against the decision. An enquiry into the appeal was heard. The inspector recommended that planning permission be refused. However, the Secretary of State disagreed with the inspector's recommendation. The Secretary of State took the view that concerns about atmospheric pollution could be satisfactorily addressed by HMIP in terms of the EPA regulatory regime. The former, therefore, granted outline planning permission, subject to conditions. GMBC applied to the High Court, under s 288 of the TCPA 1990, for an order that the decision of the Secretary of State be quashed. However, the application was dismissed. GMBC then appealed to the Court of Appeal.

The key issue that the Court of Appeal was required to determine was whether the Secretary of State was entitled to decide that the controls under the EPA were adequate to deal with the concerns about air pollution from the plant that had been raised by the inspector. In dismissing the appeal, Glidewell LJ held, first, that potential pollution from a proposed development was a material consideration.[131] The judge also held that when the Secretary of State was determining the planning application, they could legitimately take into account the powers that HMIP possessed under the EPA. The judge went on to conclude that the Secretary of State was justified in deciding that the issues that had been raised at the planning inquiry in relation to atmospheric pollution from the plant could be addressed by HMIP and, furthermore, could also be adequately dealt with by that body.[132] Therefore, the decision of the Secretary of State could not be impugned.

The inter-relationship between pollution, planning controls and the relevant pollution regulatory regime came to be discussed again in *R v Bolton MBC ex p Kirkman*.[133] In that case, the claimant (K) was a local resident. He applied for judicial review of a decision by the defendant planning authority, namely, Bolton Metropolitan Borough Council (BMBC) to grant planning permission for the installation of an incinerator. K contended, *inter alia*, that when BMBC was determining the planning application it had failed to address potential pollution from the incinerator. At first instance, Carnwath J (as he then was) held that the impact of discharges from the incinerator ranked as a material consideration in terms of planning law. Furthermore, in considering that issue, the planning authority was entitled to take into account the system of controls available under integrated pollution control (IPC) unless it appeared to the planning authority that the discharges in question either would, or would probably, be unacceptable to the Environment Agency.[134] It was therefore, legitimate for BMBC to leave the regulation of potential pollution from the waste incinerator to the Environment Agency.

The relationship between planning and pollution control was discussed in *Hopkins Development Ltd v First Secretary of State and North Wiltshire DC*.[135] The claimant (H) applied to the second defendant (NWDC) for planning permission in relation to the construction of a concrete plant on an industrial estate. NWDC failed

[131] [1995] Env LR 37 at 44.
[132] [1995] Env LR 37 at 50.
[133] [1998] JPL 787.
[134] [1998] JPL 787 at 795.
[135] [2007] Env LR 14.

to determine the planning application in the required period. H, therefore, appealed to the first defendant (FSS). NWDC argued that the proposed development would be contrary to existing planning policy in that it would have a serious effect on the amenities of the area. The inspector refused the appeal on the basis that despite the application of existing pollution control measures, the proposed development would have a detrimental effect on the amenities of local residencies and businesses due to a significant increase in dust, noise and visual intrusion. H challenged the inspector's decision under s 288 of the TCPA 1990, *inter alia*, on the ground that the relevant controls under the pollution prevention control regime would provide sufficient protection for those who might be affected by pollution from the plant.

In dismissing the appeal, the court endorsed the approach of the courts in the *Gateshead* and *Bolton* cases (above) to the effect that the impact of emissions from a proposed development could rank as a material consideration in terms of the TCPA 1990.[136] Furthermore, a planning authority could take account of the pollution control regime. Therefore, the planning authority could leave pollution control to the pollution control authorities. However, the planning authority was not obliged, as a matter of law, to do so. In the last analysis, by focusing on whether the development itself was an acceptable use of the land and the impacts that it would have, rather than on the control processes or emissions, the inspector had acted in accordance with the law.[137]

Finally, the weighting that a planning authority attaches to a material consideration is a question of planning judgement for the planning authority or the Secretary of State, and subject to review only on *Wednesbury* principles.[138]

Planning conditions

A planning authority can control the potential negative impact of a proposed development by attaching conditions on granting planning permission. Under s 70(1) of the TCPA 1990 a local planning authority can attach conditions as it thinks fit. Whereas a planning authority has fairly wide discretion as to both the nature and content of a condition that it may impose, such discretion is not unfettered.[139] The limits of the powers of planning authorities in imposing planning conditions were set out in the leading House of Lords case of *Newbury DC v SoS for the Environment*.[140] The House of Lords held that for a planning condition to be valid, first, the relevant condition required to be imposed for a planning purpose and not for an ulterior one; second, the condition required to fairly and reasonably relate to the relevant development; and finally, the condition was required not to be so unreasonable that no reasonable planning authority could have imposed it.[141]

136 [2007] Env LR 14 at [11].

137 [2007] Env LR 14 at [13]. See also *James v Dover DC* [2022] EWHC 961.

138 [1995] 1 WLR 759.

139 *Pyx Granite Co Ltd v Ministry of Housing and Local Government* [1958] 1 QB 554.

140 [1981] AC 578.

141 [1981] AC 578 at 599 (per Viscount Dilhorne). See also Circ. 11/95, *Use of Conditions in Planning Permission* (Department of Environment, 1995). The circular suggests that a planning condition should meet six tests, namely that a planning condition is necessary; relevant to planning relevant to the development to be permitted; enforceable; precise and reasonable in all other respects: *ibid* at para 14.

An important Scottish case that illustrates the application of the requirements that were set out in *Newbury* is the Inner House case of *British Airports Authority v SoS for Scotland*.[142] In that case, the British Airports Authority (BAA) had applied to Aberdeen County Council to carry out certain developments at Aberdeen Airport, including the erection of a new terminal building and a new aircraft apron. The Secretary of State confirmed the grant of planning permission by the planning authority, subject to two conditions that were designed to restrict the operational hours at the airport and also regulate the direction of both take offs and landings of aircraft there. Both conditions were imposed in order to reduce noise impact from the premises.

An application for planning permission had also been made by British Airways Helicopters Ltd (BAHL) for the erection of a one storey building in order to provide an office for its flight operations headquarters at its terminal. In this case, planning permission had been granted to BAHL, subject to a condition that was designed to restrict its operational hours at the terminal.

Bristow Helicopters (BH) had also applied for planning permission to build an extension to its terminal building at the airport in order to provide freight-handling facilities and additional office accommodation. Again, the planning authority had attached a condition to the grant of planning permission that restricted operational hours at the terminal.

All three parties appealed to the Court of Session under s 233 of the Town and Country Planning (Scotland) Act 1972[143] against the conditions that had been attached to their respective planning permissions.

As far as the appeal by BAA was concerned, the court held that both of the conditions that had been imposed fairly and reasonably related to the proposed development. However, as far as the condition that sought to regulate the direction of take offs and landings from the airport was concerned, such a function fell to be exercised not by the Secretary of State but, rather, by the Civil Aviation Authority. The second condition was, therefore, *ultra vires*.

As far as the appeal by BAHL was concerned, the court held that the condition that related to operational hours was *ultra vires* on two grounds. First, the condition did not fairly and reasonably relate to the development in question, in that no helicopter took off or landed from any land that was occupied by BAHL. Second, and in any case, such a condition was unnecessary in that, since all aircraft took off and landed from runways at the airport, operational hours in relation to such aircraft fell to be regulated by the valid relevant planning condition that had been imposed on BAA.

In the case of the BH appeal, it was held that the condition that sought to restrict operational hours was *ultra vires* since it did not fairly and reasonably relate to the development in question, and also because the proposed increase in office/freight accommodation would not directly lead to an increase in air traffic and, therefore, more noise. The condition was both pointless and unnecessary.[144]

See also Planning Circular 4/98, *The Use of Conditions in Planning Permissions* (Scottish Government, 1998): *Ibid* para 2.

142 1979 SC 200.

143 Repealed.

144 The Airports (Noise-related Operating Restrictions) (England and Wales) Regulations 2018

Scotland

The law relating to the control of development in Scotland is roughly similar to that in England.[145] Planning is a devolved function under the Scotland Act 1998.

Scottish Government

As far as central government's role in planning is concerned, the Scottish Ministers have overall responsibility for the planning system in Scotland.[146] This includes initiating new planning legislation in the Scottish Parliament; drawing up national planning policies; determining appeals against planning decisions (a function normally delegated to a reporter)[147]; issuing guidance on planning policy in the form of Scottish Planning Policy (SPP); issuing Planning advice notes (PANs)[148] and circulars; and preparing the NPF.

The National Planning Framework 3 (NPF3) was approved and published by the Scottish Parliament in 2014.[149] The NPF provides a statutory framework for Scotland's long-term spatial development for the next twenty to thirty years. A NPF4 is currently[150] in the course of preparation.

The current government's SPP sits side by side with the NPF. The legal significance of the SPP is that planning policy ranks as a material consideration that a planning authority requires to take into account when it determines a planning application for the development of land.

(SI 2018/785) apply to airports that have more than 50,000 civil aircraft movements per year. The 2018 Regulations make the relevant planning authority responsible as the competent authority for the purposes of implementing the provisions of EU Regulation 598/2014 (which makes provision for the establishment of rules and procedures in relation to the introduction of noise-related operating restrictions at airports within a balanced approach). A local planning authority is the competent authority for the purposes of the 2014 Regulations in relation to a proposal for it to impose, modify or discharge an operating restriction under the Town and Country Planning Act 1990 or an operating restriction imposed under the 1990 Act: reg 3(1). See also the Airports (Noise-related Operating Restrictions) (Scotland) Regulations 2019 (SSI 2019/409). The Scottish Ministers are made the competent authority for the purposes of the 2014 Regulation in relation to Scotland: reg 3. See the *Guidance on the introduction of noise-related operating restriction at major airports* (Department for Transport, 3 October 2019).

145 For a discussion of planning in Scotland, see N. Collar, *Planning*, 4th edn (W Green, 2016); A.M. Slater, *Planning Law Essentials* (Dundee University Press, 2010); R. McMaster, A. Prior and J. Watchman, *Scottish Planning Law*, 3rd edn (Bloomsbury, 2014) and F. McManus, 'Planning and Pollution Control' in F. McManus, *Environmental Law in Scotland* (Edinburgh University Press, 2016) Ch 10.

146 For a general overview of the role of the Scottish Government in relation to planning, see R. McMaster et al, *Scottish Planning Law* (fn 141) paras 2.34–2.37.

147 The Directorate for Planning and Environmental Appeals is responsible for administering planning appeals and the public inquiries system (both for planning and other regimes). A wide range of planning appeals have been delegated by the Scottish Ministers to reporters for decisions. 90 per cent of appeals are now decided by reporters.

148 See Scottish Government Planning Advice Note 1/2011 (published 3 March 2011), which provides guidance on the role of the planning system in helping to limit the adverse effects of noise.

149 Scottish Government, June 2014.

150 February 2022.

Local government

At local level, planning authorities implement the policies of the Scottish Ministers, prepare development plans,[151] determine applications for planning permission and enforce planning controls.

As far as the control of development is concerned, the TCPSA 1997 s 37(2) requires a planning authority, when it is determining a planning application, to take into account the relevant development plan so far as it is material to the application, and to any other material considerations. As is the case with the TCPA 1990, the TCPSA 1997 does not define the term 'material consideration'. Therefore, the courts in Scotland have been required to fill the legislative gap. The decided cases south of the border on the meaning of 'material considerations', whilst technically are non-binding on the Scottish courts, are highly persuasive and indeed, are invariably followed.

Planning conditions

Under s 37(1) of the TCPSA 1997 on granting planning permission, a planning authority can *inter alia* attach such conditions as it thinks fit.[152] Section 41A makes special provision for noise-sensitive developments in terms of the conditional grant of planning permission. A noise-sensitive development is defined as a development that is the subject of a planning application for planning permission if residents or occupiers of the development are likely to be affected by significant noise from an existing activity in the vicinity of the development (a 'noise source').[153] When considering whether to grant planning permission for a noise-sensitive development under s 37 a planning authority is required to take particular account of whether the development includes sufficient measures to mitigate, minimise or manage the effect of noise between the development and any existing cultural venues or facilities (including, in particular, but not limited to, live music venues) or dwellings or businesses in the vicinity of the development.[154] Furthermore, a planning authority may not, as a condition of granting planning permission, for a noise-sensitive development, impose on a noise source additional costs relating to acoustic design measures to mitigate, minimise or manage the effects of noise.

---

[151] Under s 13(2) of the Planning (Scotland) Act 2019, which amends s 24 of the TCPSA 1997, the NPF becomes part of the development plan for an area.

[152] See Scottish Government Circ. 4/1998'The Use of Conditions in Planning Permission' (published 27 February 1998).

[153] Town and Country Planning (Scotland) Act 1997 s 41A(1).

[154] TCPSA 1997 s 41A(2).

Chapter 11

Noise in the Workplace

A worker's health and welfare can be seriously prejudiced unless appropriate measures are taken to ensure that the relevant employee is not unduly exposed to noise and vibration. As far as the legal controls over noise in the workplace are concerned, the relevant controls take the form of both common law and statutory controls. Each is now dealt with, in turn.

COMMON LAW

Place of work

An employer's common law duty to protect their employee from excessive noise is derived from the ordinary rules of employer's liability. An employer is under a duty at common law to ensure that their employees have a safe place of work and that a safe place of work is maintained.[1] Such a duty embraces an obligation to ensure that the employee does not sustain injury, as a result of exposure to noise and vibration in the workplace.[2]

The duty incumbent on the employer to provide a safe place of work for the employee remains when the employee is sent to work away from the premises that are under the control of the employer.[3] However, the employer's duty in such circumstances is much lower. In determining the extent of the duty that is owed, each situation requires to be decided on its own facts. In some circumstances, the law will require an employer to carry out an inspection of the relevant premises to which their employee is sent to ascertain its condition. If the premises to which the relevant employee is sent presents an obvious potential risk to the employee, the employer is under a duty to inspect the relevant premises to ascertain its safety.[4] However, there is no relevant case law on the application of this general principle in relation to a situation in which the relevant danger emanates from noise. However, in most situations in which noise could present a risk to the employee's health the relevant

---

1 *Naismith v London Film Productions Ltd* [1939] 1 All ER 794.

2 See *McDonald v Indigo Sun Retail Ltd* [2022] SAC (Civ) 15 where it was held that the defender company, which had allowed an employee to be exposed to excessive noise from a fire alarm for two hours on a single occasion, by reason of which the employee had suffered damage to her ears, had breached its common law duty to the employee.

3 *Wilson v Tyneside Window Cleaning Co* [1958] 2 QB 110.

4 [1958] 2 QB 110.

state of affairs would be readily identifiable, normally by virtue of the existence of the relevant plant, etc. capable of creating the noise, or by virtue of the nature of the operations that are being carried out on the premises. In such a case, the law would, it is suggested, impose a duty on the employer to inspect the premises and also take such measures to ensure that the employee did not suffer injury by way of exposure to noise or vibration.

System of work

An employer is under a duty to ensure that all systems of work that the employee is required to perform within the scope of their employment are safe.[5] The significance of such an obligation, in the current context, is that the various systems of work must be of such a nature that the employee suffers no injury by reason of being exposed to noise or vibration. However, the expression 'system of work' has never been comprehensively defined and is somewhat elusive. In *Speed* it was held that the phrase included the physical layout of the job, the sequence in which the work is to be carried out, as well as the provision, where necessary, of warnings, notices and issue of special instructions.[6]

Under general principles of the law of negligence, the appropriate precautions that the employer is obliged to take requires to be proportionate to the relevant risk.[7] In *Stokes v Guest, Keen and Nettlefold (Bolt and Nuts) Ltd*[8] Stanwick J stated that the test of an employer's liability for common law negligence was to be assessed on the basis of the conduct of the reasonable and prudent employer, taking positive thought for the safety of their workers in the light of what they know or ought to know. An employer was also required to keep up with developing knowledge and was required to weigh up the risk in terms of the likelihood of injury occurring and the potential consequences if it does. Against this, the employer was required to balance the probable effectiveness of the precautionsthat can be taken to meet it, and the expense and inconvenience that they involve. The employer is also required to take into account any relevant government guidance, such as codes of practice.[9]

Of practical significance, in the present context, is the extent to which the employer is under a duty to give warnings to the employee about the risks that are inherent in the relevant system of work. If the risk is insidious, which would seem from decided cases to be a question of fact and degree, there would be a duty to warn the employee of the relevant danger.[10] The risk presented to the employee by noise or vibration is not readily apparent. Therefore, the employer would be under a duty to warn the employee of the relevant danger.

Another important issue, in practical terms, is the extent to which an employer is required to ensure, by taking affirmative action, that the employee takes the relevant preventative measures in relation to their own safety, for example, by wearing ear

5 *Speed v Thomas Swift and Co* [1943] KB 557.
6 [1943] KB 557 at 563 (per Lord Greene MR).
7 *Bolton v Stone* [1951] AC 850.
8 [1968] 1 WLR 1776 at 1783. See also *Thompson v Smith's Ship Repairers (North Shields) Ltd* [1984] QB 405.
9 *Baker v Quantum Clothing Group Ltd* [2011] 1 WLR 1003; *Thompson* (above).
10 *Pape v Cumbria CC* [1992] ICR 132.

protectors. As explained in the last paragraph, the requisite measures must be commensurate with the degree of risk involved. The law requires the employer to ensure that the relevant preventative measures are taken by the employee, notwithstanding the fact that the risk of an accident occurring is small but, at the same time, any injury would be grave if such an accident did occur.[11] Furthermore, in determining the precautions that must be taken, the ramifications of any accident to any particular employee must also be taken into account.[12]

Finally, in the present context, in the House of Lords case of *Qualcast (Wolverhampton) Ltd v Haynes*[13] Lord Denning stated that when considering if a particular employer has breached their duty of care at common law (including a duty to give appropriate warnings to the employee) one must guard against elevating decisions based on the facts of the relevant decided case into propositions of law that are of general application. Therefore, the conclusion should be avoided that in relation to certain types of work, the employer is bound to provide the employee with specific safety measures

Plant and machinery

Every employer has a duty, under common law, to provide their employees with plant, materials and resources for the performance of their work that are safe.[14] The duty is a continuing one, and encompasses ensuring that the relevant plant, etc. is kept in a safe condition while available for use by the employee.[15] The duty the common law imposes, in relation to plant and equipment, would include ensuring that plant and machinery cannot cause the employee harm, by virtue of being exposed to noise and vibration.

Protective equipment

An employer is under a duty to ensure that employees who are exposed to the risk of injury, are provided with suitable protective equipment, for example, ear protectors.[16] Depending on several factors, including the risk of injury and also the gravity of potential harm, the duty on the part of the employer extends to ensuring that the employee is personally issued with protective equipment. In certain circumstances, an employer is under a common law duty to instruct the employee as to how such equipment should be used, and also persuade or insist upon the use of such equipment. This depends on the facts of a particular case.[17] However, in certain circumstances (for example, where the employee is experienced) the employer can simply rely on the employee to use the protective equipment.[18]

---

[11] *Nolan v Dental Manufacturing Co* [1958] 1 WLR 936.

[12] *Paris v Stepney BC* [1951] AC 367.

[13] [1959] AC 743 at 759.

[14] *Lovell v Blundells and T Albert Crompton and Co Ltd* [1944] KB 502; *McIntyre v Strathclyde RC* 1944 SLT 933.

[15] *Wilson and Clyde Coal Co Ltd v English* [1938] AC 57 at 84 (per Lord Wright).

[16] *Crouch v British Rail Engineering Ltd* [1988] IRLR 404.

[17] *Bux v Slough Metals Ltd* [1973] 1 WLR 1358 at 1367 (per Edmund-Davies LJ).

[18] *Qualcast (Wolverhampton) Ltd v Haynes* [1959] AC 743.

Statutory control of noise in the workplace

Statutory law has also an important role to play in relation to noise in the workplace. The relevant controls are now discussed.

Health and Safety at Work etc. Act 1974

Section 2(1) of the Health and Safety at Work Act 1974 provides that "[i]t shall be the duty of every employer to ensure, so far as is reasonably practicable, the health safety and welfare of all his employees".

Section 2(2)(a) provides that without prejudice to the generality of an employer's duty under s 2(1), the duty extends to provision and maintenance of plant and systems of work that are, so far as is reasonably practicable, safe and without risks to health.

Noise that affects the relevant employee's health, safety and welfare would, therefore, fall within the scope of the Act.[19] The duty to ensure the employee's welfare is of practical importance, in that noise that is simply annoying to the employee could be dealt with under the Act. Therefore, it is suggested, in the absence of authority, the persistent sound of 'piped' music (or 'muzak') if it proved to be annoying to the staff of premises in which they are at work, could fall within the scope of s 2(1).

The Act is frequently used to found criminal health and safety prosecutions, though noise prosecutions are extremely rare. It should also be stated that no direct right of action for damages arises under the Act.[20]

The Control of Noise at Work Regulations 2005[21]

The Control of Noise at Work Regulations 2005 (the 2005 Regulations) implement Directive 2003/10/EC as respects England, Wales and Scotland.[22] The aim of the Regulations is to protect persons against risk to their health and safety, arising from exposure to noise[23] at work.[24] The duties the Regulations impose are in addition to those contained in the Health and Safety at Work Act 1974.[25]

Risk assessment

An employer who carries out work that is liable to expose any employees to noise, at or above a lower exposure action value,[26] is required to make a suitable and sufficient

---

[19] Under 1974 Act s 3(1) every employer is placed under a duty to ensure so far as is reasonably practicable that persons not in their employment who may be affected thereby are not affected thereby exposed to the risks to their health or safety.

[20] 1974 Act s 47(1).

[21] SI 2005/1643.

[22] Similar regulations (SR 2006 No 1) apply in Northern Ireland.

[23] 'Noise' is defined as any audible sound: SI 2005/1643 reg 2(1).

[24] SI 2005/1643 reg 3(1).

[25] See generally *Controlling Noise at Work: The Control of Noise at Work Regulations 2005. Guidance on Regulations*, 3rd edn (L108, (HSE, 2021). See also *Noise at Work: A brief guide to controlling the risks* (HSE, November 2012). See also *Sound Advice: Control of noise in music and entertainment* (HSE, 2008) and *Sound solutions for the food and drinks industry*, 2nd edn (HSE, 2013).

[26] 'Lower exposure action value' means the lower of the two levels of daily or weekly personal noise exposure or of peak sound pressure set out in reg 4 that, if reached or exceeded, require specific action to be taken to reduce risk: SI 2005/1643 reg 2(1). 'Daily personal noise exposure' means the level

assessment of the risk from that noise to health and safety of those employees.[27] The risk assessment is required to identify the measures that are needed to meet the requirements of the regulations. In conducting the risk assessment, the employer is required to assess the levels of noise to which workers are exposed by means of: (a) observation of specific working practices; (b) reference to relevant information on the probable levels of noise, corresponding to any equipment used in the particular working conditions; and (c) if necessary, measurement of the level of noise to which their employees are likely to be exposed.[28] The employer is required to assess whether any employees are likely to be exposed to noise at or above a lower exposure action value, an upper exposure action value[29] or an exposure limit value.[30]

The risk assessment is required to include consideration of a variety of factors.[31] Such factors include:

(i) the level, type and duration of exposure, including any exposure to peak sound pressure[32];
(ii) the effects of exposure to noise on employees, or groups of employees, whose health is at particular risk from such exposure;
(iii) so far as is practicable, any effects on the health and safety of employees;
(iv) any information provided by the manufacturers of work equipment; and
(v) the availability of personal hearing protectors with adequate attenuation characteristics.

The risk assessment requires to be reviewed regularly, and forthwith if:

(a) there is reason to suspect that the risk assessment is no longer valid; or
(b) there has been a significant change in the work to which the assessment relates.[33]

---

of personal noise exposure of an employee as ascertained in accordance with Sch 1 Part 1 taking account of the level of noise and the duration of exposure and covering all noise: SI 2005/1643 reg 2(1). 'Weekly noise exposure' means the level of weekly personal noise exposure as ascertained in accordance with Sch 1 Part 2 taking account of the level of noise and the duration of exposure and covering all noise. The lower exposure action values are: (a) a daily or weekly personal noise exposure of 80dB(A-weighted); and (b) a peak sound pressure of 135 dB (C-weighted): SI 2005/1643 reg 4(1). In *McDonald* (fn 2above) a part-time employee had been exposed to an average noise level of 82.3 dB(A) LEPd over a period of two hours on one occasion. It was held that one required to employ a daily, as opposed to a weekly, personal noise exposure action value to determine whether the employer was in breach of the Regulations. See Chapter 3 for a discussion of the measurement of noise.

27 SI 2005/1643 reg 5(1).

28 SI 2005/1643 reg 5(2).

29 An upper exposure action value means the higher of two levels or weekly personal noise exposure, or of peak sound pressure set out in reg 4(2), which, if reached or exceeded, require specific action to be taken to reduce risk: SI 2005/1643 reg 2(1). Under reg 4(2) the upper exposure action values are: (a) a daily or weekly personal noise exposure of 85dB(A-weighted); and a peak sound pressure of 137 dB (C-weighted).

30 Under reg 4(3) the exposure limit values are: (a) a daily or weekly personal noise exposure of 87 dB (A-weighted); and (b) a peak sound pressure of 140 dB(C-weighted). In applying the exposure limit values account requires to be taken of the protection given to the employee by any personal hearing protectors provided by the employer provided in accordance with reg 7(2): SI 2005/1643 reg 4(5).

31 SI 2005/1643 reg 5(3).

32 'Peak sound pressure' means the maximum sound pressure to which an employee is exposed, ascertained in accordance with Schedule 2: SI 2005/1643 reg 2(1).

33 SI 2005/1643 reg 5(4).

Where, as a result of the review, changes to the risk assessment are required, those changes are required to be made.

The employees concerned, or their representatives, are required to be consulted on the assessment of risk in terms of the Regulations.[34] The employer is required to record: (a) the significant findings of the risk assessment as soon as is practicable after the risk assessment is made or changed; and (b) the measures that they have taken and that they intend to take to meet the requirements of regs 6, 7 and 10 (below).[35]

Elimination or control of exposure to noise at the workplace

The employer is required to ensure that risk from the exposure of their employees to noise is either eliminated at source or, where that is not reasonably practical, reduced to as low a level as is reasonably practicable.[36] If any employee is likely to be exposed to noise either at, or above, an upper exposure action value, the employer is required to reduce the noise to as low a level as is reasonably practicable by establishing and implementing a programme of organisational and technical measures, excluding the provision of personal hearing protectors, that is appropriate to the activity.[37]

The actions taken by the employer in order to secure compliance with the above provisions are required to be based on the general principles of prevention, which are set out in Schedule 1 to the Management of Health and Safety at Work Regulations 1999 and are required to include consideration of, *inter alia*, the following:

(i) other working methods which reduce exposure to noise;
(ii) choice of appropriate work equipment emitting the least possible noise, taking account of the work to be done;
(iii) the design and layout of workplaces, workstations and rest facilities;
(iv) suitable and sufficient information and training for employees, such that work equipment may be correctly used in order to minimise their exposure to noise; and,
(v) the limitation of the duration and intensity of exposure to noise.[38]

The employer is required to ensure that their employees are not exposed to noise above an exposure limit value; or if an exposure limit value is exceeded, the employer is required forthwith:

(i) reduce exposure to noise to below the exposure limit value;
(ii) identify the reason for that exposure limit value being exceeded; and
(iii) modify the organisational technical measures taken in accordance with paras (1) and (2) and regs 7 and 8(1) to prevent it being exceeded again.[39]

---

34 SI 2005/1643 reg 5(5).
35 SI 2005/1643 reg 5(6).
36 SI 2005/1643 reg 6(1). For a discussion of the expression 'reasonably practicable' under reg 6(1), see *Goldscheider v Royal Opera House Covent Garden Foundation* [2020] ICR 1 at [41]–[48]. In that case, the claimant had sustained injury after having been exposed to excessive noise from the playing musical instruments.
37 SI 2005/1643 reg 6(2).
38 SI 2005/1643 reg 6(3).
39 SI 2005/1643 reg 6(4).

The employer is required to adapt any measures taken in compliance with the requirements of reg 6 to take account of any employee, or group of employees, whose health is likely to be particularly at risk from exposure to noise.[40]

Hearing protection

An employer who carries out work that is likely to expose any employees to noise either at, or above, a lower exposure action value is required to make personal hearing protectors available, on request, to any employee who is so exposed.[41] If the employer is unable by other means to reduce the levels of noise to which an employee is likely to be exposed to below an upper exposure action value, he is required to provide personal hearing protectors to any employee who is so exposed.[42]

If in any area of the workplace under the control of the employer, the employee is likely to be exposed to noise, at or above an upper exposure action value for any reason the employer is required to ensure that:

- (i) the area is designated a hearing protection zone;
- (ii) the area is demarcated and identified by means of the sign specified for the purpose indicating that ear protection must be worn in the Health and Safety (Safety Signs and Signals) Regulations 1996; and
- (iii) access to the area is restricted, where this is practicable, and the risk from exposure justifies it.[43]

The employer is also required to ensure so far as is reasonably practicable that no employee enters that area unless that employee is wearing personal hearing protectors.[44] Any personal hearing protectors, either made available or provided under reg 7(1) or (2), requires to be selected by the employer:

- (a) so as to eliminate the risk to hearing or to reduce the risk to as low a level as is reasonably practicable; and
- (b) after consultation with the employees concerned or their representatives.[45]

Any personal hearing protectors are required to comply with any legal requirement[46] that is applicable to them.

Maintenance and use of equipment

The employer is required to ensure, so far as is practicable, that anything provided by them in compliance with their duties under the Regulations either to, or for, the benefit of an employee, other than personal hearing protectors provided under

[40] SI 2005/1643 reg 6(6).
[41] SI 2005/1643 reg 7(1).
[42] SI 2005/1643 reg 7(2).
[43] SI 2005/1643 reg 7(3).
[44] In *Goldscheider* (above) the court accepted the fact that it was not reasonably practicable for players in an orchestra pit to perform if they were required to wear personal hearing protectors at all times.
[45] SI 2005/1643 reg 7(4).
[46] 'Legal requirement' means any requirement of the Personal Protective Equipment Regulations 2002 or Regulation (EU) 2016/425 of the European Parliament and of the Council on personal protective equipment and repealing Council Directive 89/686/EEC: SI 2005/1643 reg 7(5).

reg 7(1), is fully and properly used.[47] The employer is also required to ensure that anything provided by them in compliance with their duties under the Regulations is maintained in an efficient state, in efficient order, and in good repair.[48] Every employee is required to make full and proper use of personal hearing protectors provided to them by their employer, in compliance with reg 7(2), and of any other control measures provided by their employer in compliance with their duties under the Regulations. If the employee discovers any defect in any personal hearing protectors, or other such control measures, the employee is required to report it to their employer as soon as is practicable.

Health surveillance

If the risk assessment indicates that there is a risk to health of their employees who are, or are liable to be, exposed to noise, the employer is required to ensure that such employees are placed under suitable health surveillance, which is required to include testing of their hearing.[49] The employer is also required to ensure that a heath record in respect of each employee is made and maintained and that the record, or a copy thereof, is kept available in a suitable form.[50] The employer is required, on reasonable notice being given, to allow an employee access to their personal health record, and also provide the enforcing authority with copies of such health records as it may require.

Where, as a result of a health of health surveillance, an employee is found to have identifiable hearing damage, the employer is required to ensure that the employee is examined by a doctor and, if the doctor or any specialist to whom the doctor considers it necessary to refer the employee, considers that the damage is likely to be the result of the exposure to noise, the employer is *inter alia* required to:

(i) review the risk assessment;
(ii) review any measures taken to comply with regs 6, 7 and 8, taking into account any advice given by a doctor or occupational health professional or by the enforcing authority;
(iii) consider assigning the employee to alternative work where there is no risk to further exposure to noise, taking account any advice given by a doctor or occupational health professional; and
(iv) ensure continued health surveillance and also provide for a review of the health of any other employee who has been similarly exposed.[51]

An employee to whom the above provisions apply, must, when required by their employer, and at the cost of their employer, present themselves during their working hours for such health surveillance procedures as may be required for the purposes of reg 9(1) above.[52]

[47] 2005 Regulations reg 8(1).
[48] 2005 Regulations reg 8(2).
[49] 2005 Regulations reg 9(1).
[50] 2005 Regulations reg 9(2).
[51] 2005 Regulations reg 9(4).
[52] 2005 Regulations reg 9(5).

Information, instruction and training

Where employees are exposed to noise that is likely to be at or above a lower exposure action value, the employer is required to provide these employees, and their representatives, with suitable and sufficient information, instruction and training.[53] Such information, instruction and training requires to include *inter alia*:

(i) the nature of risks from exposure to noise;
(ii) the exposure limit values and upper and lower exposure action values set out in reg 4;
(iii) the significant findings of any risk assessment, including any measurements taken, with an explanation of those findings;
(iv) the availability and provision of personal hearing protectors under reg 7 and their correct use in accordance with reg 8(2);
(v) why and how to detect and report signs of hearing damage;
(vi) the entitlement to health surveillance under reg 9 and its purposes; and
(vii) safe working practices to minimise exposure to noise.[54]

The information, instruction and training required under reg 10(1) requires to be updated to take account of significant changes in the type of work carried out or the working methods used by the employer.[55]

The employer is required to ensure that any person, whether or not their employee, who carries out work in connection with their employer's duties under the Regulations, has suitable and sufficient information, instruction and training.

Exemption certificates from hearing protection

The Health and Safety Executive (HSE) may, by a certificate in writing, exempt any person, or class of person, from the provisions of reg 6(4) (exposure to noise above a limit value) and reg 7(1), (2) (hearing protectors) where because of the nature of the work, the full and proper use of personal protectors would be likely to cause greater risk to health or safety, than not using the protectors.[56] Any such exemption may be granted subject to conditions and to a limit of time. It may also be revoked by a certificate in writing at any time. However, the HSE may not grant such an extension unless:

(a) it consults the employers and the employees or their representatives concerned;
(b) it consults such other persons as it considers appropriate;
(c) the resultant risks are reduced to as low a level as is reasonably practicable; and
(d) the employees concerned are subjected to increased health surveillance.[57]

[53] 2005 Regulations reg 10(1).
[54] 2005 Regulations reg 10(2).
[55] 2005 Regulations reg 10(3).
[56] 2005 Regulations reg 11(1).
[57] 2005 Regulations reg 11(2).

Emergency services

The HSE may, by a certificate in writing, exempt any person, or class of persons, from the provisions of reg 6(4) and reg 7(1)–(3) in respect of activities carried out by the medical services that conflict with the requirements of any of those provisions.[58] Any such exemption may be granted subject to conditions and to a limit of time. Furthermore, the exemption may be revoked by a certificate in writing at any time. An exemption may not be granted unless the HSE is satisfied that the health and safety of the employees concerned is ensured as far as possible in the light of the objectives of the Regulations.[59]

Exemptions relating to the Ministry of Defence

The Secretary of State for defence may, by a certificate in writing, exempt any person, or class of persons, from the provisions of regs 6(4) and 7(1)–(3) in respect of activities carried out in the interests of national security that conflict with the requirements of the Regulations.[60] Any such exemptions may be granted subject to conditions and to a limit of time. However, the Secretary of State may not grant an exemption unless they are satisfied that the health and safety of the employees concerned is ensured, as far as possible in the light of the objectives of the Regulations.[61]

[58] 2005 Regulations reg 12(1).
[59] 2005 Regulations reg 12(2).
[60] 2005 Regulations reg 13(1).
[61] 2005 Regulations reg 13(2).

APPENDIX I

Chapter summaries and discussion questions

CHAPTER 1 INTRODUCTION

Noise can have a serious effect on human health. During the nineteenth century there was no national legislation dealing with noise. As far as the twentieth century was concerned, the Noise Abatement Act 1960 made noise pollution a statutory nuisance. The 1970s witnessed a growing interest in the effect of pollution, in general, on the environment. The Control of Pollution Act 1974 introduced the concept of noise abatement zones. The 1980s witnessed growing awareness that environmental noise was getting worse. In 1993 the Noise and Statutory Nuisance Act 1993 gave local authorities the power to deal, *inter alia*, with noise from burglar alarms and loudspeakers in streets and roads. The Noise Act 1996 *inter alia* made the creation of noise an offence, if it exceeded a given limit at night. As far as the twenty-first century was concerned, neighbourhood noise was being viewed, not as a free-standing problem but, rather, as part of the wider problem of antisocial behaviour. Antisocial behaviour legislation was made by both the UK and Scottish Parliaments. The EU's END Directive (2002), which dealt with ambient noise, was transposed into UK law. The UK government issued a Noise Policy Statement for England in 2010. The Environment Act 2021 makes provisions for the preparation of targets, plans and policies for improving the natural environment. Such targets, etc. could contain provisions relating to noise.

CHAPTER 2 BASIC ACOUSTICS AND HUMAN PERCEPTION

Concepts important for the understanding of acoustics are introduced together with basic terminology starting with sound pressure level and its associated unit, the decibel (dB). The important difference between sound pressure level and sound power level are explained together with the concept of frequency or pitch and how sound travels from the source (whatever makes the noise) to the receiver (the person who hears the sound). A simple explanation of the way sound behaves in buildings is then provided, including the way in which it travels between rooms, and also from inside to outside and vice versa. The hearing mechanism is described, including different types of hearing impairment and what can be done to alleviate this with the use of hearing aids. The factors that influence sound perception in humans is discussed, including the importance of 'non-acoustic factors' and the concept of 'noise', which is used to describe unwanted sound.

Question

Is it correct to refer to noise as pollution?

CHAPTER 3 THE MEASUREMENT AND ASSESSMENT OF NOISE

The basic objective noise measurement tool, the sound level meter, is introduced including its basic function, which is to convert a fluctuating pressure signal into its decibel value. The way sound level meters compensate for the differing sensitivity of ear at different frequencies by using 'weighting curves' (A-weighting, C-weighting, etc.) is explained together with the way decibel readings are aggregated over different time periods. Various noise 'indices' that are required to quantify noise are described, which are rarely steady as they vary over time. The significance of 'tones' in the noise (frequency analysis) and variation in noise level (temporal analysis) and the way they are assessed is described together with other 'acoustic features' and the way they are dealt with in noise assessment. Different approaches to assessment are discussed, including assessing the absolute or relative noise levels and the concept of noise 'dose'. Finally, relevant noise assessment guidance and standards are described including BS4142, Methods for Rating and Assessing Industrial and Commercial Sound.

Question

Is it correct to have a British Standard that is very flexible in approach and with an outcome that depends on 'context'?

CHAPTER 4 COMMON LAW NUISANCE

The law of nuisance protects the occupier of land from the unreasonable interference with their enjoyment of that land. The courts take a variety of factors into account when determining if a given state of affairs ranks as a nuisance, including social utility, motive of the defender, locality, duration and intensity, time of day, sensitivity of the claimant, social utility of the thing interfered with and whether the state of affairs complained of is typical of modern life. The author of the nuisance can be sued for the creation of a nuisance, as can the occupier of land, the landlord (in certain limited circumstances) and the licensor of the nuisance. There are certain defences to a nuisance action, including the defence of statutory authority, prescription and acquiescence. The remedies for nuisance are injunction/interdict, delaration/declator and damages.

Question

Should planning law have any role to play in the development of the law of nuisance? See *Lawrence v Fen Tigers Ltd* [2014] UKSC 13.

CHAPTER 5 STATUTORY NUISANCE

The Environmental Protection Act 1990 (EPA) designates a variety of adverse circumstances, including noise nuisance, as a nuisance. A local authority is placed under a duty to investigate complaints of a nuisance. If a local authority is satisfied that a nuisance exists, it is required to serve an abatement notice. The EPA specifies on whom the notice is to be served. Provision is made for appeals against the notice. It is an offence to fail to comply with the notice. The EPA makes provision for penalties and non-compliance with the notice. Provision is also made to allow private individuals to take proceedings in respect of a statutory nuisance.

Question

Should the creation of a statutory nuisance simply be made an offence of strict liability, subject to specified statutory defences?

CHAPTER 6 NEIGHBOURHOOD NOISE

The legislation dealing with neighbourhood noise is piecemeal. The Control of Pollution Act 1974 gives local authorities extensive powers to deal with noise from construction sites and loudspeakers in streets and roads. The Civic Government (Scotland) Act 1982 makes provision for noise from musical instruments, etc. and dogs. The Noise Act 1996 makes provision for night-time noise. Provision is made for the service of warning notices and offences. The Antisocial Behaviour etc. (Scotland) Act 2004 makes provision for the service of antisocial behaviour orders in relation to antisocial behaviour, which includes the creation of noise. The Act also makes special provision in relation to neighbourhood noise. Provision is made for the service of warning notices, offences and fixed penalty notices, and also the power to seize equipment. The Anti-social Behaviour, Crime and Policing Act 2014 makes provision for a wide range of antisocial behaviour, including such behaviour that causes noise. The Act makes provision for the granting of injunctions, the closure of premises and offences. The Licensing Act 2003 provides a unified system in England and Wales for the licensing of the sale of alcohol, the provision of 'regulated entertainment' and the provision of late-night refreshments. The licensing system is achieved through the provision of, *inter alia*, authorisations, personal licenses and premises licences. A licensing authority has power to attach conditions to grant of a premises license and club premises certificates. As far as Scotland is concerned, the Licensing (Scotland) Act 2005 allows a licensing board to impose conditions *inter alia* relating to the control of noise from premises that sell alcohol. The Civic Government (Scotland) Act 1982 gives a licensing authority power to attach conditions to premises used as a place of public entertainment. The Criminal Justice and Public Order Act 1994 makes special provision relating to raves. The Fireworks Regulations 2004 regulate the use and supply of fireworks. The Pyrotechnic Articles (Safety) Regulations 2015 make provision relating to the traceability of pyrotechnic articles. The Local Government Act 1972 and the Local Government (Scotland) 1973 allow local authorities to make byelaws to control noise in their areas. The EU Industrial Emissions Directive 2010/75/EU which has been implemented in the UK by subordinate legislation (namely the Pollution Prevention and Control Regulations (Scotland) 2012 and the Environmental Permitting (England and Wales) Regulations 2016), which make provision for the permitting of industrial installations. A permit could contain a requirement relating to noise from relevant premises. Waste management activities are regulated in England and Wales under the 2016 Regulations. In Scotland SEPA regulates waste treatment facilities under a licensing system, in terms of regulations made under the EPA. A licence could contain a provision relating to noise. Certain waste management facilities in Scotland are regulated under the 2012 Regulations. Landfill sites are regulated in Scotland by means of a licensing system under the Licensing (Scotland) Regulations 2003 in terms of which SEPA can regulate the emission of noise from such sites. Building regulations contain provisions relating to sound insulation of domestic premises. The Noise Emission in the Environment by Equipment for Use Outdoors Regulations 2001 makes provision for the control of noise from machinery and equipment. The Household Appliances (Noise Emission) Regulations 1990 prohibit the manufacturer or importer of any appliance that has either been manufactured or imported by them from doing so, unless the requirements of the Regulations have been complied with.

Question

'The law relating to neighbourhood noise is fragmented and requires to be consolidated and simplified in a single statute.'

Discuss.

CHAPTER 7 NOISE AND HUMAN RIGHTS

Article 8 and art 1 of the First Protocol of the European Convention of Human Rights have been invoked on a number of occasions by individuals affected by various forms of pollution, including noise. Whether art 8 has been engaged depends on all the circumstances of the case, including whether the noise has contravened national legislation, its intensity, duration, the physical and mental effects of the noise, and whether the noise exceeds WHO environmental noise guidelines and those of other European countries.

In certain circumstances, the state comes under a positive duty to protect its citizens from noise pollution. However, in such circumstances, the state enjoys a certain margin of appreciation in striking a balance between the competing interests of the individual and the community as a whole.

Question

Compare the law of nuisance with the ECHR in terms of the protection of individuals from exposure to excessive noise.

CHAPTER 8 TRANSPORT NOISE

The Rules of the Air Regulations 2015 prohibit the take-off or landing of aircraft within a congested area of any city, town or settlement except an aerodrome in accordance with procedures notified by the CAA. The noise provisions contained in Volume 1 of Annex 16 of the Chicago Convention requires aircraft to be certified before being allowed to operate. Noise certificates are issued by the CAA under the Civil Aviation Act 1982. The CAA is under a duty in terms of the Act, in exercising its aerodrome or licensing functions, to have regard to the need to minimise, so far as is reasonably practicable, any adverse effect on the environment and any disturbance to the public from, *inter alia*, noise and vibration from the aerodrome. The Air Navigation Order 2016 allows the Secretary of State to prescribe the conditions under which noise and vibration may be caused by aircraft on aerodromes. The Act gives the Secretary of State wide-ranging control over aircraft noise from designated aerodromes. An important device to reduce the impact of noise on the ground of those living in the vicinity of airports from aircraft taking off at the airport, is the use of noise preferential routes (NPRs) at airports. NPRs have been established under the Act for designated aerodromes. Some local authorities have established NPRs under the Town and Country Planning Act 1990. Some NPRs have been established voluntarily. An airport operator may establish a noise control scheme under the Act to reduce the impact of noise from aircraft taking off or landing at a non-designated aerodrome. As far as road traffic noise is concerned, the Road Vehicles (Construction and Use) Regulations 1986 make provision for minimising noise from vehicles. The defence of statutory authority may apply in relation to rail traffic noise.

Question

Noise from aircraft is immune from civil action, in terms of the law of nuisance, if the aircraft has complied with the relevant provisions of the Civil Aviation Act 1982 and regulations made under the Act.

Discuss whether you consider such immunity justified.

CHAPTER 9 NOISE MAPPING

Environmental noise mainly consists of noise from transport sources such as road, rail and aviation. Directive 2002/49/EU (the END Directive) addresses this problem. The END's main objective is to establish a common approach intended to avoid, prevent or reduce, on a prioritised basis, the harmful effects, including annoyance, caused by exposure to environmental noise. That policy is to be implemented *inter alia* by the determination of exposure to environmental noise through noise mapping and ensuring that information on environmental noise and its effects is made available to the public. The END makes provision for strategic noise mapping and action plans. The END has been implemented in the UK by subordinate legislation. In England the END has been implemented by Environmental Noise (England) Regulations 2006. The Secretary of State has general responsibility for measures relating to the assessment, management and control of environmental noise. The Secretary of State is made the competent authority for the making, review and revision of strategic noise maps for sources other than non-designated airports. The Regulations make provision for the drawing up of action plans that are required to be kept under review and, if appropriate, revised. An action plan is required *inter alia* to prevent and reduce environmental noise and also preserve environmental noise quality where it is good. The Secretary of State is the competent authority for the drawing up and revision of action plans. The airport operator is the competent authority for major airports and non-designated (other airports) in certain circumstances. The Regulations make provision for public participation. The Secretary of State has the responsibility for adopting strategic noise maps and action plans.

Question

Assess the general importance of noise mapping.

CHAPTER 10 PLANNING AND NOISE

Environmental impact assessment (EIA) enables decision-makers (mainly planning authorities) to take account of the environmental impact of their decisions. The Town and Country Planning (Environmental Impact Assessment) Regulations 2017 prohibit either a planning authority, the Secretary of State, or an inspector, from granting planning permission (or subsequent consent) for an EIA development unless an EIA has been carried out. An EIA development consists either a Schedule 1 or a Schedule 2 development, which is likely to have significant effects on the environment. EIA includes the preparation of an environmental statement (ES). The ES is a statement that allows the planning authority to assess the environmental effects of a project. A person who intends to develop land may request the planning authority to adopt a screening opinion. A person who intends to submit an EIA application can also request the planning authority for a scoping opinion, as to the scope and level of detail of the information, which requires to be included in the ES. The ES is required to contain certain information. The Regulations make provision for the publicity of the ES. Strategic environmental assessment (SEA) is an assessment of the potential environmental impacts of plans and programmes on the environment. An SEA is required for plans and programmes that are prepared *inter alia* for town and country planning and land use and set the framework for the future development consent of projects, which require an EIA. If an SEA is required, an environmental report must be prepared. The SEA is implemented in England by the Environmental Assessment of Plans and Programmes Regulations 2004. The Regulations make provision for consultation procedures. The responsible body is required to monitor the significant environmental effects of the plan or programme. Town and country planning has an important role to play in relation to the control of noise. Central government has the overall responsibility for town and country planning in England. The National Planning Policy Framework (NPPF) sets out the government's planning policy for England and how the government expects such policies to be applied. Local planning authorities are responsible for the preparation of development plans and also for granting development consent. In the UK the planning system is plan-led. Under the Town and Country Planning Act 1990, in deciding whether or not to grant planning permission, a planning authority is required to have regard *inter alia* to the provisions of the development plan that are relevant to the application and to any other material considerations. Under the Planning and Compulsory Purchase Act 2004 a local planning authority is required to determine a planning application in accordance with the development plan unless material considerations indicate otherwise. Noise from a proposed development can constitute a material consideration, as can relevant regulatory controls. The weighting that a planning authority attaches to a material consideration is a matter of planning judgement. Under the 1990 Act a planning authority can attach conditions on granting planning permission.

Question

Assess the general importance of town and country planning in terms of noise control.

CHAPTER 11 NOISE IN THE WORKPLACE

An employer is under a duty at common law to protect their employee from excessive noise in the workplace. The duty remains during the period the employee is sent to work elsewhere. An employer is under a duty to ensure that all systems of work that the employee is required to perform, within the scope of their employment, are safe. This includes a duty to ensure the employee is not exposed to the risk of injury by being exposed to excessive noise or vibration. The appropriate precautions that the employer is required to take must be proportionate to the relevant risk. An employer is under a duty to provide their employees with plant, materials and resources that are safe. This duty would include ensuring that plant and machinery cannot cause the employee harm by virtue of being exposed to noise and vibration. An employer is under a duty to provide their employees who are at risk to injury with suitable protective equipment, for example, ear protectors. The Health and Safety at Work etc Act 1974 provides that it shall be the duty of every employer to ensure, so far as is reasonably practicable, the health safety and welfare of all their employees. The duty extends to the provision and maintenance of plant and systems of work that are, so far as is reasonably practicable, safe and without risks to health. The Control of Noise at Work Regulations 2005 make provision for the protection of persons against risk to their health and safety arising from exposure to noise at work. An employer who carries out work that is liable to expose any employees to noise, at or above a specified action value, is required to make an appropriate assessment of that risk. The employer is required to ensure that the risk from the exposure of their employees to noise is either eliminated at source or, where that is not reasonably practicable, reduced to as low a level as is reasonably practicable. The employer who carries out work which is likely to expose any employees to noise above a specified action value is required to make personal hearing protectors available to any employee who is so exposed. The Regulations make provision for the maintenance and use of equipment, health surveillance, information, instruction and training.

Question

Assess the general importance of the Control of Noise at Work Regulations 2005.

Index

References to footnotes are represented as page number followed by note number (eg 3n15). Page numbers for figures appear in italics.

absolute noise level assessment, 24
acoustic features, 24, 25–6
acoustic reflex, 13
acquiescence, 42–3
action plans *see* **noise mapping**
aircraft and airport noise
aerodromes and airports, 114–19
assessment of noise, *10*, 20, 21
civil aircraft, 29, 101–2, 111–20
military aircraft, 33, 100–1, 111, 120, 176
see also **noise mapping**
airport developments *see* **environmental impact assessment (EIA); strategic environmental assessment (SEA)**
antisocial behaviour, 4, 73–83

Batho Report (1990), 3–4
best practicable means, defence of, 56–7, 60–1
Brexit, 7
British Standards
BS 4142 (industrial and commercial sound), 2, 20, 21, 26, 26–7
BS 5228 (construction noise), 20, 27–8, 66
BS 7445 (environmental noise), 27
BS 8233 (sound insulation for buildings), 27, 97
BS EN 61672 (sound level meters), 17, 18
burglar alarms, 4
byelaws, 2, 93–4

children's hearing, 13
civil aviation *see* **aircraft and airport noise**
clay target shooting, 29
closure orders, 80–3
cochlea, 13–14
Code of Practice on Environmental Noise Control at Concerts, 28
common law nuisance, 31–43
defences, 41–3
factors taken into account, 32–8
good neighbourliness principle, 31–2
notion of reasonableness, 31–2
persons liable, 38–40
remedies, 43
vehicle noise, 121
concerts and performances, 12, 28, 37, 40, 43
conductive hearing loss, 14–15
constant bandwidth filtering, 22
construction sites, 20, 27–8, 56, 57, 63–6
see also **machinery and outdoor equipment**
cumulative noise, 26

day-evening-night noise level, 21
day-night noise level (USA), 21
decibel (dB) scale, 10, *10*, 20
DEFRA Contract Report NANR 45 (low frequency noise), 29
DEFRA Contract Report NANR 163 (pubs and clubs), 28
development plans, 161
dogs, noise by, 68

emergency services, exemptions, 176
environmental impact assessment (EIA), 141–51

Environmental Noise Guidelines for the European Region **(WHO)**, 29
equivalent continuous sound level, 20
ETSU-R-97 (wind farm noise), 20, 26, 28
EU noise policy, 5–7
see also **environmental impact assessment (EIA); noise mapping; strategic environmental assessment (SEA)**
eustachian tube, 13

Fast Fourier Transform (FFT), 22, *23*
fireworks, *10*, 89–93
frequency analysis, 21–2, 23–4, *23*
frequency of sound, 11, 15

grommets, 13
Guidelines for Community Noise **(WHO)**, 29

hair cells, 14
health and safety at work *see* **workplace noise**
Health and Safety Executive (HSE), 175–6
hearing loss, causes, 13, 14–15
hearing mechanism, 13–15, *14*
helicopter noise, *10*, 111–12
household appliances, 98
hovercraft noise, 120
human rights law, 99–110

impulsive noise, 24
industrial/commercial noise, 20, 26–7, 34–5, 41, 67, 94–5
see also **machinery and outdoor equipment; workplace noise**
injunctions, 79–80
inner ear, 13
Institute of Acoustics, 28
instruments, playing of, 2, 34, 67–8, 94
ISO 1996 (environmental noise), 27
ISO 9613 (attenuation of sound during propagation outdoors), 30

landfill sites, 95–6
landlords, 40
licensed premises
closure orders, 80–3
DEFRA guidelines (pubs and clubs), 28
licensing system, 83–6
see also **concerts and performances; music, amplified**
local authorities
abatement of statutory nuisances, 50–6, 57–9
action against vehicle noise, 122
byelaws, 2, 93–4
noise from construction sites, 63–6
powers under antisocial behaviour legislation, 4, 73–83
reluctance to use NAZs, 3
role in planning system, 161, 166
testing of building works, 97
loudspeakers in streets and roads, 4, 66–7

machinery and outdoor equipment, 97–8
see also **construction site noise**
measurement of sound, 17–30
acoustic features, 24, 25–6
frequency analysis, 21–2, 23–4, *23*
impulsive noise, 24
sound level meters, 17–19, *19*
temporal analysis, 22–4
varying noise levels, 20–1
microlight aircraft, 114
middle ear, 13
military aviation, 33, 100–1, 111, 120, 176
mineral extraction, 28
Ministry of Defence, exemptions, 176
motor cycles, 123
see also **road traffic noise**
motor sport, 35–6, 43
music, amplified, 4, 12, 15, 25, 28, 56, 67–8
see also **concerts and performances; instruments, playing of**

National Planning Framework (NPF), 155, 165
National Planning Policy Framework (NPPF), 155, 160
National Society for Clean Air (NSCA), 3n15
Night Noise Guidelines for Europe **(WHO)**, 29
night-time flights, 117–18
night-time noise, 20, 29, 36, 68–73
Noise Abatement Society, 2
noise abatement zones (NAZs), 3

Noise Council, 28
noise insulation *see* **sound insulation**
noise mapping, 129–39
***Noise Policy Statement for England* (2010) (NPSE)**, 5
noise rating (NR) curves, 25–6, *25*
nuisance *see* **common law nuisance; statutory nuisance**

octave bands, 22, *23*
outer ear, 13
oversensitivity, 37

***Partnership for a Better Scotland* (2003)**, 4, 73
pitch, 11
planning law *see* **environmental impact assessment (EIA); strategic environmental assessment (SEA); town and country planning**
plant and machinery, 67
see also **industrial/commercial noise**
prescription, 42
public entertainment licences, 86
public works, compensation for loss, 124
pubs and clubs *see* **licensed premises**
pyrotechnic articles, 92–3
see also **fireworks**

radios, 67–8
see also **music, amplified**
rail developments, 154–5
see also **environmental impact assessment (EIA); strategic environmental assessment (SEA)**
rail traffic noise, 29, 30, 126–8
see also **noise mapping**
raves, 86–9
relative noise level assessment, 24–5
residential property *see* **household appliances; sound insulation**
reverberation time, 12
road developments, 153–4
see also **environmental impact assessment (EIA); strategic environmental assessment (SEA)**
road traffic noise, 1, *10*, 11, 15, 21, 29, 30, 121–5
see also **noise mapping**
Robust Details Scheme, 97
schools, design of, 96
seizure of equipment, 77–8
sensori-neural hearing loss, 14–15
sleep disturbance *see* **night-time noise**
social utility, 33, 37
sound
effects of unwanted sound, 16
perception of, 15
propagation of, 11–12
terminology, 15–16
sound exposure level (SEL or LAE), 21
sound insulation for buildings
BS guidance, 27, 97
building regulations, 96–7
poor insulation of domestic property, 32, 47, 52
rail traffic noise, 126–8
road traffic noise, 124–5
see also **sound transmission in buildings**
sound level meters, 17–19, *19*
sound power level, 10–11
sound pressure level, 9–10, *10*, 11
sound transmission in buildings, 12–13
statistical indices, 21, *22*
statutory authority, defence of, 41
statutory nuisance, 45–61
abatement by local authority, 50–6, 57–9
defences, 56–7, 60–1
noise from premises, 46–9, 52, 59–60
noise from vehicles, machinery, equipment, 49–50, 53–4, 57–8, 60
penalties, 56
proceedings by private individuals, 59–61
where more than one person responsible, 57–8, 60
strategic environmental assessment (SEA), 151–9
strategic noise maps, 129–39

televisions, 67–8
temporal analysis, 22–4
temporary deafness, causes, 13
town and country planning, 159–66
development plans, 161
planning conditions, 163–4, 166
planning permission
and law of nuisance, 35–6
and pollution control, 161–3
role of local and national government, 160–1, 165–6
traffic noise *see* **road traffic noise**

waste management activities, 95–6
Wilson Report (1963), 2, 16, 26
wind chimes, 16
wind turbine noise, 20, 26, 28, 29
workplace noise, 167–76
  applicable legislation, 170
  common law duties, 167–9
  evaluation of, 20
  exemptions, 175–6
  exposure to noise, 172–3
  health surveillance, 172–3
  hearing protection, 169, 173–4
  information, instruction and training, 175
  risk assessments, 170–2
  safety of plant and equipment, 169, 173–4
World Health Organisation (WHO), 1, 20, 29–30

EU Authorised Representative:
Easy Access System Europe Mustamäe tee 50, 10621 Tallinn, Estonia
gpsr.requests@easproject.com

Printed and bound by CPI Group (UK) Ltd, Croydon, CR0 4YY
14/09/2026
02216780-0003